MATHEMATICS

A

SMART TECHNIQUE TO SOLVE

Useful for all academic classes &competitive exams like banking, railway,Defense various recruitments, NDA, CDS, SSC, State Service Commission etc.

Tusar kumar sahoo

B.Tech.(mech.)

PREFACE

The challenge is to learn the new technique will help us to solve the question in high speed and better accuracy. Preparation required for competitive examination is fundamentally different from that of qualifying ones like Board based examination. Now each and every competitive exams, ask the question to judge the candidate accuracy of solving the problem with shortest possible time. That means they create an atmosphere for the candidate to do it under pressure. As a human, even the known thing can go wrong in hurrying situation. So it is a silly excuse for the student "to know the things better but it goes wrong in exams".

This book becomes the key of the above problem to overcome such type of situation. Many students, teacher and expert advice are placed on this book to make success of the student. In each topic, applies smart technique to solve it in quick and error free. All questions are simplified by mental calculation method which another key factor to minimize the mistake while writing in hurry. Each technique placed in shortest explanation form with example which helps better to memorize the rules easily. The questions which are placedalready asked in different competitive exams and also likely to ask in similar type of question in incoming competitive exams. This book covers some of the question which follows reverse technique i.e. from given options to question for solving the problems.

This book consists of many smart techniques which starts from basic calculation to typical trigonometrically solutions. It is applicable for every student, guardians, teacher, engineer and competitors. It gives not only immense pleasure to read and understand but also improve psychological and mental alertness.The utmost care has been taken to make this book error free. If still have some error come to your notice, kindly bring it to my notice for helping me better. Any suggestion, amendment, appreciation are most welcome to all.

CONTENT

MULTIPLICATION

Multiplication is a basic part of any type of mathematical application. It starts from lower class to any top level calculation. It takes much time to solve a problem in addition to the application of easy technique. So it is important to apply smart technique for multiplication method to save time and better accuracy. In this chapter we use different technique to multiply the numbers in easiest way with shortest possible time. let's have some clip before going to details process

Q. Find the value of 41x81?

Solve

41x81
= 4x8 /4+8 / 1
= 32 /12 / 1
= 3321

Ex. Find the value of 6317 x 5.
Solution:
 6317 x 10/2
=3158.5 x 10
= 31585
Q. Find the value of 24 x 99
Solution
  24 x 99
= 24-1 /99-23
=2376
Q. find the value of 113 x 107
Solve:
113 x 107
 = 113 +07/13 x 7
= 12091
Q. Find the value of 46x49.
Solve:
        46x49
= 46x(50-1)
=(46x50) –(46x1)
=2300-46
=2354.

MULTIPLICATION OF NUMBER HAVING UNIT DIGIT 1

Q.1 Find the value of 41x 31

Solve.

Regular Method	Smart Technique
41 x 31 = 41 31 = 41 123 1271	The smart technique to find the multiplication value of any number can be obtained by three simple steps. 41x31 **Step I** multiply the 10th digit of the number I.e. 4 x3 =12 **Step II** add 10th digit and place after that i.e. 4+3 = 7 = 4x3 /4+3 **Step III** place unit digit i.e. 1 after the above number = 4 x3 /4+3 /1 =1271

Q. Find the value of 31x91

Solve.

STEP1 3x9

STEP2 3x9 /3+9 = 27 /12

STEP 32 8 / 2 /1

Hence the value is 3x9/3+9 /1= 2821

Q. Find the value of 71x61?

Solve

71x61
= 7x6 /7+6 / 1
= 42 /13 / 1
=4331

Q. Find the value of 41x81?

Solve

41x81
= 4x8 /4+8 / 1
= 32 /12 / 1
= 3321

Q. Find the value of 61x51?

Solve

61x51
= 6x5 /6+5 / 1
= 30 /11 / 1
= 3111

Q. Find the value of 91x101?

Solve

91x101
= 9x10 /9+10 / 1
= 90 /19 / 1
= 9191

Q. Find the value of 41x101?

Solve

41x101
= 4x10 /4+10 / 1
= 40 /14 / 1
= 4141

<u>TECHNIQUE#</u>

<u>MULTIPLICATION OF NUMBERS WITH 5</u>

Q. 1 Find the value of 436 x 5?

<u>SOLVE</u>

Regular Method	Smart Technique
436 x 5 = 436 <u> 5</u> = 2180	Multiplication of any number with 5 can be done muchfaster without any paperwork by taking 5 as 10/2 436 x 5 = 436 x 10/2 = 218 x 10 = 2180

Ex. Find the value of 524 x 5

Solution.
524 x 10/2

= 262 x 10/

=2620

Ex. Find the value of 6317 x 5.

Solution:

6317 x 10/2

=3158.5 x 10

= 31585

Ex. Find the value of 444 x 5.

Solution:

444 x 10/2

=222 x 10 = 2220

TECHNIQUE

MULTIPLICATION OF NUMBERS WITH 25

Q. Find the value of 116x25

Solution.

Regular Method	Smart Technique

116 x 25
= 116
    25
= 580
332
2900
	Multiplication with 25 can be done much faster without any paperwork by taking 25 as 100/4
	116 x 25 = 116 x 100/4
	        = 29 x 100
	        = 2900

Q. 876x25
Solution.

876 x 25

= 876 x 100/4

= 219 x 100

= 2190

Ex. Find the value of 420 x25.

Solution:

420 x 100/4

=105 x 100 = 10500

Ex. Find the value of 684 x25.

Solution:

684 x 100/4

=171 x 100 = 17100

<u>__TECHNIQUE__</u>#

<u>__MULTIPLICATION OF NUMBERS WITH 9,99 and 999__</u>

Q. Find the value of 15 x 99

Solution

Regular Method	Smart Technique
15 x 99 = 15 x (100- 1) = 15000- 15 = 1485	15 x 99 =15-1 /9 9-14 =14 /85 =1485

Q.Find the value of 24 x 99
<u>**Solution**</u>
24 x 99
=24-1 /99-23
=2376

Q. Find the value of 723 x 999

<u>**Solution**</u>

723 x 999
=723-1 /999-722
=722277

Q. Find the value of 43 x 999

<u>**Solution**</u>

43 x 999
=43-1 /999-42
=42957

Q. Find the value of 256 x 999

Solution

    256 x 999
=256-1 /999-255
=255744

Q. Find the value of 185 x 9999

Solution

    185 x 9999
=185-1 /9999-184
=1849815

Q. Find the value of 381 x 999

Solution

    381 x 999
=381-1 /999-380
=380619

Q. Find the value of 77 x 99

Solution

    77 x 99
=77-1 /99-76
=7623

TECHNIQUE

MULTIPLICATION OF NUMBERS JUST OVER 100

Q. Find the value of 103x104

Solve by smart technique

Regular Method	Smart Technique
103x104 = 103 x (100+ 4) = 10300 + 412 = 10712	103 X 104 = 103+4 /3x4 = 10712

Q. find the value of 113 x 107
Solve:
113 x 107
 = 113 +07/13 x 7
= 12091

Q. Find the value of 109 x 106
Solve:
   109 x 106
 = 109 + 06   / 9x6
= 115 /54
= 11554.

Q. Find the value of 110 x 116
Solve:
   110 x 116
 = 110 + 16   / 10x16
= 126 /160
= 12760.

Q. Find the value of 115 x 106
Solve:
   115 x 106

$= 115 + 06 \quad /15 \times 6$
$= 121 \quad /90$
$= 12190.$

Q. Find the value of 112 x 103
Solve:

112×103
$= 112 + 03 \quad / 12 \times 3$
$= 115 \quad /36$
$= 11536.$

Q. Find the value of 113 x 112
Solve:

113×112
$= 113 + 12 \quad / 13 \times 12$
$= 125 \quad /156$
$= 12656.$

TECHNIQUE

MULTIPLICATION OF NUMBERS WITH 11

Q.1 find the value 3721 x 11

Solve by smart technique

Regular Method	Smart Technique
3721x 11 = 3721 x (10+ 1) = 37210 + 3721 = 40931	3721 x 11 =1x3 /1x3+7 /1x7+2 /1x2+1 /1x1 = 3 /10 /9 /3 /1 = 40931

Q. Find the value of 8735 x 11.

Solve:
 8735 x11
= 8x1 /8x1+7 /7x1+3 /3x1+5 /5x1
= 8 /15 /10 /8 /5
= 96085.

Q. Find the value of 563 x 11.

Solve:
   563 x11
= 5x1 /5x1+6 /6x1+3 /3x1
 = 5 /11 /9 /3
= 6193.

Q. Find the value of 76928 x 11.

Solve:
   76928 x11
= 7x1 /7x1+6 /6x1+9 /9x1+2 /2x1+8 /8x1
 = 7 /13 /15   /11 /10   /8
 = 846208.

Q. Find the value of 3702 x 11.

Solve:
    3702 x11
= 3x1 /3x1+7 /7x1+0 /0x1+2 /2x1
 = 3 /10 /7 /2 /2
 = 40722.

Q. Find the value of 3729 x 11.

Solve:
    3729 x11
= 3x1 /3x1+7 /7x1+2 /2x1+9 /9x1
 = 3 /10 /9 /11 /9
 = 41019.

TECHNIQUE

MULTIPLICATION OF NUMBERS WITH 12

Q. Find the value of 121 x 12.

Solve by smart technique

Regular Method	Smart Technique
121 x 12 = 121 x (10+ 2) = 1210+ 242 = 1452	121x12 = 1x1 /2x1+2 /2x2+1 /2x1 = 1 /4 /5 /2 = 1452

Q. Find in the value of 2364x12.
 Solve:
   2364x12
= 2x1 /2x2+3 /3x2+6 /6x2+4 /2x4
= 2 /7 /12 /16 /8
= 28368.

Q. Find in the value of 1673x12.
 Solve:
   1673x12
= 1x1 /2x2+6 /6x2+7 /7x2+3 /2x3
= 1 /10 /19 /17 /6
= 20076.

Q. Find in the value of 5036x12.
 Solve:
   5036x12
= 5x1 /5x2+0 /0x2+3 /3x2+6 /6x2
= 5 /10 /03 /12 /12
= 60432.

Q. Find in the value of 276x12.

Solve:

276x12

= 2x1 /2x2+7 /7x2+6 /6x2

= 2 /11 /20 /12

= 3312.

Q. Find in the value of 732x12.

Solve:

732 x12

= 7x1 /7x2+3 /3x2+2 /2x2

= 7 /17 /8 /4

= 8784.

Q. Find in the value of 4726x12.

Solve:

4726x12

= 4x1 /4x2+7 /7x2+2 /2x2+6 /6x2

= 4 /15 /16 /10 /12

= 56712.

Q. Find in the value of 3425x12.

Solve:

3425x12

= 3x1 /3x2+4 /4x2+2 /2x2+5 /5x2

= 3 /10 /10 /9 /10

= 41100.

Q. Find in the value of 93276x12.

Solve:

93276x12

= 9 /21 /08 /11 /20 /12

= 1119312.

TECHNIQUE

MULTIPLICATION OF NUMBERS WITH 13

Q. Find the value of 259 x 13.

Solve by smart technique

Regular Method	Smart Technique
259x13 = 259 x (10+ 3) = 2590+ 777 = 3367	259x13 = 1x2 /3x2+5 /3x5+9 /3x9 = 2 /11 /24 /27 = 3367

Q. Find in the value of 372x13.
 Solve:
372x13
= 1x3 /3x3+7 /3x7+2 /3x2
= 3 /16 /23 /6
= 4836.

Q. Find in the value of 3240x13.
 Solve:
3240x13
= 1x3 /3x3+2 /3x2+4 /3x4+0 /3x0
= 3 /11 /10 /12 /0
= 42120.

Q. Find in the value of 5326x13.
 Solve:
5326x13
= 5 /18 /11 /12 /18
= 69238.

Q. Find in the value of 9283x13.
 Solve:
9283x13
= 9 /29 /14 /27 /09= 120679.

<u>TECHNIQUE#</u>

<u>MULTIPLICATION OF NUMBER NEAREST TO 100</u>

Q. Find the value of 97x98.

Solve by smart technique

Regular Method	Smart Technique

97x98
= 97
  98
 776
873
9506
	97x98
	
	97 (-3)
	            (Both have less than 100 by
	98 (-2) 3 and 2 respectively)
	
	98-3 = 97-2= 95 (if we subtracts diagonally
	                  Both should have equal
	                  value)
	
	95x100= 9500
	         +6 (the result of -3x -2)
	
	      =9506

Q. Find the value of 92x96.

Solve:

```
      92 x 96
92   (-8) =96-8=88          (both subtract diagonally)
96   (-4) =92-4=88
88x100=8800                 (the result multiply with 100)
        +32
      =8832.
```

Q. Find the value of 83x94.

Solve:

83 x 94

83   (-17) =94-17=77   (both subtract diagonally)

94   (-6) =83-6=77
77x100=7700   (the result multiply with 100)
            +102
          =7802

Q. Find the value of 118x92.

Solve:

118 x 92
118   (+18) =92+18=110 (both subtract diagonally)
92   (-8) =118-8=110
110x100=11000   (the result multiply with 100)
            -144   +18x(-8)=-144

          =10856.

Q. Find the value of 95x103.

Solve:

95x 103
95   (-5) =103-5=98   (both subtract diagonally)
103   (+3) =95+3=98
98x100=9800   (the result multiply with 100)
            -15   +3x(-5)=--15

          =9785.

Q. Find the value of 103x107.

Solve:

103x 107
103   (+3) =107+3=110 (both subtract diagonally)
107   (+7) =103+7=110
110x100=11000   (the result multiply with 100)
            +21

          =11021.

TECHNIQUE

MULTIPLICATION OF COMPLIMENTARY NUMBERS

Complimentary numbers are the number which unit digits are same and the sum of the value of tenth digit is 10 i.e. 34 and 74

Q. Find the value of 34x74.

Solve by smart technique

Regular Method	Smart Technique

34x74
 	
  34
  <u>74</u>
 136
<u>238</u>
2516
	34x74
	Step I (3x7)+4= 25
	Step II 4x4 =16
	Hence result
	  25 /16
	=2516

Q. Find the value of 77x37.

Solve:
77x 37
= (7x3) +7 /7x7
= 28 /49
= 2849.

Q. Find the value of 75x35.

Solve:
75x 35
= (7x3) +5 /5x5
= 26 /25
= 2625.

Q. Find the value of 65x45.

Solve:

65x 45
= (6x4) +5 /5x5
= 29 /25
= 2925.

Q. Find the value of 86x26.

Solve:
86x26
= (8x2) +6 /6x6
= 22 /36
= 2236.

Q. Find the value of 38x78.

Solve:
38x78
= (7x3) +8 /8x8
= 29 /64
= 2964.

Q. Find the value of 43x63.

Solve:
43x63
= (4x6) +3 /3x3
= 27 /09
= 2709.

Q. Find the value of 66x46.

Solve:
66x46
= (6x4) +6 /6x6
= 30 /36
= 3036.

TECHNIQUE
MULTIPLICATION OF COMPLIMENTARY NUMBERS

Complimentary numbers are the number which tenth digits are same and the sum of the value of unit digit is 10 i.e. 43 and 47

Q. Find the value of 43x47.

Solve by smart technique

Regular Method	Smart Technique
43x47 43 <u> 47</u> 301 <u>172</u> 2021	43x47 **Step I** (4x5)= 20 (Multiply tenth digit with next higher one) **Step II** (3x7) =21(Multiply both unit digits) Hence result 20 /21 =2021

Q. Find the value of 68x62.

Solve:
68x62
= (6x7) /8x2
= 42 /16
= 4216.

Q. Find the value of 77x73.

Solve:
77x73
= (7x8) /7x3
= 56 /21
= 5621.

Q. Find the value of 59x51.

Solve:
59x51

= (5x6) /9x1
= 30 /09
= 3009.

Q. Find the value of 68x62.

Solve:
68x62
= (6x7) /8x2
= 42 /16
= 4216.

Q. Find the value of 64x66.

Solve:

Smart Technique	Alternate method
64x66 =(6x7) /4x6 = 42 /24 = 4224	64x66 = (65-1)x (65+1) = $65^2 - 1^2$ =4225-1 =4224

Q. Find the value of 93x97.

Solve:
93x97
= (9x10) /3x7
= 90 /21
= 9021.

TECHNIQUE#

MULTIPLICATION OF NUMBER WITH SPLIT AND MERGE METHOD

Q. Find the value of 12x23.

Solve by smart technique

Regular Method	Smart Technique
12x23 12 <u>23</u> 36 <u>24</u> 276	12X23 =12 x(20+3) =(12x20) +(12x3) = 240 +36 =276 OR (10+2)x23 =10x23) +(2x23) =230 +46 =276

Q. Find the value of 46x49.

Solve:

     46x49
= 46x(50-1)
=(46x50) –(46x1)
=2300-46
=2354.

Q. Find the value of 114x15.

Solve:

     114x(10+5)
= 114x(10+5)
=(114x10) +(114x5)
=1140+570
=1710.

Q. Find the value of 345x22.

Solve:

Smart Technique	Alternate method
345x22	345x22
=345x (20+2)	=345x (11+11)
= (345x20)+(345x2)	=(3/3x1+4 /4x1+5 /5x1)+(345x11)
= 6900+690	= 3795 +3795 **as discussed previous techinque**
=7590	=7590

Q. Find the value of 775x25.

Solve:

Smart Technique	Alternate method
775x25	775x25
= 775x(20+5)	= 775x100/4
=(775x20) +(775x5)	=19375.
=15500+3875	
=19375.	

Q. Find the value of 72x68.

Solve:

$$72 \times 68$$
$$= (70+2) \times (70-2)$$
$$= (70^2 - 2^2)$$
$$= 4900 - 4$$
$$= 4896.$$

Q. Find the value of 24x36.

Solve:

$$24 \times 36$$
$$= (30-6) \times (30+6)$$
$$= (30^2 - 6^2)$$
$$= 900 - 36$$
$$= 864.$$

TECHNIQUE

REVERSE TECHNIQUEto SOLVE LARGMULTIPLICATION

Q. Find the value of 2486x137.

(a)438402 (b)654023 (c)340582 (d)386052

 Solve by smart Technique:

2486x137

= (2+4+8+6)x (1+3+7)=20 x11 =(2+0) x (1+1)=2x2 =4

In the given option, we should find the same answer by applying above method. Out of the four option, one should have the correct number. Lets try

- (a) 438402=4+3+8+4+0+2=21=2+1=3 (not matched)
- (b) 564023=6+5+4+0+2+3=20=2+0=2 (not matched)
- (c) 340582=3+4+0+5+8+2=22=2+2=4 (matched)
- (d) 386052=3+8+6+0+5+2=26=2+6=8 (not matched)
  Hence correct answer is (c)

Q. Find the value of 3597x684.

(a)2460448 (b) 2640948 (c)2758038 (d)2460348

 Solve by smart Technique:

3597x648

= (3+5+9+7)x(6+4+8)=24 x18 =(2+4) x (1+8)=6x9 =54=5+4=9

In the given option, we should find the same answer by applying above method. Out of the four options, one should have the correct number. Lets try

- (a) 2460448=2+4+6+0+4+4+8=30=3+0=3 (not matched)
- (b) 2640948=2+6+4+0+9+4+8=31=3+1=4 (not matched)
- (c) 2758038=2+7+5+8+0+3+8=33=3+3=6 (not matched)
- (d) 2460348=2+4+6+0+3+4+8=27=2+7=9 (matched)
  Hence correct answer is (d)

SQUARE AND SQUARE ROOT

To find square or square root of any number is quite difficult in shortest possible time unless it is remembered. Again remembering such a large number is not that much easy unless a special technique. We cannot solve some mathematics without using this. So we have to do this practice without any excuse. For better understanding and easy memories, we use various special techniques. Lets some examples placed ...

Q. Find the square of 64

Solve:

```
        64x64
Step I      64      x 64
-4 +4
60      x 68  =  4080
Step II              4x4   =      16
                           = 4096
```

Q. Find the square of 85.

Solve.

 85x85

$= (8 \times 9) / (5 \times 5)$

 $= 7225$

Q. Find the square of 57.

Solve.

57^2

Step I: 25+7=32

Step II: 7^2=49

 =3249.

Q. Find the square root of 3249.

(a) 67 (b) 73 (c) 57 (d) 67 (e) 83

Solution: <u>Smart Technique</u>

Step I: $\overline{3249}$

$$\overline{3249} < \genfrac{}{}{0pt}{}{3}{7}$$

Step II:

Step III:

$\overline{32}\overline{49} < \dfrac{3}{7}$

5^2 30 6^2

Ans: 57

TECHNIQUE
BASIC RULE TO FIND THE SQUARE OF ANY NUMBER

Q. Find the square of 63.

Solve

Regular Method	Smart Technique
63^2 $= (60+3)^2$ $= 60^2 +2\times60\times3 +3^2$ $= 3600 +360 +9$ $= 3969$ Note: $(a+b)^2=a^2+2ab+b^2$ apply here to find the answer.	The basic smart technique to find the square of any number can be obtained two simple steps. The square of 63= 63x63 **Step I** convert the number into nearest zero unit digit number. i.e. $= (63-3)(63+3)$ $= 60 \times 66$ $= 3960$ **Step II** the unit digits of both have multiplied and add the result of step I i.e. 3x3 =9 =3960 +9 =3969

Q. Find the square of 47.

(a) 2209 (b)3039 (c) 3729 (d) none of these

Solve:

```
        47x47
Step I      47     x 47
+3        -3
50      x 44  =  2200
Step II           3x3  =     9
                    = 2209
```

Q.Find the square of 86.

(a)7236 (b) 7396 (c) 7426 (d) 77666 (e)none of these

Solve. 86x86

Step I   86   x 86

$$\frac{+4-4}{90} \quad x82 \ = \ 7380$$

Step II   4x4   =   16

     = 7396

Q. Find the square of 64

Solve:

    64x64

Step I   64   x 64

$$\frac{-4\ +4}{60} \quad x\ 68 \ = \ 4080$$

Step II   4x4   =   16

    = 4096

Q. Find the square of 39.

Solve:

    39x39

Step I   39   x 39

$$\frac{+1\ -1}{40} \quad x\ 38 \ = \ 1520$$

Step II   4x4   =   01

    = 1521.

Q. Find the square of 86.

Solve:

    86x86

Step I   86   x 86

$$\frac{+4\ -4}{90} \quad x\ 82 \ = \ 7380$$

Step II   4x4   =   16

$$= 7396$$

SMART TECHNIQUE FOR MEMORISING THE SQUARE OF A NUMBER

SQUARE TABLE

NUMBER	SQUARE	NUMBER	SQUARE	NUMBER	SQUARE	NUMBER	SQUARE	NUMBER	SQUARE
		50^2	2500			100^2	10000		
1^2	1	49	2401	51^2	2601	99	9801	101^2	10201
2	4	48	2304	52	2704	98	9604	102	10404
3	9	47	2209	53	2809	97	9409	103	10609
4	16	46	2116	54	2916	96	9216	104	10816
5	25	45	2025	55	3025	95	9025	105	11025
6	36	44	1936	56	3136	94	8836	106	11236
7	49	43	1849	57	3249	93	8649	107	11449
8	64	42	1764	58	3364	92	8464	108	11664
9	81	41	1681	59	3481	91	8281	109	11881
10	100	40	1600	60	3600	90	8100	110	12100
11	121	39	1521	61	3721	89	7921	111	12321
12	144	38	1444	62	3844	88	7744	112	12544
13	169	37	1369	63	3969	87	7569	113	12769
14	196	36	1296	64	4096	86	7396	114	12996
15	225	35	1225	65	4225	85	7225	115	13225
16	256	34	1156	66	4356	84	7056	116	13456
17	289	33	1089	67	4489	83	6889	117	13689
18	324	32	1024	68	4624	82	6724	118	13924
19	361	31	961	69	4761	81	6561	119	14161
20	400	30	900	70	4900	80	6400	120	14400
21	441	29	841	71	5041	79	6241	121	14641
22	484	28	784	72	5184	78	6084	122	14884
23	529	27	729	73	5329	77	5929	123	15129

24	576	26	676	74	5476	76	5776	124	15376
25	625			75	5625			125	15625

Follow the above Square task table

Memorizing the square of a number is very difficult task for a student. Again without memorizing the square of a number, they cannot solve the problem in given time. For such a difficult task, if we memorize some simple smart technique, you can easily remember up to 125 square numbers and it's remember for ever

Observe the above table, we find some similarity like:

1 to 24, 26 to 49, 51 to74, 76-99 I.e., the last two digits are same in sequential order. It will help you a bit to memorize the square of a number.

Again for any square of a number, widely used shortest application is

$$(36)^2 = (30+6)^2 = 30^2 + 2 \times 30 \times 6 + 6^2$$
$$= 900 + 360 + 36$$
$$= 1296$$

You can find out any square of a number by using this technique .But it's not that much easy what smart technique has going to explain.

THECHNIQUE

SQUARE OF A NUMBER HAVING UNIT DIGIT 5

Q.Find the value of 15^2

Solve by smart technique

We obtain the square of a number having unit digit 5, is very easy and without paper and pen, get the result with 2 simple steps. 15x15

<u>STEP 1</u>Multiply the tenth digit with the next higher digit i.e. 1x2=2
<u>STEP 2</u>Multiply the unit digits i.e., 5x5=25
Hence the result is 225

Q. Find the square of 65.

Solve.

65^2

$\qquad\qquad$ =65x65

Step1 $\qquad$ 6x7=42

Step2 $\qquad$ 5x5=25

$\qquad\qquad$ =4225

Q. Find the square of 85.

Solve.

85x85

= (8x9) /(5x5)

=7225

Q. Find the square of 105.
Solve.
105x105
= (10x11) /(5x5)=11025.

<u>TECHNIQUE #</u>

<u>SQUARE OF A NUMBER HAVING UNIT DIGIT 1</u>

Q. Find the square of 21.
<u>solve</u>
21x21
STEP-1 Multiply the tenth digit i.e. 2x2= 4

STEP-2 Add the tenth digit number and place after that i.e.2+2=4

STEP-3 Place unit digits at last i.e. (2x2) (2+2)1=441

Q. Find the square of 41.

Solve.

$$41 \times 41$$

Step1	4x4=16
Step2	4+4=8
Step3	1

$$16\ /08\ /01$$
$$=1681$$

Q. Find the square of 71.
Solve.

71x71
= (7x7) / (7+7) /1
= 49 /14 / 1

=5041   (note: when addition of tenth digit number is more than one digit, tenth digit to be added to the next number)

Q. Find the square of 101.
Solve.
 101X101
= (10x10) (10+10) 1
= 100 /20 /1
= 10201.

Q. Find the square of 131.
Solve.
131x131
= (13x13) (13+13) 1
= 169 /26 /1
=17161.

Q. Find the square of 121.

Solve.

121x121

= (12x12) (12+12) 1

= 144 /24 /1

=14641.

Q. Find the square of 111.

Solve.

111x111

= 11x11 /11+11 / 1

= 121 /22 /1

=12321.

TECHNIQUE

SQUARE OF A NUMBER HAVING UNIT DIGIT 0

Q. Find the square of 20.

Solve

  20x20

= 2x2 /0x0

=400.

Q. Find the square of 500

Solve

500x500

= 5x5 /0000

=250000.

Q. Find the square of 70.
Solve.

70x70

=(7x7)(0x0)

=4900.

Q. Find the square of 90.
Solve.

90x90

=9x9 /0x0

=8100.

Q. Find the square of 150.
Solve.

150x150

=15X15 /0x0

= 22500.

TECHNIQUE

SQUARE OF A NUMBER FROM 41-49

Q. Find the square of 47.

Solve by smart technique

The square of a number from 41-47 can obtained in the following 3 simple steps. After a few practice, you can obtain the result without using paper and pen. Such steps are:-

Step I: Subtract the number from 50 **i.e.50-47=03**
Step II: Subtract the result of step I from 25 **i.e.25-3= 22**
Step III: Square the result of step I i.e. $(03)^2$=09 and place after step II

Hence the square of 47= 2209

Q. Find the square of 48.

Solve.

48^2
Step I: 50-48=02
Step II: 25-02=23
Step III: $(02)^2$= 04
Hence the result is 2304.

Q. Find the square of 49.
Solve.
=50-49/$(01)^2$
=25-01/ $(01)^2$ (Try to calculate the value in mind and place the final result)
=2401.

Q. Find the square of 43.
Solve.

=50-43/ (07)^2
=25-07/ (07)^2=1849.

TECHNIQUE#
SQUARE OF A NUMBER FROM 51 TO 59

Q. Find the square of 54.

solve by smart technique

The square of a number from **51 to 59** can be obtained in simple **2** steps. It is very easy and obtains the result in few second. The steps are

Step I: Add 25 to the unit digit i.e. 25+4=29
Step II: Square the unit digit i.e. 4^2=16
$$=2916$$

Q. Find the square of 57.
Solve.
57^2
Step I: 25+7=32
Step II: 7^2=49
$$=3242.$$

Q. Find the square of 59.
Solve.
59^2
Step I: 25+9=34
Step II: 9^2=81
Hence the result is 3481.

Q. Find the square of 52.
Solve.
52^2
Step I: 25+2=27
Step II: 2^2=04
Hence the result is 2704.

Similarly other Numbers I.e.**53, 55, 56, 58** and **59** are following the same rule.

<u>TECHNIQUE #</u>
<u>SQUARE OF A NUMBER FROM 91 TO 99</u>

Q. Find the square of 97.

<u>**SOLVE BY SMART TECHNIQUE**</u>

The square of a number from **91 to 99** can be obtained by 3 simple steps which are easy to remember and obtain the result without using paper and pen. Such steps are;-

Step I: Subtract the number from 100 **i.e.100-97=03**
Step II: The result of step I multiply with 2 and subtract from 100 **i.e. 100-(3x2) =94**
Step III: Square the result of step 1 **i.e. $(03)^2$=09**
Hence the answer is **9409.**

Q. Find the square of 94.
Solve.
$$94^2$$
Step I: 100-94=06.
Step II: 100-(6x2) =88
Step III: $(06)^2$=36
=8836

Q. Find the square of 99.
Solve.
99^2
Step I: 100-99=1
Step II: 100-(1x2) =98
Step III: $(01)^2$= 01
Hence the result 9810.

Q. Find the square of 96.
Solve.
96^2
Step I: 100-96=4
Step II: 100-(4x2) =92

Step III: $(04)^2$= 16Hence the result 9216.

TECHNIQUE

THE SQUARE OF A NUMBER FROM 101 TO 109

Q. Find the square of 103

SOLVE BY SMART TECHNIQUE

To find the square of a number from 101 to 109 is very easy and can be obtained two simple step and with this method, you can obtain the result up to square of 125 also.

Let us learnthe step:

103^2

Step I: Add the unit digit with number **i.e. 103+3=106**

Step II: Square the unit digit **i.e. $(03)^2$= 09**

      Hence the resultis**10609**.

Q. Find the square of 105.
Solve.
105^2

Step I: 105+5=110

Step II: $(05)^2$= 025

Hence the result is 11025.

Q. Find the square of 113.
Solve.
113^2

Step I: 113+13=126

Step II: $(13)^2$= 169

Hence the result is 12769.

Q. Find the square of 106.

Solve.

106^2

$= 106 \times 106$

$= 106+6 \,/\, 6 \times 6$

$= 11236.$

Q. Find the value of $98^2 + 106^2$

(a) 20449 (b) 20840 (c) 28444 (d) 24804

Solution:

Smart Technique	Alternate Method
By applying unit digit method $98^2 = \ldots\ldots\ldots 4$ $106^2 = \ldots\ldots\ldots 6$ So unit digit become '0' The option 'b' only have the unit digit 0. Hence Answer is (b) 20840	$98^2 + 106^2$ $= 100 - 2 \times 2 \,/\, 2^2 + 106+6/6^2$ $= 9604 + 11236$ $= 20840$

Q. Find the value of $57^2 + 103^2 + 71^2$

(a) 19899 (b) 19989 (c) 18899 (d) 10899

Solution:

$57^2 + 103^2 + 71^2$

(Apply different technique for quick solving)

$=(25+7/7^2)+(103+3/3^2)+ (7\times7/7+7/1)$

$=3249 + 10609 + 5041$

$= 18899.$

TECHNIQUE

SQURE ROOT OF THE GIVEN PERFECT SQAURE NUMBER

Q. Find the square root of 3721.

(a) 69(b) 61 (c) 71 (d) 73 (e) none of these

Solution:

Regular method	Smart Technique
6 | 3721 | 61 36 12 | 121 121 0 Itis a long division method. Chance of error while calculating.	Square root of a perfect square number can be obtained in 3 simple steps without any possibility of error. Step I: Unit place of a given number is 1. Hence the square number ends in either 1 or 9. As $1^2 = 1$ and $9^2 = 81$ Step II: separate the number by grouping of two digit from unit digit side. i.e. 3721 Step III: the digit 37 is nearest square digit number 6 i.e. $6^2 = 36$ So the number became 61 or 69 To obtain correct answer, compare the number with nearest Zero digit or 5 digits number i.e. $60^2 = 3600$ $70^2 = 4900$ 3721 is nearest to 3600, so answer is 6.

Q. Find the square root of 1849.

   (a) 67 (b) 33 (c) 43 (d) 53 (e) none of these.

Solution: <u>Smart Technique</u>

Step I: $\overline{1849}$

Step II:
$$\overline{1849} < \frac{3}{7} >$$ unit digit

Step III:
$$\overline{18}\underset{\wedge}{}\overline{49} < \frac{3}{7}$$ (18 fall between 4^2 (16) and 5^2 (25)

4^2 20 5^2

=43   (When number is less than multiplication of both nearest square digit before 5 is used otherwise digit after 5 to be put)

Q. Find the square root of 6889?

(a) 87 (b) 83 (c) 73 (d) 79 (e) 93

Solution: <u>Smart Technique</u>

Step I: $\overline{6889}$

Step II:
$$\overline{6889} < \frac{3}{7}$$

Step III:
$$\overline{68}\underset{\wedge}{}\overline{89} < \frac{3}{7}$$

$8^2$72 9^2

Ans: 83

Q. Find the square root of 3249.

(a) 67 (b) 73 (c) 57 (d) 67 (e) 83

Solution: <u>Smart Technique</u>

Step I: $\overline{3249}$

Step II:
$$\overline{3249} < \frac{3}{7}$$

Step III:
$$\overline{32}\underset{V}{}\overline{49} < \frac{3}{7}$$

5^2 30 6^2

Ans: 57

Q. Find the square root of 19044.

(a) 136 (b) 138 (c) 128 (d) 132 (e) 142

Solution:<u>Smart Technique</u>

Step I: $\overline{19044}$

Step II:
$$\overline{19044} < \frac{2}{8}$$

$$\overline{190}\underset{V}{}\overline{44} < \frac{2}{8}$$

Step III:
$$13^2 \ 182 \ \ 14^2$$

Ans: 138.

Q. Find the square root of 3364.

(a) 48 (b) 52 (c) 58 (d) 62

Solution:<u>Smart Technique</u>

Step I: $\overline{3364}$

Step II:
$$\overline{3364} < \frac{2}{8}$$

$$\overline{33}\underset{V}{}\overline{64} < \frac{2}{8}$$

Step III:
$$5^2 306^2$$

Ans: 58.

Q. Find the square root of 7524.

(a) 87 (b) 83 (c) 73 (d) 79 (e) 93

Solution:<u>Smart Technique</u>

Step I: $\overline{7524}$

Step II:
$$\overline{7524} < \frac{2}{8}$$

$$\overset{\overline{75}\underline{24}}{\underset{\vee}{}} < \frac{2}{8}$$

Step III:

8^2 72 9^2

Ans: 88.

Q. Find the square root of 15129.

(a) 121 (b) 127 (c) 123 (d) 133

Solution: <u>Smart Technique</u>

Step I: $\overline{15129}$

Step II:
$$\overline{15129} < \frac{3}{7}$$

$$\overset{\overline{151}\underline{29}}{\underset{\wedge}{}} < \frac{3}{7}$$

Step III:

12^2 155 13^2

Ans: 123.

Q. Find the square root of 5329.

(a) 87 (b) 83 (c) 73 (d) 79 (e) 93

Solution: <u>Smart Technique</u>

Step I: $\overline{5329}$

Step II:
$$\overline{5329} < \frac{3}{7}$$

$$\overset{\overline{53}\underline{29}}{\underset{\vee}{}} < \frac{3}{7}$$

Step III:

7^2 568^2

Ans: 73.

TECHNIQUE

CUBE ROOT OF THE GIVEN PERFECT CUBE

Q. Find the cube root of 328509.

(a) 63 (b) 61 (c) 69 (d) 83

Solution:

Regular Method	Smart Technique

<table>
<tr><td>

3|328509
3|109503
3|36501
23|12167
23|529
23

= 3 x 23
= 69

</td><td>

Cube root of a perfect cube can be obtained in two simple steps in few second.

Step I: Unit place of the given number (328509) is 9. Hence cube of 9 is 729 i.e. unit digit is 9.

Step II: Leave the last three digits of the number i.e. $\overline{509}$ and the remaining 3 digit number i.e. 328 is highest perfect cube of less than 328 is 216 be 6^3. Hence the tenth place of the cube root is 6. Hence Answer is 69.

</td></tr>
</table>

Q. Find the cube root of 19683?

(a) 37 (b) 27 (c) 73 (d) 28 (e) 33

Solution: <u>Smart Technique</u>

Step I: $\overline{19\,683}$

Step II: $\overline{19}$ $\overline{683}$ (Unit digit is 3, 7^3 is 343 so the unit digit is taken as 7)

   $2^3 = 8$ $3^3 = 27$ (19 is the cube between 2 and 3 so use 2 as the cube root)

Hence answer is 27

Q. Find the cube root of 79507.

(a) 41 (b) 43 (c) 53 (d) 47 (e) 53

Solution: <u>Smart Technique</u>

Step I: $\overline{79507}$
Step II: $\overline{79507}$

   $4^3 = 64$ $5^3 = 125$ 3^3 (27)
   Ans. 43.

Q. Find the cube root of 970299.

(a) 89 (b) 99 (c) 999 (d) 109

Solution: <u>Smart Technique</u>

Step I: $\overline{970299}$
Step II: $\overline{970299}$
$10^3 = 1000$ $9^3 = 729$ $9^3 = 729$ (Unit digit 9)
Hence Ans is 99.

Q. find the cube root of 614125.

(a) 85 (b) 95 (c) 105 (d) 125

Solution: <u>Smart Technique</u>

Step I: $\overline{614125}$
Step II: $\overline{614}$ $\overline{125}$(Unit digit 5)$8^3 = 812$ $9^3 = 729$ $5^3 = 125$
Hence answer is 85.

Q. Find the cube root of 1728.

(a) 12 (b) 08 (c) 22 (d) 16 (e) none of these

Solution: <u>Smart Technique</u>

Step I: $\overline{1728}$
Step II: $\overline{1728}$
        $1^3 = 1$ $2^3 = 8$
        Hence answer is 12.

<u>TECHNIQUE#</u>
<u>SMART TECHNIQUE FOR DIVISION</u>

Q. 5378216 ÷ 4

Solution: <u>Smart Technique</u>

Smart Technique	Rule I: Single Step Division

4) $5_1 3_1 7_1 8_2 2_2 1_1 6 \vert$ 1344554	The following steps should be observed Step I: Write the number in horizontal way with leaving same space between the numbers. Step II: Divide the number with divisor. Place the quinteton bottom and reminder should be write before the next number as shown above.

Q. 83246789 ÷ 9

Solution:<u>Smart Technique</u>

4) $8\ 3_2 2_4 4_8 6_5 7_3 8_2 9 \vert$

$9249643\dfrac{2}{9}$

Q. 897 ÷ 3

Solution:

Smart Technique	Rule II: Spilt / Merge Method
$897 \div 3$ => $(900\text{-}3) \div 3$ => $900 \div 3 - 3 \div 3$ = 300-1 = 299	The following steps should be observed Step I: Spilt / merge the number with zero unit digit nos. Step II: Division become easy and do if on memory write the result only.

Q. 756 ÷ 4

Solution:<u>Smart Technique</u>

$756 \div 4$

$(800 - 44) \div 4$

$$= \frac{800}{4} - \frac{44}{4}$$

$$= 200 - 11$$

$$= 189.$$

Q. 2376÷ 8

Solution: <u>Smart Technique</u>

$2376 \div 8$

$= (2400 - 24) \div 8$

$$= \frac{2400}{8} - \frac{24}{8}$$

$= 300 - 3$

$= 297$

Q. 135 ÷ 3

Solution:

Smart Technique	**Alternate Method**
$(150 - 15) \div 3$	$135 \div 3$
$= \dfrac{150}{3} - \dfrac{15}{3}$	$= (120 + 15) \div 3$
$= 50 - 5 = 45$	$= \dfrac{120}{3} + \dfrac{15}{3}$
	$= 40 + 5 = 45$

Q. 285 ÷ 5

Solution:

Smart Technique	**Alternate Method**
$(150 - 15) \div 3$	$135 \div 3$
$= \dfrac{150}{3} - \dfrac{15}{3}$	$= (120 + 15) \div 3$
	$= \dfrac{120}{3} + \dfrac{15}{3}$

Q. 345 ÷ 3

Solution:

$= 50 - 5 = 45$

Smart Technique	Rule III: Grouping Method
$(3)(45) \div 3$ $= 115$	Step I: Make the number into groups. Step II: Divide independent by in each group.

Q. $485 \div 4$

Solution:

Q. $485 \div 4$

solution

$(4) (8) (5) \div 4$

$121\dfrac{1}{4}$ (Note: Reminder to make fraction at the end)

Q. $432 \div 36$

Solution:

Smart Technique	**Alternate Method**
$(4) (32) \div 4 \times 3 \times 3$	$432 \div 36$
$= 108 \div 3 \times 3$	$= 432 \div 2 \times 2 \times 9$
$= 36 \div 3$	$= 216 \div 2 \times 9$
$= 12$	$= 108 \div 9$
	$= 12$

Q. $984 \div 8$

Solution:

Smart Technique	**Alternate Method**
$984 \div 8$	$984 \div 8$
$= 984 \div 2 \times 2 \times 2$	$= (1000 - 16) \div 8$
$= 492 \div 2 \times 2$	$= 125 - 2$
$= 123$	$= 123$

Q. Find the value of $73435 \div 5 + 8436 \div 4 + 378 \div 9$

Solution:

$7_23_34_43_35 \div 5 + 8436 \div 4\,387 \div 9$

$= 14687 + 2109 + 43$

$= 16839.$

Q. Find the value of $2496 \div 4 + 8775 \div 15 + 384 \div 24$

Solution:

$2496 \div 4 + 8775 \div 15 + 384 \div 24$

$= (2500 - 4) \div 4 + \dfrac{8_27_07_15}{3 \, x \, 5} + \dfrac{3\,8_24}{6 \, x \, 4}$

$= (625 - 1) + \dfrac{29_425}{5} + \dfrac{64}{4}$

$= 624 + 585 + 16$

$= 1275.$

<u>TECHNIQUE #</u>

SMART TECHNIQUE FOR ADDITION OF LARGE NUMBER

Q. Find the value of

769283 + 34872 + 863428 + 97028 + 2314 + 167102

(a) 1934307 (b) 1934037 (c) 1934027 (d) 1984026

Solution: Smart Technique

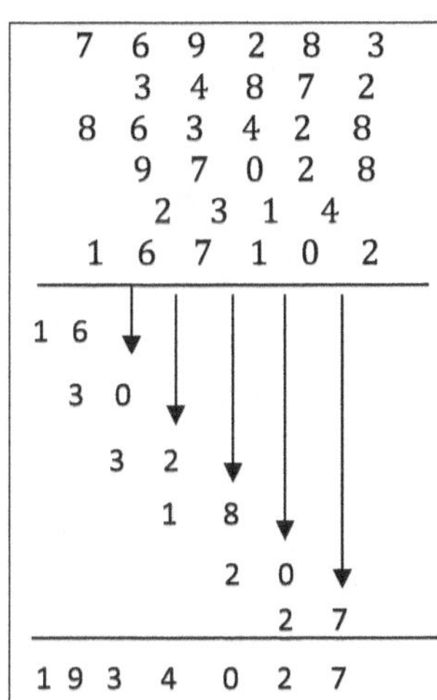

Such a large number of addition is to take much time to get answer and also have the chance of error. But in the Smart Technique, it is quite easy and no chance of error, for this follow the rules.

Step I: Write the number vertically according to their place value.
Step II: Start calculate from left place value digit.
Step III: Write the result according as shown above.
Step IV: Calculate all number and get answer.

Q. Find the value of
582346 + 127342 + 67285 + 392463

(a) 1169436 (b) 6191446 (c) 369142 (d) 1693246

Solution: Smart Technique

<table>
<tr>
<td>

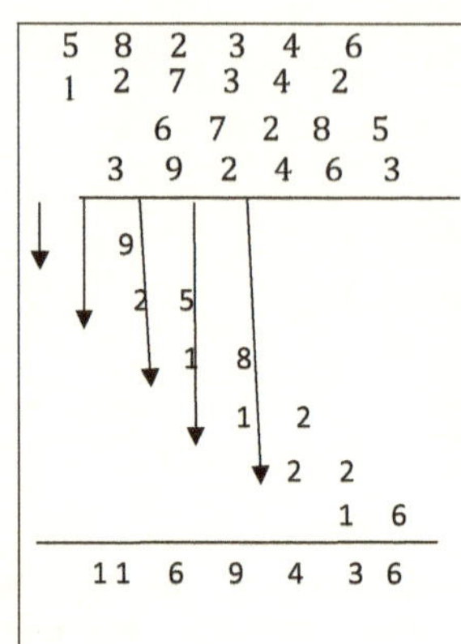

</td>
<td>

<u>For checking correctness or get result by option</u>

Step I: Add all digit horizontally and divide by 9. The reminder be the unit digit.

Step II: Add all rows unit digit and the result is match with obtained result unit digit. If equal, the answer is correct.

(Note: Without doing calculation, if follow the reverse technique on the above, you can get result.)

</td>
</tr>
</table>

Q. Find the value of

$32196 + 2343 + 72986 + 3724 + 81639$

Solution

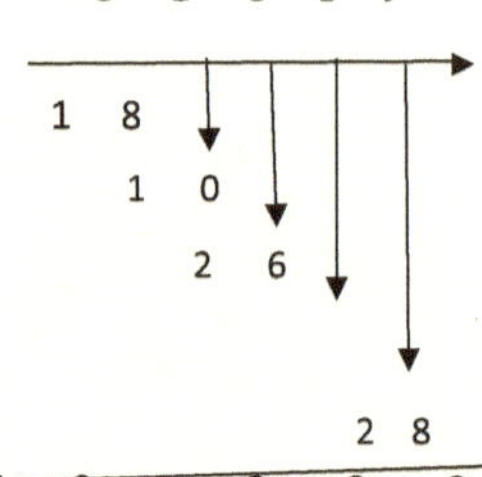

Q. Find the value

23409 + 86210 + 63245 + 19213

Solution: <u>Smart Technique</u>

Add the numbers without writing in vertical way

<pre>
          1 7
             2   1
                1   0
                   0   6
                      1   7
          ____
          1 9   2   0   7   7
</pre>

Q. Find the Value   of

645690 + 671234 + 235106 + 359127

Solution: <u>Smart Technique</u>

<pre>
       1 7
          1 2 0
             1   0
                1 4
                   1 7
       ____
       1 9 1 1 1 5 7
</pre>

<u>NUMBER SYSTEM</u>

Number system is an important part of arithmetic. It is also an important portion of all type of competitive examination. Sound knowledge of number system is very important for all students. Use different mathematical formula, its correct application and different smart techniques to solve in shortest possible time are important of this chapter. Let some synopsis for number system

1. The standard formula for the sum of the square of the number is

$$1^2 + 2^2 + 3^2 \ldots\ldots + n^2 = \frac{n(n + 1)(2n + 1)}{6}$$

2. Standard rule for sum of the average of even number from 1 to n is $\dfrac{n + 2}{2}$

3. Geometric mean of x, y $= \sqrt{xy}$

4. The sum of the cube of first 'n' natural number is

$$\left[\frac{n(n + 1)}{2}\right]^2$$

5. Lets

$$\sqrt{X \pm \sqrt{X \pm \sqrt{X \pm \ldots}}}$$

    Suppose a and b are the two consecutive factors of x(b > a)

    Rule I: If +ve sign in the expression, the answer is 'b'.

    Rule II: If –ve sign in the expression, the answer is 'a' (The Smaller Factor)

6. If root goes up to ∞ , the result of the sum is the number it self

i.e. $\sqrt{7 + \sqrt{7 + \sqrt{7 + \sqrt{7 + \ldots}}}}_{\infty} = 7$

7. $a^n + b^n$ is exactly divisible by (a + b) when 'n' is odd.

8. $a^n - b^n$ is exactly divisible by both (a + b) and (a − b) when 'n' value is even.

TECHNIQUE

NUMBER SYSTEM RELATED SUM SOLVED BY SMART TECHNIQUE

Q. The sum $11^2 + 12^2 + \ldots\ldots\ldots + 21^2 =$?

    (a) 2926 (b) 3017 (c) 3215 (d) 3311

Solution:

The standard formula for the sum of the square of the number is

$$1^2 + 2^2 + 3^2 .... + n^2 = \frac{n(n+1)(2n+1)}{6}$$

$$11^2 + 12^2 + ... + 21^2 = (1^2 + 2^2 + 3^2 .... + 21^2) - (1^2 + 2^2 + 3^2 .... + 10^2)$$

$$= \frac{21(21+1)(42+1)}{6} - \frac{10(10+1)(20+1)}{6}$$

$$= \frac{21 \; X \; 22 \; X \; 43}{6} - \frac{10 \; X \; 11 \; xX21}{6}$$

$$= 3311 - 385 = 2926$$

Q. $\dfrac{2.3^3 - 0.027}{(2.3)^2 + 0.69 + 0.09}$

(a) 0 (b) 2.0 (c) 1.6 (d) 3.4

Solution: $\dfrac{2.3^3 - 0.027}{(2.3)^2 + 0.69 + 0.09}$

If we change into $a^3 - b^3 = (a - b)(a^2 + ab + b^2)$

Then $\dfrac{(2.3)^3 - (0.3)^3}{(2.3)^2 + 0.69 + 0.09}$

$$= \frac{(2.3 - 0.3)(2.3)^2 + 0.69 + 0.09}{(2.3)^2 + 0.69 + 0.09}$$

$$= 2$$

Q. The average of the even number from 1 to 30 is

(a) 15 (b) 17 (c) 19 (d) 16

Solution:

Standard rule for sum of the average of even number from 1 to n is $\dfrac{n+2}{2}$

Hence the average $= \dfrac{30+2}{2}$

$= 16$

Q. Find the average of the first 97 natural number

(a) 47 (b) 37 (c) 48 (d) 49

Solution: Smart Technique

Standard rule

The sum of the average 1 to n natural number $= \dfrac{n+1}{2}$

Hence the average of 1 to 97 $= \dfrac{97+1}{2}$

$= 49.$

Q. The geometric mean of 4, 5, 20 and 25 is

(a) 1000 (b) 100 (c) 10 (d) none of these

Solution: Standard Rule

Geometric mean of x, y $= \sqrt{xy}$

Hence geometric of 4, 5, 20, 25 $= \sqrt[4]{4,\, 5,\, 20,\, 25}$

$= \sqrt[4]{2 \times 2 \times 5 \times 5 \times 2 \times 2 \times 5 \times 5}$

$= 2 \times 5$

$= 10$

Q. Find the sum of the $1^3 + 2^3 + 3^3 \ldots\ldots + 12^3$

(a) 3564 (b) 6884 (c) 6084 (d) 7804

Solution:

The sum of the cube of first 'n' natural number is

$$\left[\frac{n(n+1)}{2}\right]^2$$

Acc.to the formula $\left[\frac{12(12+1)}{2}\right]^2$

$$= \left[\frac{12 \times 13}{2}\right]^2 = (6 \times 13)^2$$

$$= (78)^2 = 6084.$$

Q. The product of two numbers is $15\frac{3}{16}$ and their quotient is 3. The smaller number is

(a) $\frac{3}{4}$ **(b)** $\frac{15}{2}$ **(c)** $\frac{9}{4}$ **(d) 3**

Solution: Let the two number be x and y.

$$xy = 15\frac{3}{16}$$

$$xy = \frac{243}{16} \quad \ldots\ldots\ldots \text{(I)}$$

$$\frac{x}{y} = 3$$

$$\Rightarrow x = 3y \ldots\ldots \text{(II)}$$

If we put the value of x in equation 1.

$$3y^2 = \frac{243}{16}$$

$$y^2 = \frac{81}{16}$$

$$y = \frac{9}{4}$$

As per equation 1.

$$xy = \frac{243}{16}$$

$$x\frac{9}{4} = \frac{243}{16}$$

$$x = \frac{27}{4}$$

Hence the smallest number is $\frac{9}{4}$.

Q. A person distribute some sweets among four friends A, B, C and D in the ratio $\frac{1}{3}$: $\frac{1}{4}$: $\frac{1}{5}$: $\frac{1}{6}$. What is the minimum number of sweets that the person should have?

(a) 57 (b) 65 (c) 75 (d) 47

Solution:

LCM of 3, 4, 5, and 6 is 60

A's ratio $\frac{1}{3} = \frac{20}{60}$

B's ratio $\frac{1}{4} = \frac{15}{60}$

C's ratio $\dfrac{1}{5} = \dfrac{12}{60}$

D's ratio $\dfrac{1}{6} = \dfrac{10}{60}$

Hence the minimum of the sweets is $20 + 15 + 12 + 10 = 57$

Q. If $1^3 + 2^3 + 3^3 \ldots\ldots + 10^3 = 3025$, then the value of $2^3 + 4^3 + 6^3 \ldots\ldots + 20^3$

    (a) 6050 (b) 9075 (c) 12100 (d) 24200 (e) 27200

Solution:

$2^3 + 4^3 + 6^3 \ldots\ldots + 20^3$ (Note: $1^3 + 2^3 + 3^3 \ldots\ldots + n^3 = \left[\dfrac{n(n+1)}{2}\right]^2$)

$= 2^3(1^3 + 2^3 + 3^3 \ldots\ldots + 10^3) = 2^3 \times 3025 = 8 \times 3025 = 24200$

Q. Two numbers are 30% and 40% more than the third number respectively. The first number is x% of the second. The value of x is

    (a) $105\dfrac{2}{13}$ (b) 140 (c) $405\dfrac{5}{7}$ (d) $92\dfrac{6}{7}$ (e) $92\dfrac{8}{3}$

Solution:

    Let the number be 100

1st number is 130

2nd number is 140

$130 = x\%$ of 140

$\dfrac{x}{100} X\ 140 = 130$

$x = \dfrac{1300}{14}$

$x = 92\dfrac{6}{7}.$

Q. 15 litters of mixture contain alcohol and water in the ratio 1:4. It 3 litters of water is mixed in it, the percentage of alcohol in the new mixture will be

(a) 15 (b) $16\dfrac{2}{3}$ (c) 17 (d) $18\dfrac{1}{2}$ (e) $20\dfrac{1}{2}$

Solution:

$$\frac{Alcohol}{Water} = \frac{x}{4x} = \frac{3}{12}$$

3ltrs of water added, new ratio

$$\frac{Alcohol}{Water} = \frac{3}{12 + 3} = \frac{3}{15}$$

Alcohol % $= \dfrac{\frac{3}{18} X\,100}{}$

$$= \frac{\frac{100}{6}}{}$$

$$= 16\frac{2}{3}\,\%.$$

Q. 2.5% of 478 is what percent of 50

(a)23.4 (b) 23.9 (c) 23.1 (d) 23.2

Solution:

Let   2.5% of 478 = x % of 50

$$\frac{x}{2.5} = \frac{478}{50}$$

$$x = \frac{478}{50} \times \frac{2.5}{10} = 23.9$$

(Always use split method to get answer instead of multiplying)

Q. $\sqrt{236 - \sqrt{400 \, X \, \sqrt{20 - \sqrt{20 - \sqrt{20 - \sqrt{20 \ldots \ldots \ldots \infty}}}}}}$ **is**

(a) 10 (b) 12 (c) 14 (d) 16

Solution:

$= \sqrt{236 - \sqrt{400 \, X \, 4}}$

$= \sqrt{236 - 40}$ (As you know $\sqrt{20 - \sqrt{20 - \sqrt{20 - \sqrt{20 \ldots \ldots \ldots \infty}}}} = 4$)

$= \sqrt{196} = 14.$

Q. if x $= (2\frac{1}{100})^3 + (0.99)^3 + 3(2\frac{1}{100})^2 .(0.99) + 3(2\frac{1}{100}) \, (0.99)^2$

Then the value of 'x'

(a) 9 (b) 25 (c) 5.00² (d) 27 (e) $\dfrac{27}{5}$

Solution: <u>Smart Technique</u>

$X = (2\frac{1}{100})^3 + (0.99)^3 + 3 \, (2\frac{1}{100})^2(0.99) + 3 \, (2\frac{1}{100}) \, (0.99)^2$

= it follow the formula of $(a+b)^3 = a^3 + b^3 + 3a^2b + 3ab^2$

$= \{(2\frac{1}{100}) + 0.99\}_3$

$= (\frac{201}{100} + 0.99)^3$

$$=(2.01+0.99)^3$$

$$= 3^3 = 27.$$

Q. The 25th terms of these series

2, 5, 10, 17, 26 ….. is

(a) 525 (b) 626 (c) 323 (d)424 (e) 759

Solution: Smart Technology

n^{th} term $= n^2 + 1$

25th term $= 25^2 + 1$
$$= 625 + 1$$
$$= 626.$$

Q. The average of the first nine integer multiple of 3 is

(a) 12 (b) 15 (c)18 (d)21

Solution:

Regular method	Alternate method
Numbers are 3, 6, 9, 12…… Arithmetic progression, if a = 3 n = 9 d = 3 n^{th} term $= \dfrac{n}{2}\{2a + (n-1)d\}$ $= \dfrac{9}{2}\{2X3 + (9-1)3\}$ $= \dfrac{9}{2}(6 + 8X3)$ $= 9 \times 15$ Average of the number $= \dfrac{9 X 15}{9}$ $\qquad = 15$	Numbers are 3, 6, 12…… $= 3(1 + 2 + 3 +… 9)$ Average of the numbers $= \dfrac{3}{9} X \dfrac{9 X 10}{2}$ $= 15$ (Note: Sum of n natural number $\dfrac{n(n+1)}{2}$ Average of n natural number $\dfrac{(n+1)}{2}$)

Q. if a and b are two distinct natural numbers, which one of the following condition is true.

(a) $\sqrt{a+b}$ (b) $\sqrt{a}+\sqrt{b}$ (c) $\sqrt{a+b} > \sqrt{a}+\sqrt{b}$ (c) $\sqrt{a+b} < \sqrt{a}+\sqrt{b}$

(d) ab = 1

Solution:

Regular method	Smart Technique
By seeing the action, $\sqrt{a+b} = (\sqrt{a+b})^2 = a+b$ L.H.S $\sqrt{a}+\sqrt{b} = (\sqrt{a}+\sqrt{b})^2 = a+b+2\sqrt{a}+\sqrt{b}$ R.H.S Hence L.H.S < R.H.S $\sqrt{a+b} < \sqrt{a}+\sqrt{b}$ $(a = b \neq 0)$	Lets two natural number 9 & 16 $\sqrt{a+b} = \sqrt{a+b} = \sqrt{25} = 5$ $\sqrt{9}+\sqrt{16} = 3+4 = 7$ $5 < 7$ $\sqrt{a+b} < \sqrt{a}+\sqrt{b}$

Q. The arithmetic mean (Average) of first 10 whole numbersis

    (a) 5 (b) 4 (c) 5.5 (d) 4.5

Solution:

The arithmetic mean of first 10 whole number = $\dfrac{10 \times 11}{2}$

Average of first 10 whole number = $\dfrac{55}{10} = 5.5$.

Q. if the Sum of two numbers, one of which is $\dfrac{2}{5}$ times the other is 50. Then the numbers are:

(a) $\dfrac{115}{7}, \dfrac{235}{7}$ (b) $\dfrac{150}{7}, \dfrac{200}{7}$ (c) $\dfrac{240}{7}, \dfrac{110}{7}$ (d) $\dfrac{250}{7}, \dfrac{100}{7}$

Solution:

Let one of the number is x.

Other number is $\dfrac{2x}{5}$

As per the question $x + \dfrac{2x}{5} = 50$

$$7x = 250$$

$$x = \dfrac{250}{7}$$

Other number $= \dfrac{2x}{5} = \dfrac{2}{5} x \dfrac{250}{7}$

Two numbers are $\dfrac{250}{7}, \dfrac{100}{7}$.

Q. The ratio of expenditure to saving is 3:2. If the income increased by 15% and saving increase by 6%, then what percentage does expenditure increase?

(a) 16% (b) 21% (c) 14% (d) 12.5% (e) 15%

Solution:

Let the expenditure be 3x Saving be 2x Income be 5x Now, new income $= 5x \times \dfrac{115}{100} = 5.75x$ New saving $= 2x \times \dfrac{106}{100} = 2.12x$ New Exp. $= 5.75x - 2.12x = 3.63x$ % increase in Exp. $= \dfrac{3.63x - 3x}{3x} \times 100$	Alternate Method Let the expenditure be 300 Saving be 200 Income be 500 Now new income 15% of 500 = 575 New saving 6% of 200 = 212 New Exp. = 575 – 212 = 363 % increase in Exp. $= \dfrac{363 - 300}{300} \times 100$ $= \dfrac{63}{300} \times 100$ $= 21\%$

= 21%	(Note: In % calculation, always assume the value as 100 instead of x to solve easily.)

TECHNIQUE

FIND THE VALUE OF X FROM SQUARE ROOT / CUBE

Q. Find the value of $\sqrt{12 + \sqrt{12 + \sqrt{12 + \ldots}}}$

    (a) 12 (b) 3 (c) 4 (d) 5 (e) 6

Solution.

Regular Method	Alternate Method
Let x = $\sqrt{12 + \sqrt{12 + \sqrt{12 + \ldots}}}$ Squaring both sides, $x^2 = 12 + x$ => $x^2 - x - 12 = 0$ => $x^2 - 4x + 3x - 12 = 0$ => $x(x - 4) + 3(x - 4) = 0$ => $(x - 4)(x + 3) = 0$ x = 4 because x ≠ -3 Hence answer is 4.	Lets $\sqrt{X \pm \sqrt{X \pm \sqrt{X \pm \ldots}}}$ Suppose a and b are the two consecutive factors of x(b > a) Rule I: If +ve sign in the expression, the answer is 'b'. Rule II: If −ve sign in the expression, the answer is 'a' (The Smaller Factor) $\sqrt{12 + \sqrt{12 + \sqrt{12 + \ldots}}}$ Two consecutive factor of 12 are 3 and 4 Hence answer is 4 (The Bigger Factor)

Q. $\sqrt{20 - \sqrt{20 - \sqrt{20 - \ldots}}}$ **is equal to**

    (a) 16 (b) 5 (c) 4 (d) 20 (e) None of these

Solution:

If we apply the above formula, the two consecutive factors of 20 are 4 and 5 and –ve sign in the expression.

Hence answer is 4 (the smaller factor)

Q. $\sqrt{6 + \sqrt{6 + \sqrt{6 + \cdots}}}$ **is equal to**

(a) 2 (b) 3 (c) 4 (d) 5 (e) $3^{\frac{1}{2}}$

Solution:

In the above expression, have +ve sign and two consecutive factors of 6 is 2 and 3 If the condition are fulfilled as per Rule I.

The answer is 3 (the bigger factor)

Q. $\sqrt{7 + \sqrt{7 + \sqrt{7 + \sqrt{7 + \cdots \infty}}}}$ **is equal to**

(a) 7 (b) $\dfrac{7}{2}$ (c) $7\dfrac{1}{2}$ (d) 49 (e) **None of the above.**

Solution:

Regular Method	Smart Technique
Lets x= $\sqrt{7 + \sqrt{7 + \sqrt{7 + \sqrt{7 + \cdots \infty}}}}$ $x^2 = 7x$ $\Rightarrow x^2 - 7x = 0$ $\Rightarrow x(x - 7) = 0$ $\Rightarrow x = 7$	In smart Technique: if root goes up to ∞, the result of the sum is the number it self i.e. $\sqrt{7 + \sqrt{7 + \sqrt{7 + \sqrt{7 + \cdots \infty}}}}$ $= 7$

Q. If $\sqrt{7 + \sqrt{7 + \sqrt{7 + \sqrt{7 + \cdots\infty}}}} = (343)^{y-1}$, **then y is equal to**

(a) $\dfrac{2}{3}$ (b) 1 (c) $\dfrac{4}{3}$ (d) $\dfrac{3}{4}$ (e) **None of the above.**

Solution:

$\sqrt{7 + \sqrt{7 + \sqrt{7 + \sqrt{7 + \cdots\infty}}}} = (343)^{y-1}$ (As per the above solution

$\sqrt{7 + \sqrt{7 + \sqrt{7 + \sqrt{7 + \cdots}}}} = 7$)

$7^1 = (7)^{3(y-1)}$

$1 = 3y - 3$

$\Rightarrow 3y = 4$

$\Rightarrow y = \dfrac{4}{3}$

Q. Find the value of

$\sqrt{30 + \sqrt{30 + \sqrt{30\ldots}}}$

(a) 5 (b) $3\sqrt{10}$ (c) 6 (d) 7 (e) **None of these**

Solution:

If we apply smart technique for the above condition sum

i.e. $\sqrt{30 + \sqrt{30 + \sqrt{30\ldots}}} = 6$

Two consecutive factors of 30 are 5and 6, the larger one is 6.

Hence the answer is 6.

Q. Find the value of

$$\sqrt{72 - \sqrt{72 - \sqrt{72}\ldots}}$$

(a) 8 (b) (c) 12 (d) 6 (e) None of these

Solution:

If we apply Smart technique for the above condition

Sum, i.e. $\sqrt{72 - \sqrt{72 - \sqrt{72}\ldots}} = 8$

$\therefore$ The consecutive factors of 72 are 8 and 9. Through sign is $-$ve, the smaller factor become the answer.

Hence answer is 8.

Q. If $(3x - 2y) : (2x + 3y) = 5 : 6$, then one of the value of $\left(\dfrac{\sqrt[3]{X} + \sqrt[3]{Y}}{\sqrt[3]{X} - \sqrt[3]{Y}}\right)^2$ is

(a) $\dfrac{1}{25}$ (b) 25 (c) $\dfrac{1}{5}$ (d) 5

Solution:

$$\frac{3x - 2y}{2x + 3y} = \frac{5}{6}$$

$\Rightarrow 6(3x - 2y) = 5(2x + 3y)$

$\Rightarrow 18x - 12y = 10x + 15y$

$\Rightarrow 8x = 27y$

$\Rightarrow \dfrac{x}{y} = \dfrac{27}{8}$ Consider $x = 27$ and $y = 8$

Put the value accordingly

$$\left(\frac{\sqrt[3]{X}+\sqrt[3]{Y}}{\sqrt[3]{X}-\sqrt[3]{Y}}\right)^2 = \left(\frac{\sqrt[3]{27}+\sqrt[3]{8}}{\sqrt[3]{27}-\sqrt[3]{8}}\right)^2$$

$$=\left(\frac{3+2}{3-2}\right)^2$$

$$=25.$$

Q. The value of $(\sqrt{5}+\sqrt{3})\left[\dfrac{3\sqrt{3}}{(\sqrt{5}+\sqrt{2})}-\dfrac{\sqrt{5}}{(\sqrt{3}+\sqrt{2})}\right]$

Solution:

$$(\sqrt{5}+\sqrt{3})\left[\frac{3\sqrt{3}(\sqrt{5}-\sqrt{2})}{(\sqrt{5}+\sqrt{2})(\sqrt{5}-\sqrt{2})}-\frac{\sqrt{5}(\sqrt{3}-\sqrt{2})}{(\sqrt{3}+\sqrt{2})(\sqrt{3}-\sqrt{2})}\right]$$

$$=(\sqrt{5}+\sqrt{3})\left[\frac{3\sqrt{3}(\sqrt{5}-\sqrt{2})}{3}-\frac{\sqrt{5}(\sqrt{3}-\sqrt{2})}{1}\right]$$

$$=(\sqrt{5}+\sqrt{3})\{(\sqrt{15}+\sqrt{6})-(\sqrt{15}+\sqrt{10})\}$$

$$=(\sqrt{5}+\sqrt{3})(\sqrt{15}-\sqrt{6}-\sqrt{15}+\sqrt{10})$$

$$=(\sqrt{5}+\sqrt{3})(\sqrt{10}-\sqrt{6})$$

$$=\sqrt{50}+\sqrt{30}+\sqrt{30}-\sqrt{18}$$

$$=5\sqrt{2}+3\sqrt{2}$$

$$=2\sqrt{20}.$$

TECHNIQUE

FIND THE UNIT DIGIT OF THE NUMBER OF A GIVEN PRODUCT

Q. Find the unit place of $(134647)^{553}$.

(a) 7 (b) 9 (c) 1 (d) 0 (e) None of these

Solution: Smart Technique

Such a large digit power is very difficult to obtain until and unless we made a standard formula to solve this sum, we have to remember simple steps

Step I: power value of the number divided by 4, the reminder become the new poweri.e $553 \div 4$ gives 1 as a reminder, the new power of the sum.

Step II: The unit digit of base number become the new base number of the obtained power in above step.   i.e. $(134647)^{553} = (*****7)^1 = *****7^1 = ******7$

Hence the unit place digit is 7.

Q. Which is the unit digit in the expansion of $(222)^{222}$

(a) 2 (b) 4 (c) 6 (d) 8 (e) 0

Solution:

Step I: $222 \div 4$ gives 2 as a reminder, thus reminder is taken a new power.

i.e. $(222)^{222} = (222)^2$

Step II: $(222)^{222} = (**2)^2$

Hence the unit digit is 4.

Q. The unit digit in the product $(2467)^{153} \times (431)^{72}$ is

    (a) 9 (b) 3 (c) 7 (d) 1

Solution:

$153 \div 4$ gives 1 as a reminder. Thus reminder is taken as new power

$(2467)^{153} = (***7)^1 = ****7$

$72 \div 4$ gives 0 as a reminder. Thus the reminder is taken as new power $(341)^{72} = (**1)^4 = ***1$

(Note: the reminder is o as consider as 4)

Hence the unit digit of the product $= ****7 \times ***1$

$$= ******7$$

Q. The digit in the unit's place of

$[(251)^{98} + (21)^{29} - (106)^{100} + (705)^{35} - (16)^4 + 259]$ **is**

    (a) 1 (b) 4 (c) 5 (d) 6 (e) 0

Solution:

To obtain the result, the power should be divided by 4, the reminder became the new power.

$[(251)^{98} + (21)^{29} - (106)^{100} + (705)^{35} - (16)^4 + 259]$

$= [(251)^2 + (21)^1 - (106)^4 + (705)^3 - (16)^1 + 259]$

The unit digit $= 1 + 1 - 6 + 5 - 6 + 9$

$$= 4.$$

Q. Solve for x as $3^x - 3^{x-1} = 486$

   (a) 6 (b) 7 (c) 9 (d) 5

Solution:

Regular Method	Smart Technique

Let $3^x = a$
 	
 $\Rightarrow a - \dfrac{a}{3} = 486$
 $\Rightarrow 3a - a = 486 \times 3$
 $\Rightarrow 2a = 1458$
 $\Rightarrow a = 729$
 $\Rightarrow 3^x = 3^6$
 $= x = 6$
	If we follow the unit digit method and apply reverse technique.
	 Let us try
	 Let $x = 6$
	    (a) $3^6 - 3^5$
	     $= 3^2 - 3^1 = 9 - 3 = 6$ match with 486
	 Let $x = 7$
	    $= 3^7 - 3^6$
	    $= 3^3 - 3^2$
	    $= *7 - 9 = 8$ not match with 486
	 Like this calculation, we get the answer without using paper and pen.

Q. When 2^{33} is divided by 10, the reminder will be

   (a) 2 (b) 3 (c) 4 (d) 8

Solution:

The unit digit of 2^{33} is

$$= 2^{4 \times 8 + 1}$$ (to obtain new power, the present power divided
$$= 2$$ by 4, the reminder will be the new power)

Any unit digit 2, when divided by 10, the reminder will be 2.

[Ex. $12 \div 10 = 2$ (Reminder)

$22 \div 10 = 2$ (Reminder)

And so on]

Q. The reminder, when $17^{37} + 29^{37}$ is divided by 23 is

   (a) 0 (b) 1 (c) 17 (d) 29

Solution:

Acc. to the formula,

> **$a^n + b^n$ is exactly divisible by $(a + b)$ when 'n' is odd.**
>
> **$a^n - b^n$ is exactly divisible by both $(a + b)$ and $(a - b)$ when 'n' value is even.**

Acc. to the given question,

$17^{37} + 29^{37}$ where n = 37 (odd)

Is divided by $(17 + 29) = 46$ i.e. also divisible by 23.

Hence the reminder is **Zero**.

Q. Find the reminder of 2^{1000} when divided by 3

   (a) 1 (b) 2 (c) 4 (d) 6

Solution:

$2^{1000} = 2^{1000 \div 4} = 2^4 = 16$ (Note: when no reminder after divided by   four, it is consider as 4)

The reminder when divided by 3 is 1.

Q. The unit's digit in the expression

$3^{43} \times 6^{43} \times 7^{43}$ **is**

   (a) 4 (b) 7 (c) 3 (d) 6

Solution:

Regular Method	Smart Technique
$3^{43} \times 6^{43} \times 7^{43}$ The new power will be after divided by 4. $= 3^3 \times 6^3 \times 7^3$	$a^n \times b^n \times c^c = (a \times b \times c)^n$ Hence $(3 \times 6 \times 7)^{43}$ Unit digit of base ….6 Hence unit digit of the expression

=***7 x ***6 x***3 = ****6	$(....6)^3 = ...6$

TECHNIQUE

USE UNIT PLACE DIGIT TO FIND THE VALUES OF SQUARE OR CUBE ROOT SUM.

Q. $X^2 + 65^2 = 160^2 - 90^2 - 7191$

    (a) 75 (b) 77 (c) 79 (d) 81 (e) None of these

Solution:

Regular Method	Smart Technique

$x^2 + 65^2 = 160^2 - 90^2 - 7191$
$\Rightarrow x^2 + 4225 = 25600 - 8100 - 1791$
$\Rightarrow x^2 = 25600 - 8100 - 1791 - 4225$
$\Rightarrow x^2 = 6084$
$\Rightarrow x = \sqrt{6084} = 78$
Use unit value to find the answer in place of calculating the whole value. Let us by.
	$65^2 = ...5$
	$160^2 = ...0$
	$90^2 = ...0$
	$7191 = ...1$
	We get $x^2 = ...0 - ....0 - .....5 - ....1$
	    $x^2 = ...0 - .....6$
	    $x^2 = ...4 \Rightarrow x = \sqrt{....4}$
	When Unit digit of a square root number is 4 the unit digit of that number either 2 or 8.
	Hence the answer of above options unit digit is either 2 or 8. In the option, no such unit digit number is given. Hence answer is none of these.

Q. $x^2 + 79^2 = 172^2 - 88^2 - 8203$

    (a) 93 (b) 89 (c) 83 (d) 81 (e) None of these.

Solution:

We find the solution by calculating only unit digit in smart technique.

Lets us $79^2 = ...1$

$\qquad 172^2 = ...4$

$\qquad 88^2 = ...4$

$\qquad 8203 = ...3$

So $x^2 = ...4 - ....4 - ....3 - ....1$

$\quad x^2 = ...4 - .....8$

$\quad x^2 = ...6$

$\quad x = \sqrt{....6}$ Unit digit either 4 or 6.

$x = ...4$ or $....6$

Hence answer is None of these.

Q. Find the value of x when

$\sqrt{3249} + 75^2 + \sqrt{x} = 5745$

$\qquad$ **(a) 3721 (b) 4096 (c) 3481 (d) 3969 (e) 3364**

Solution:

$\qquad \sqrt{3249} + 75^2 + \sqrt{x} = 5745$

$\qquad => \sqrt{x} = 5745 - 57 - 5625$

$\qquad => \sqrt{x} = 5745 - 5682$

$\qquad => \sqrt{x} = 63$

$\qquad => x = (63)^2$ Unit digit is 3 square number of unit digit became 9. On the option except 3969, no other option unit digit is 9.

Hence Answer is 3969 (Without doing any calculation).

Q. The unit digit in 3 x 38 x 537 x 1256 is

$\qquad$ **(a) 1 (b) 2 (c) 4 (d) 6 (e) 8**

Solution:

To find the unit digit of the above sum, we need not to calculate the whole number. Only multiply the unit digit on your mind and leave the tenth place in every step and get result. Let us.

3 x 38 x 537 x 1256	In Lengthy Calculation
= 3 x ..8 x ..7 x ..6	= 3 x ...8 x ...7 x ...6
= 24 x ...7 x ...6	= 24 x 7 x 6
= ...4 x ...7 x 6	=168 x 6
= 28 x ...6	= 1008
= ...8 x ...6	(to the avoid such type of calculation
=48	in exam)
=...8	

Q.$(9.8)^2 + x^2 = (149)^2 - (78)^2 - 737$

(a) 6084 (b) 76 (c) 82 (d) 6724 (e) None of these

Solution:

It is a very large calculation sum. As the choice is given so for finding the answer, we use the unit digit method.

$(98)^2 + x^2 = (149)^2 - (78)^2 - 737$

$=>***4 + x^2 =***1 - ***4 - **7$

$=> x^2 = ****1 - ***4 - **7 - ***4$

$\quad = **1 - *5$

$\quad x^2 = *6$

$\quad x =$ either 4 or 6 be the unit digit

Hence the option (a) (b) or (d) can be possible. As we know, the square root of any option should be the answer so, (b) and (d) be the rules out.

Hence answer either (b) or (e) .For again conformation, we have to do the total calculation which is not possible in short period but, the answer is (b).

Q. $\sqrt[3]{12167} + (112)^2 = 191 - x$. Find value of x.

(a) 13 (b) 21 (c) 24 (d) 15 (e) 28

Solution:

Use unit place rather to make full calculation.

$\sqrt[3]{12167} + (112)^2 = 191 - x$

$\Rightarrow x = 191 - \sqrt[3]{12167} - (12)^2$ (Use mental calculation only)

$\Rightarrow x = **1 - **3 - **4$

$\quad = **1 - **7$

$\quad = *4$

Unit place 4 is in the option of (c)

Hence Answer (c).

Q. 3463 x 295 – 18611 = x + 5883

    (a)997091 (b) 997071 (c) 997070 (d) 98072 (e) 997094

Solution:

Regular Method	Smart Technique
3463 x 295 – 18611 – 5883 = x => 1021585 – 24494 = x => x = 997091	Follow the given option to get the result quickly 3463 <u>x 296</u> <u>***15</u> ***7 ***85 Result of multiplication <u>-***94</u> ***91 final result We calculate up to two digit because in the give option, both (a) and (b) has unit digit 1. To find exact answer only after two digit. Some times it may calculate three places also.

<u>**TECHNIQUE #**</u>

<u>**UNIT PLACE USED TO FIND THE VALUE FROM LARGE FRACTION**</u>.

Q. $\dfrac{343 \times 49}{216 \times 16 \times 81} = ?$

(a) $\dfrac{7^5}{6^5}$ (b) $\dfrac{7^5}{6^7}$ (c) $\dfrac{7^6}{6^7}$ (d) $\dfrac{7^4}{6^8}$

Solution:

Regular Method	Smart Technique
$\dfrac{343 \times 49}{216 \times 16 \times 81}$ $= \dfrac{16,807}{2,79,936} = \dfrac{7^5}{6^7}$	If we look at the given option, it asks the power of 7 and 6. So we can convert accordingly rather than doing lengthy, multiplication. $\dfrac{343 \times 49}{216 \times 16 \times 81}$ $= \dfrac{7^3 \times 7^2}{6^3 \times 2^4 \times 3^4} = \dfrac{7^5}{6^3 \times (2 \times 3)^4} = \dfrac{7^5}{6^7}$

Q. $1.4 \times 3.5 + 1.5 \times 2.4 = ?$

(a) 8.3 (b) 6.8 (c) 8.5 (d) 7.4

Solution:

$1.4 \times 3.5 + 1.5 \times 2.4$
$= 4.90 + 3.60$
$= 8.5$

<u>Smart Technique</u>
In smart technique, use split method to calculate in mind and get the result.

	Split like
	$= 1.4 \times (3 + 0.5) + 1.5 \times (2 + 0.4)$
	$= 4.2 + 0.70 + 3.0 + 0.60$ (Add in memory only)
	$= 8.5$

Q. Find the value of $(1001)^3$ is

(a) 103003001 (b) 1003003001 (c) 100303001 (d) 10030001

Solution:

Regular Method	Smart Technique
$(1001)^3$	$(1001)^3$ [apply $(a + b)^3$ formula]
$= 1001 \times 1001 \times 1001$	$= (1000+1)^3$ i.e. $a^3 + b^3 + 3ab (a + b)$
$= 10002001 \times 1001$	$= (1000)^3 + 1^3 + 3 \times 100 \times 1(1000 + 1)$
$= 1003003001$	$= 1000000000 + 1 + 3000 (10001)$
	$= 1003003001$

Q. if $P = 99$, then the value of $P(P^2 + 3P + 3)$ is

(a) 10000000 (b) 999000 (c) 999999 (d) 990000

Solution:

Regular Method	Smart Technique
	$P (P^2 + 3P + 3)$
	$= P^3 + 3P^2 + 3P$
$P (P^2 + 3P + 3)$	In the above equation if we add 1 and
$= 99 (99^2 + 3 \times 99 + 3)$	subtract 1, it will be a algebraic
$= 99 (9801 + 297 + 3)$	formula without changing any value.
$= 99 (10101)$	$= P^3 + 3P^2 \times 1 + 3P \times 1^2 + 1^3 - 1$
$= 999999.$	$= ((a + b)^3 = a^3 + 3a^2b + 3ab^2 + b^3)$
	$= (P + 1)^3 - 1$
	$= (99 + 1)^3 - 1$
	$= (100)^3 - 1$

	= 1000000 − 1
	= 999999.

Q. The average of first five multiply 7 will be

    (a) 14 (b) 21 (c) 17.5 (d) 24.5 (e) None of these.

Solution:

Regular Method	Smart Technique

First five multiple of 7 are
7, 14, 21, 28, 35
Average of 5 multiple
 	
$= \dfrac{7 + 14 + 21 + 28 + 35}{5}$
 	
$= 21$
As per Smart Technique, the average number of any sequence in the middle of the number.
Hence Number is 21
	First five multiple of 7 are
	7, 14, 21, 28, 35
	7(1+2+3+4+5)
	$\underline{7 \times (5+1)}$
	  2(Avg. of conjugative no
	        $\dfrac{(n+1)}{2}$
	$=21$

Q. Find the smallest among the numbers

    $2^{250}, 3^{150}, 5^{100}$ **and** 4^{200}

    (a) 4^{200} **(b)** 5^{100} **(c)** 3^{150} **(d)** 2^{250}

Solution:

If we make the power equalof all the number,i.e

$2^{250} = (2^5)^{50} = (32)^{50}$

$3^{150} = (3^3)^{50} = (27)^{50}$

$5^{100} = (5^2)^{50} = (25)^{50}$

$4^{200} = (4^4)^{50} = (256)^{50}$

So the smallest number is 5^{100}

Q. The greatest number among

$$3^{50}, 4^{40}, 5^{30} \text{ and } 6^{20}$$

(a) 6^{20} (b) 5^{30} (c) 3^{50} (d) 4^{40}

Solution:

To make equal power of all number

Then, $\quad (3^5)^{10} = (243)^{10}$

$$(4^4)^{10} = (256)^{10}$$

$$(5^3)^{10} = (125)^{10}$$

$$(6^2)^{10} = (36)^{10}$$

Hence the greatest number 4^{40}.

Q. The greatest number among

$$\sqrt{5}, \sqrt[3]{4}, \sqrt[5]{2}, \sqrt[7]{3}$$

(a) $\sqrt[3]{4}$ (b) $\sqrt[7]{3}$ (c) $\sqrt{5}$ (d) $\sqrt[5]{2}$

Solution:

$$5^{\frac{1}{2}}, 4^{\frac{1}{3}}, 2^{\frac{1}{5}}, 3^{\frac{1}{7}}$$

For finding the greatest number, we have to make the surds equal.

So LCM of 2, 3, 5 and 7 is 210

$$5^{\frac{1}{2}} = 5^{\frac{105}{210}} = (5^{105})^{\frac{1}{210}}$$

(Note: $5^{\frac{1}{2}} = 5^{\frac{105}{210}} = (5^{105})^{\frac{1}{210}}$ multiply the same value

$$4^{\frac{1}{3}} = 4^{\frac{70}{210}} = (4^{70})^{\frac{1}{210}}$$

in number and denominator)

$$2^{\frac{1}{5}} = 2^{\frac{42}{210}} = (2^{42})^{\frac{1}{210}}$$

$$3^{\frac{1}{7}} = 3^{\frac{30}{210}} = (3^{30})^{\frac{1}{210}}$$

Hence the largest number is $(5^{105})^{\frac{1}{210}} = \sqrt{5}$.

Q. Find the value of

$$999\tfrac{1}{7} + 999\tfrac{2}{7} + 999\tfrac{3}{7} + 999\tfrac{4}{7} + 999\tfrac{5}{7} + 999\tfrac{6}{7} \text{ is}$$

(a) $1000\tfrac{9\,2}{7}$ (b) $5994\tfrac{6}{7}$ (c) $9999\tfrac{2}{7}$ (d) 5997

Solution:

$$999\tfrac{1}{7} + 999\tfrac{2}{7} + 999\tfrac{3}{7} + 999\tfrac{4}{7} + 999\tfrac{5}{7} + 999\tfrac{6}{7}$$

$$= 999 \times 6 + \frac{1+2+3+4+5+6}{7}$$

$$= 5994 + 3 \qquad \text{(use split method } (1000-1)6 = 6000 - 6 = 5994)$$

$$= 5997$$

Q. Solve for x: $x^3 - 3^{x-1} = 486$

Solution:

$$x^3 - \frac{x^3}{3} = 486$$

Let $x^3 = a$

$$a - \dfrac{a}{3} = 1986$$

$\Rightarrow 3a - a = 1986 \times 3 \qquad$ (Avoid multiply here)

$\Rightarrow 2a = 486 \times 3$

$\Rightarrow x^3 = 3^5 \times 3$

$\Rightarrow x = 6$

Q. $\dfrac{243^{\frac{n}{5}} \times 3^{2n+1}}{9^n \times 3^{n-1}}$

(a) 12 (b) 9 (c) 6 (d) 3

Solution:

$$\dfrac{(243)^{\frac{n}{5}} \times 3^{2n+1}}{9^n \times 3^{n-1}}$$

$$= \dfrac{(3^5)^{\frac{n}{5}} \times 3^{2n+1}}{(3^2)^n \times 3^{n-1}}$$

$$= \dfrac{3^{n+2n+1}}{3^{2n+n-1}}$$

$$= 3^{3n+1-3n+1}$$

$$= 3^2 = 9.$$

Q. $\dfrac{6^2 + 7^2 + 8^2 + 9^2 + 10^2}{\sqrt{7 + 4\sqrt{3}} - \sqrt{4 + 2\sqrt{3}}}$ **is equal to**

(a) 330 (b) 355 (c) 305 (d) 366

Solution:

Regular Method	Smart Technique
$$\dfrac{36+49+64+81+100}{\sqrt{(2+\sqrt{3})^2}-\sqrt{(1+\sqrt{3})^2}}$$ $$=\dfrac{330}{2+\sqrt{3}-1-\sqrt{3}}$$ $$=330$$	To avoid large calculation, follow unit digit method and get result. $$\dfrac{*6+*9+*4+*1+**0}{\sqrt{(2+\sqrt{3})^2}-\sqrt{(1+\sqrt{3})^2}}$$ $$=\dfrac{**0}{1}=**0$$ In the option only 330 having the unit digit is 0, Hence the answer is 330.

Q. If $\sqrt{1+\dfrac{27}{169}}=1+\dfrac{x}{13}$, **then x equals**

(a) 1 (b) (c) $3\sqrt{3}$ (d) 27

Solution:

Regular Method	Smart Technique
$$\sqrt{1+\dfrac{27}{169}}=1+\dfrac{x}{13}$$ $$\left(\sqrt{1+\dfrac{27}{169}}\right)^2=(1+\dfrac{x}{13})^2$$ $$1+\dfrac{21}{169}=1+\dfrac{x^2}{169}+\dfrac{2x}{13}$$ $$=>\dfrac{27}{169}=\dfrac{x^2}{169}+\dfrac{26x}{13}$$ $$=> x^2+26x-27=0$$ $$=> x^2+27x-x-27=0$$ $$=> x(x+27)-1(x+27)=0$$	$$\sqrt{1+\dfrac{27}{169}}=1+\dfrac{x}{13}$$ $$\sqrt{\dfrac{169+27}{169}}=1+\dfrac{x}{13}$$ $$\sqrt{\dfrac{196}{169}}=1+\dfrac{x}{13}$$ $$\dfrac{14}{13}=1+\dfrac{x}{13}$$ $$\dfrac{x}{13}=\dfrac{14}{13}-1$$ $$\dfrac{x}{13}=\dfrac{1}{13}$$ $$X=1$$ Right approach and strong mental

=> (x + 27) (x − 27) = 0 => x = -27, x = 1 $\therefore$ x = 1	calculation helps to get answer.

Q. if a = 2 +$\sqrt{3}$ then the value of

$$\frac{a^6 + a^4 + a^2 + 1}{a^3} \text{ is}$$

(a) 45 (b) 42 (c) 56 (d) 65

Solution:

Right approach of the sum is the key to obtain quick and accurate result.

Let's try

Given a = 2 +$\sqrt{3}$

$$\frac{1}{a} = \frac{1}{2 + \sqrt{3}} \times \frac{2 - \sqrt{3}}{2 + \sqrt{3}} = \frac{2 - \sqrt{3}}{4 - \sqrt{3}} = 2 - \sqrt{3}$$

Simply $= \dfrac{a^6 + a^4 + a^2 + 1}{a^3}$ into $\dfrac{a^6}{a^3} + \dfrac{a^4}{a^3} + \dfrac{a^2}{a^3} + \dfrac{1}{a^3}$

(Note: Use mental calculation and avoid steps)

$$= a^3 + a + \frac{\frac{1}{a} + \frac{1}{a^3}}{}$$

$$= a^3 + \frac{1}{a^3} + a + \frac{1}{a}$$

$$= \left(a + \frac{1}{a}\right)^3 - 3 \times (a + \frac{1}{a}) + (a + \frac{1}{a})$$

$$= (2 + \sqrt{3} + 2 - \sqrt{3})^3 - 3(2 + \sqrt{3} + 2 - \sqrt{3}) + (2 + \sqrt{3} + 2 - \sqrt{3})$$

$$= 4^3 - 3 \times 4 + 4$$

$= 64 - 12 + 4 = 56.$

Q. $\dfrac{1}{30} + \dfrac{1}{42} + \dfrac{1}{56} + \dfrac{1}{72} + \dfrac{1}{90} + \dfrac{1}{110}$ **is equal to**

(a) $\dfrac{5}{90}$ (b) $\dfrac{6}{55}$ (c) $\dfrac{3}{29}$ (d) $\dfrac{6}{47}$

Solution:

<u>Regular Method</u>

$$\frac{1}{30} + \frac{1}{42} + \frac{1}{56} + \frac{1}{72} + \frac{1}{90} + \frac{1}{110}$$

$$= \frac{1}{5 \times 6} + \frac{1}{6 \times 7} + \frac{1}{7 \times 8} + \frac{1}{8 \times 9} + \frac{1}{9 \times 10} + \frac{1}{10 \times 11}$$

$$= \frac{1}{5} - \frac{1}{6} + \frac{1}{6} - \frac{1}{7} + \frac{1}{7} - \frac{1}{8} + \frac{1}{8} - \frac{1}{9} + \frac{1}{9} - \frac{1}{10} + \frac{1}{10} - \frac{1}{11}$$

$$= \frac{1}{5} - \frac{1}{11}$$

$$= \frac{6}{55}$$

<u>Smart Technique</u>

When any fraction given in series with denomination of complimentary number in sequence. The result will be numerical

$$= \frac{\textit{sum of the number of numerical}}{\textit{Lowest number of 1st fraction denomination} \times \textit{higher number of last fraction denimonation}}$$

$$= \frac{6}{5 \times 11} = \frac{6}{55}$$

Q.6 $\dfrac{1}{6} + \dfrac{1}{12} + \dfrac{1}{20} + \dfrac{1}{30} + \dfrac{1}{42}$ is equal to

(a) $\dfrac{3}{4}$ (b) $\dfrac{6}{19}$ (c) $\dfrac{5}{14}$ (d) $\dfrac{12}{13}$

Solution:

The above sum is continuous fraction with complementary number in denominator.

The sum of the fraction =

$$\dfrac{sum\ of\ Numerator}{Lower\ number\ of\ 1st\ fraction\ \times\ higher\ number\ of\ last\ fraction\ denominater}$$

$$= \dfrac{5}{2 \times 7}$$

$$= \dfrac{5}{14}$$

TECHNIQUE

SMART TECHNIQUE TO ADD / SUBSTRACT FRACTION

Q. $\dfrac{2}{3} + \dfrac{1}{5} = ?$

Solution:

Smart Technique	Rule
$\dfrac{2}{3} + \dfrac{1}{5}$ $= \dfrac{5 \times 2 + 3 \times 1}{15}$ $= \dfrac{10 + 3}{15}$ $= \dfrac{13}{15}$	**Step I:** Multiply crosswise of both numbers and add together i.e. $5 \times 2 = 10$ and $1 \times 3 = 3$ $\qquad 10 + 3 = 13$ **Step II:** Multiply the Denominator to get result $\qquad\quad 3 \times 5 = 15$ (Note: Applicable for the denominator which do not have common factor)

Q. $\dfrac{3}{7} + \dfrac{3}{4} = ?$

Solution:

$$\dfrac{3}{7} + \dfrac{3}{4}$$

$$= \frac{3 \times 4 + 3 \times 7}{7 \times 4}$$

(Thisstep can be avoided by calculating on your mind)

$$= \frac{12 + 21}{28}$$

$$= \frac{33}{28}$$

Q. $\frac{5}{7} + \frac{3}{4} = ?$

Solution:

$$\frac{5 \times 4 + 3 \times 7}{7 \times 4}$$

$$= \frac{20 + 21}{28}$$

$$= \frac{41}{28}.$$

Q. $\frac{6}{7} - \frac{2}{3} = ?$

Solution:

$$\frac{6}{7} - \frac{2}{3}$$

$$= \frac{18 - 14}{21}$$

$$= \frac{4}{21}.$$

Q. $\frac{4}{5} + \frac{1}{6} = ?$

Solution:

$$\frac{4}{5} + \frac{1}{6}$$

$$= \frac{24 + 5}{30}$$

$$= \frac{29}{30}.$$

Q. $\dfrac{1}{3} + \dfrac{2}{5} - \dfrac{3}{5} = \, ?$

Solution:

Smart Technique	Alternate Method
$\dfrac{1}{3} + \dfrac{2}{5} - \dfrac{3}{5}$	$\dfrac{1}{3} + \dfrac{2}{5} - \dfrac{3}{5}$
$= \dfrac{5 + 6}{15} - \dfrac{3}{5}$	$= \dfrac{1}{3} - \dfrac{1}{5}$
$= \dfrac{55 - 45}{75}$	$= \dfrac{2}{15}$
$= \dfrac{10}{75} = \dfrac{2}{15}$	

Q. $\dfrac{4}{5} + \dfrac{3}{7} + \dfrac{2}{3}$

Solution:

$$\frac{4}{5} + \frac{3}{7} + \frac{2}{3}$$

$$= \frac{28 + 15}{35} + \frac{2}{3}$$

$$= \frac{43}{35} + \frac{2}{3} = \frac{129 + 70}{105} = \frac{199}{105}.$$

Q. $\dfrac{2}{9} + \dfrac{3}{5}$

Solution

$\dfrac{2}{9} + \dfrac{3}{5}$

$= \dfrac{2 \times 5 + 3 \times 9}{45}$

$= \dfrac{37}{45}.$

Q. $\dfrac{3}{7} + \dfrac{2}{5} - \dfrac{4}{5}$

Solution:

	Alternate Method
$\dfrac{3 \times 5 + 2 \times 7}{35} - \dfrac{4}{5}$	$\dfrac{3}{7} - \dfrac{2}{5}$
$= \dfrac{29}{35} - \dfrac{4}{5}$	$= \dfrac{15 - 14}{35}$
$= \dfrac{29 - 28}{35} = \dfrac{1}{35}$	$= \dfrac{1}{35}$

TECHNIQUE

ARRANGEMENT OF FRACTION IN CORRECT ORDER

Q. Arrange the fraction in asending order

$$\frac{4}{5}, \frac{7}{8}, \frac{6}{7} \ and \ \frac{5}{6}$$

Solution:

Regular Method	Smart Technique
$\frac{4}{5} = 0.8$ $\frac{7}{8} = 0.875$ $\frac{6}{7} = 0.857$ $\frac{5}{6} = 0.833$ Ascending Order $$\frac{4}{5}, \frac{5}{6}, \frac{6}{7} \ and \ \frac{7}{8}$$	Such type of fraction can be arranged without any calculation. **Condition:** When the series of fraction asked with constant difference between numerator (N) and denominator (D), the lowest $\frac{N}{D}$ is having the lowest value. Hence ascending $$\frac{4}{5} \ \frac{5}{6} \ \frac{6}{7} \ \frac{7}{8}$$

Q. Arrange the following fraction in ascending order

$$\frac{4}{5}, \frac{7}{8}, \frac{9}{10}, \frac{11}{12} \ and \ \frac{3}{4}$$

Solution: <u>Regular Method</u>

$$\frac{4}{5} = 0.8 \qquad \frac{7}{8} = 0.875$$

$$\frac{9}{10} = 0.9 \qquad \frac{11}{12} = 0.916$$

$$\frac{3}{4} = 0.75$$

Hence the Ascending order of the fraction is $\dfrac{3}{4}, \dfrac{4}{5}, \dfrac{7}{8}, \dfrac{9}{10}$ and $\dfrac{11}{12}$.

Q. The difference of the greatest and the least fraction out of $\dfrac{6}{7}, \dfrac{7}{8}, \dfrac{9}{9}$ **and** $\dfrac{9}{10}$ **is**

(a) $\dfrac{3}{10}$ (b) $\dfrac{3}{70}$ (c) $\dfrac{1}{40}$ (d) $\dfrac{1}{12}$ (e) $\dfrac{1}{56}$

Solution: <u>Smart Technique</u>

All fraction have a common difference between numerator and denominator and in a series, so the least fraction in $\dfrac{6}{7}$ and great fraction $\dfrac{9}{10}$

$$\text{Difference} = \dfrac{9}{10} - \dfrac{6}{7} = \dfrac{63-60}{70} = \dfrac{3}{70}$$

Q. If $\dfrac{(\sqrt{7}-2)}{(\sqrt{7}+2)} = a\sqrt{7} + b$ **, then the value of a is**

(a) $\dfrac{11}{3}$ (b) $\dfrac{4}{3}$ (c) $-\dfrac{4}{3}$ (d) $\dfrac{1}{3}$ (e)) $-\dfrac{4}{3}\sqrt{7}$

Solution:

$$\dfrac{(\sqrt{7}-2)(\sqrt{7}-2)}{(\sqrt{7}+2)(\sqrt{7}+2)} = \dfrac{(\sqrt{7}-2)^2}{(\sqrt{7})^2-(2)^2}$$

$=>$ $\dfrac{7+4-4\sqrt{7}}{3} = a\sqrt{7}+b$

$$\Rightarrow \frac{11}{3} - \frac{4}{3}\sqrt{7} = a\sqrt{7} + b$$

$$\Rightarrow b = \frac{11}{3} \qquad a = -\frac{4}{3}$$

Q. Find the value of $\dfrac{7}{4} + \dfrac{7}{28} + \dfrac{7}{70+130} + \dfrac{7}{208} + \dfrac{7}{304} + \dfrac{7}{418}$

(a) $5\dfrac{1}{11}$ (b) $2\dfrac{5}{22}$ (c) $22\dfrac{1}{5}$ (d) $23\dfrac{3}{22}$

Solution:

$$\frac{7}{4} + \frac{7}{28} + \frac{7}{70} + \frac{7}{130} + \frac{7}{208} + \frac{7}{304} + \frac{7}{418}$$

$$= 7\left(\frac{1}{4} + \frac{1}{28} + \frac{1}{70} + \frac{1}{130} + \frac{1}{208} + \frac{1}{304} + \frac{1}{418}\right)$$

$$= \frac{7}{3}\left(\frac{3}{4} + \frac{3}{28} + \frac{3}{70} + \frac{3}{130} + \frac{3}{208} + \frac{3}{304} + \frac{3}{418}\right)$$

$$= \frac{7}{3}\left(1 - \frac{1}{4} + \frac{1}{4} - \frac{1}{7} + \frac{1}{7} - \frac{1}{10} + \frac{1}{10} - \frac{1}{13} + \frac{1}{13} - \frac{1}{16} + \frac{1}{16} - \frac{1}{19} + \frac{1}{19} - \frac{1}{22}\right)$$

$$= \frac{7}{3}\left(1 - \frac{1}{22}\right) = \frac{7}{3} \times \frac{21}{22} = \frac{49}{22} = 2\frac{5}{22}.$$

Q. $999\dfrac{1}{7} + 999\dfrac{2}{7} + 999\dfrac{3}{7} + 999\dfrac{4}{7} + 999\dfrac{5}{7} + 999\dfrac{6}{7}$ **simplified to**

(a) 5997 (b) 5979 (c) 59974 (d) 2997

Solution:

Regular Method	Smart Technique
$999\frac{1}{7} + 999\frac{2}{7} + 999\frac{3}{7} + 999\frac{4}{7} + 999\frac{5}{7} + 999\frac{6}{7}$ $=$ $\dfrac{6994}{7} +$ $=$ $6994 \cdot$ $= \dfrac{41979}{7} = 5997$	$999\frac{1}{7} + 999\frac{2}{7} + 999\frac{3}{7} + 999\frac{4}{7} + 999\frac{5}{7} + 999\frac{6}{7}$ $= 999$ $+ \dfrac{1}{7} + 999 + \dfrac{2}{7} + 999 + \dfrac{3}{7} + 999 + \dfrac{4}{7} + 999 +$ $= 999 \times 6 + \dfrac{1}{7} + \dfrac{2}{7} + \dfrac{3}{7} + \dfrac{4}{7} + \dfrac{5}{7} + \dfrac{6}{7}$ $= 5994 + \dfrac{21}{7}$ $= 5994 + 3 = 5997$ (This sum is a part of mental calculation only)

Q.

$$\frac{3}{1^2 \times 2^2} + \frac{5}{2^2 \times 3^2} + \frac{7}{3^2 \times 4^2} + \frac{9}{4^2 \times 5^2} + \frac{11}{5^2 \times 6^2} + \frac{13}{6^2 \times 7^2} + \frac{15}{7^2 \times 8^2} + \frac{17}{8^2 \times 9^2} + \frac{19}{9^2 \times 10^2}$$

is

(a) $\dfrac{1}{100}$ (b) $\dfrac{99}{100}$ (c) $\dfrac{101}{100}$ (d) 1

Solution:

$$\frac{1}{1^2} - \frac{1}{2^2} + \frac{1}{2^2} - \frac{1}{3^2} + \text{... ....} + \frac{1}{8^2} - \frac{1}{9^2} + \frac{1}{9^2} - \frac{1}{10^2}$$

$$= 1 - \frac{1}{10^2}$$

$$= \frac{99}{100}$$

Q. The value of $\left(1 + \frac{1}{2}\right)\left(1 + \frac{1}{3}\right)\left(1 + \frac{1}{4}\right)\text{.............}\left(1 + \frac{1}{120}\right)$ **is**

(a) 30 (b) 40.5 (c) 60.5 (d) 121

Solution:

$$\left(1 + \frac{1}{2}\right)\left(1 + \frac{1}{3}\right)\left(1 + \frac{1}{4}\right)\text{.............}\left(1 + \frac{1}{120}\right)$$

$$= \left(\frac{3}{2}\right)\left(\frac{4}{3}\right)\left(\frac{5}{4}\right)\text{......}\left(\frac{121}{120}\right)$$

$$= \frac{\frac{121}{2}}{} = 60.5$$

RATIO AND PROPORTION

Ratio: ratio is a simplest form which has no common factor other than one i.e. $\frac{P}{Q}$ where p is called as Numerator and Q is called as Denominator

$$\frac{37\ 8\ 6\ 3}{59\ 11\ 13\ 25}$$

Proportion: proportion isthe comparison of different ratio. i.e. a:b :: c:d where a, b, c and d are said to be in proportion.

If a:b = c:d then a.b = c.d

If a:b = b:c then b² = ac
$$b = \sqrt{ac}$$

In this chapter we find both ratio and proportion are applied in different mathematical equation and how is it solve in shortest possible time. It is important to solve different type of question by apply correct approaching method. Various question in different chapter related to ratio and proportion are solved in regular as well as smart technique method. We advise the students first to conversant with regular method for know the basic need of a question then follow the smart technique for saving the time and error free solving. Lets have one approach to solve

Q. An alloy contains copper, zinc and nickel in the ratio of 5:3:2. The quantity of nickel in kg. that must be added to looking of this alloy to have the new ratio 5:3:3 is
        (a) 3:5 (b) 5:3 (c) 3:7 (d) 7:3 (e) 7:5

Solution:

Regular Method	Smart Technique
Let x kg of nickel to be mixed according to question $\dfrac{20 + x}{100 + x} = \dfrac{3}{11}$ 220 + 11x = 300 + 3x 8x = 80 X = 10 kg	If we calculate this simple question in our mind, to get the answer easily. Total mixture is 100 kg and the present ratio is 5x + 3x + 2x = 10x So each ratio is 10x = 100 $\qquad\qquad\qquad$ x = 10 1 (single)part of nickel is required to obtain new ratio = 5:3:3 So 10 kg of nickel required.

Q. A sum of money is divided among A, B, C and D in the ration of 3:5:8:9 respectively. If the share of D is1872 more than the A share, then what is the total amount of money B & C together?

(a) 4156 (b) 4165 (c) 4056 (d) 4065 (e) None of these

Solution:

Regular Method	Smart Technique

Let the total amount be T

A's share = $\dfrac{3}{25} \times T$

B's share = $\dfrac{5}{25} \times T$

C's share = $\dfrac{8}{25} \times T$

D's share = $\dfrac{9}{25} \times T$

$\Rightarrow D = A + 1872$

$\Rightarrow \dfrac{9}{25} \times T = \dfrac{3}{25} \times T + 1872$

$\Rightarrow \dfrac{6}{25} \times T = 1872$

$\Rightarrow T = 1872 \times \dfrac{25}{6} = 7800$

$B + C = \dfrac{5}{25} \times 7800 + \dfrac{8}{25} \times 7800$

$= \dfrac{13}{25} \times 7800 = 4056$

A's share = 3 parts = 3x

B's share = 5x

C's share = 8x

D's share = 9x

D = 1872 + A i.e 9x = 1872 + 3x

6x = 1872

$x = \dfrac{1872}{6}$

$B + C = 5x + 8x$

$B + C = 13 \times \dfrac{1872}{6}$

$= 4056$

.

Q. A sum of money is divided among A, B, C, and D in the ratio 5:8:9:11. If the share of B is 2475 more than the share of A, then what is the total amount a money of A and C together.

(a) 9900 (b) 11550 (c) 10270 (d) 99370 (e) None of these.

Solution:

Let A = 5x, B = 8x, C = 9x, D = 11x

B – A = 8x – 5x = 2475

$$x = \frac{2475}{3} = 825$$

$$A + C = 14x$$

$$= 14 \times 825$$

$$= 11550.$$

Q. Rahim spends 60% of his monthly salary on rent, EMI and miscellaneous expenses in the respective ratio of 2:3:3. If he spends the total Rs. 16050 on rent and EMI together, how much his monthly salary.

> **(a) 50300 (b) 46750 (c) 42800 (d) 48200 (e) 57300**

Solution:

Regular Method	Smart Technique
Let the expense of rent = 2x EMI = 3x Miscellaneous = 3x 2x + 3x = 16050 $x = \dfrac{16050}{5} = 3210$ Total Expenditure = 2x + 3x + 3x = 3210 × 8 = 25680 Rahim monthly salary = $\dfrac{25680}{60} \times 100$ = Rs. 42800	To avoid repetition and much calculation, we can obtain the result by 5x = 16050 $X = \dfrac{16050}{5}$ Total => $8x = \dfrac{16050}{5} \times 8$ (do not calculate on this stage) The above amount only 60% of income 60% of income $= \dfrac{16050}{5} \times 8$ Total Income = $\dfrac{16050 \times 8 \times 100}{5 \times 60} = 42800$ On a single step calculation, we can get the result.

Q. If $\dfrac{A}{B} = \dfrac{3}{4}$ **and** $\dfrac{B}{C} = \dfrac{6}{5}$

Then C:A is

(a) 10:9 **(b)** 9:10 **(c)** 8:9 **(d)** 9:8

Solution:

Regular Method	Smart Technique
$\dfrac{A}{B} = \dfrac{3}{4} \times \dfrac{6}{6} = \dfrac{18}{24}$ $\dfrac{B}{C} = \dfrac{6}{5} \times \dfrac{4}{4} = \dfrac{24}{20}$ (To make the value of B equal in both proportion) A:B:C = 18:24:20 $\quad\quad = 9:12:10$ $\dfrac{C}{A} = 10:9$	$\dfrac{A}{C} = \dfrac{A}{B} \times \dfrac{B}{C}$ $= \dfrac{3}{4} \times \dfrac{6}{5}$ $= \dfrac{18}{20}$ $\dfrac{A}{C} = \dfrac{9}{10}$ $\dfrac{C}{A} = \dfrac{10}{9}$

Q. Three glasses of equal volume contains acid mixed with water. The ratio of acid and water of three glasses are 2:3, 3:4 and 4:5 respectively. Content of these glasses are poured in a large vessel. The ration of acid and water in the large vessel is

    (a) 401:544 (b) 411:544 (c) 417:564 (d) 407:506

        Solution:

Regular Method	Smart Technique
$\dfrac{Acid}{Water} = \dfrac{\frac{2}{5}+\frac{3}{7}+\frac{4}{9}}{\frac{3}{5}+\frac{4}{7}+\frac{5}{9}}$ The ratio of $= \dfrac{\dfrac{126+135+140}{315}}{\dfrac{189+180+175}{135}} = \dfrac{401}{544}$	$\dfrac{Acid}{Water} = \dfrac{\frac{2}{5}+\frac{3}{7}+\frac{4}{9}}{\frac{3}{5}+\frac{4}{7}+\frac{5}{9}}$ $= \dfrac{\dfrac{126+135+140}{315}}{\dfrac{\ldots\ldots}{135}} = \dfrac{\frac{401}{315}}{\frac{\ldots}{135}} = \dfrac{401}{544}$

Q. A car covers $\frac{1}{5}$ of the distance from A to B at the speed of 8 Km/hr. $\frac{1}{10}$ of the distance at 25 Km/hr and remaining at the speed of 20 Km/hr. Find the average speed of the whole journey.

(a) 12.625km/hr (b) 13.625 km/hr (d) 14.625 km/hr (d) 15.625 km/hr

Solution:

Regular Method	Alternate Method
Let the distance between A to B = x km Time taken $\frac{x}{5 \times 8} + \frac{x}{10 \times 25} + \frac{7x}{10 \times 20}$ $= x\left(\frac{25 + 4 + 35}{1000}\right)$ $= \frac{64x}{1000}$ Average Speed $= \frac{x \times 1000}{64x} = 15.625$ km.	Assume a known value in place x which is easily calculated and helps in mental calculation. Let's the distance between A to B = 1000 km 8km/hr in $\frac{1}{5}$ of 1000 = $\frac{200}{8} = 25$ hr 25km/hr in $\frac{1}{10}$ of 1000 = $\frac{100}{25} = 4$ hr Remaining 1000 − (200 + 100) = 700km in 20km/hr $\frac{700}{20} = 35$hr Average speed $= \frac{1000}{25 + 4 + 35} = \frac{1000}{64} = 25.625$km/hr (Note: it is quite easy and less calculation than the other method)

Q. An employer reduces the number of his employees in the ratio 9:8 and increases their wages in the ratio 14:15. If the original wage bill was Rs. 18,900, find the ration in which the wage bill decreased.

(a) 20:21 (b) 21:20 (c) 20:19 (d) 19:21

Solution:

Let the employee be reduced from 9x to 8x and the wages be increased from 14y to 15y.

Required ratio is $\dfrac{9x \times 14y}{8x \times 15y} = \dfrac{42}{40} = \dfrac{21}{20}$.

Q. Divide 50 into two parts so that the sum of their reciprocal is $\dfrac{1}{12}$

    (a) 28, 22 (b) 20, 30 (c) 24, 36 (d) 35, 15

Solution:

Let two parts are x and (50 – x)

$$\frac{1}{x} + \frac{1}{50 - x} = \frac{1}{12}$$

$$= \frac{50 - x + x}{x(50 - x)} = \frac{1}{12}$$

$\Rightarrow 50 \times 12 = 50x - x^2$

$\Rightarrow x^2 - 50x + 600 = 0$

$\Rightarrow x^2 - 30x - 20x + 600 = 0$

$\Rightarrow x(x - 30) - 20x(x - 30) = 0$

$\Rightarrow x = 30, 20$

(Note: In the reverse Technique, you cansolve it more quickly and easily)

Q. 75 litters of a mixture of wine and water contain 15 litters more wine than water. 6 litter of water added to it. The new ration of the wine to water in the mixture is.

(a) 3:2 (b) 4:5 (c) 5:4 (d) 1:5 (e) 3:5

Solution:

Such type of common question generally asked in the examination to confuse the student as they are conversant with the formula. So without use any formula, apply the common sense to solve the question. Let's try.

15 lt more wine in the mixture of 75 lt of wine and water.

So in the mixture contain wine 45 lt and water should be 30 lt.

6 lt of water added to the mixture. The new contain will be

$$\frac{wine}{water} = \frac{45}{30+6} = \frac{45}{36} = \frac{5}{4}$$

Hence new ratio $= \frac{5}{4}$.

Q. $\frac{2}{5}$th of a pole is in mud, $\frac{1}{3}$ of the reminder is in water and 6m is above water. The length of the pole is.

      (a) 20m (b) 25m (c) 15m (d) 10m (e) 12m

Solution:

Let the length of pole = x m

$$\text{Mud} = \frac{2x}{5}$$

$$\text{Water} = \frac{1}{3} \times \left(x - \frac{2x}{5}\right) = \frac{1}{3} \times \frac{3x}{5} = \frac{x}{5}$$

$$\text{Above water} = x - \left(\frac{2x}{5} + \frac{x}{5}\right)$$

$$6 = \frac{2x}{5}$$

$$\Rightarrow x = 15m$$

Q. A bag contains rupee, 50 paisa, and 25 paisa coins in the ration 5:6:8, if the total amount is Rs. 240, the number of 25 paisa coins is.

(a) 144 (b) 192 (c) 48 (d) 120

Solution:

Let the ratio of coins of one rupee.

50 paisa and 25 paisa be 5x, 6x and 8x respectively. $$5x + \frac{6x}{2} + \frac{8x}{4} = 240$$ (Convert given paisa into rupees as total value is given in rupees)

=> 5x + 3x + 2x = 240

=> x = 24

25 paisa coin = 8 × 24 = 192.

Q. In two types of brass, ratio of coper and zinc are 8:3 and 15:7 respectively. The ratio in which these two types of brass should be mixed, so that the ratio of copper and zinc in this new type of brass became 5:2 is

(a) 7:4 (b) 2:5 (c) 3:2 (d) 5:2 (e) 3:4

Solution:

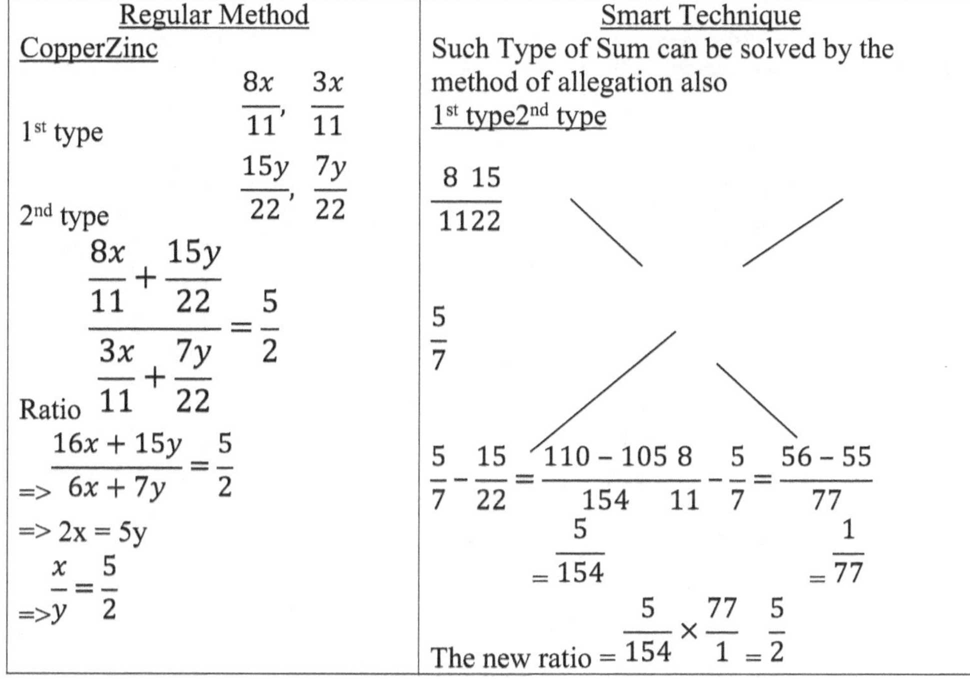

Regular Method	Smart Technique
Copper Zinc 1st type $\dfrac{8x}{11}, \dfrac{3x}{11}$ 2nd type $\dfrac{15y}{22}, \dfrac{7y}{22}$ $\dfrac{\dfrac{8x}{11} + \dfrac{15y}{22}}{\dfrac{3x}{11} + \dfrac{7y}{22}} = \dfrac{5}{2}$ Ratio $\Rightarrow \dfrac{16x + 15y}{6x + 7y} = \dfrac{5}{2}$ $\Rightarrow 2x = 5y$ $\Rightarrow \dfrac{x}{y} = \dfrac{5}{2}$	Such Type of Sum can be solved by the method of allegation also 1st type 2nd type $\dfrac{8}{11}$ $\dfrac{15}{22}$ $\dfrac{5}{7}$ $\dfrac{5}{7} - \dfrac{15}{22} = \dfrac{110 - 105}{154}$ $\dfrac{8}{11} - \dfrac{5}{7} = \dfrac{56 - 55}{77}$ $= \dfrac{5}{154}$ $= \dfrac{1}{77}$ The new ratio $= \dfrac{5}{154} \times \dfrac{77}{1} = \dfrac{5}{2}$

Q. the ratio of boys and girls in a college is 5:3. If 50 boys leave the college and 50 girls join the college the ratio become 9:7. The number of boys in the college is

(a) 300 (b) 400 (c) 500 (d) 600 (e) None of these

Solution: <u>Smart Technique</u>

The initial ratio of boys and girls is 5x and 3x.

Acc. To question $\dfrac{5x - 50}{3x + 50} = \dfrac{9}{7}$

$\Rightarrow 7(5x-50) = 9(3x + 50)$

$\Rightarrow 35x - 27x = 450 + 350$

$\Rightarrow 8x = 800$

$\Rightarrow x = 100$

Boys $= 5x = 5 \times 100 = 500$.

Q. A's expenditure and saving are in the ratio 3:2. His income increases by 10%, his expenditure also increases by 12%. His saving increases by.(a) 7% (b) 9% (c) 13% (d) 10% (e) 15%

Solution:

Regular Method	Alternate Method
Let the expenditure and saving be 3x and 2x respectively Total income = 5% Income increase 10% i.e. new income = 5.5x Increased Expenditure = 3x + 12% of 3x $\qquad = 3.36x$ Increased saving = 5.5x − 3.36x = 2.14x Increase % = $\dfrac{2.14 - 2}{2} \times 100 = 7\%$	When question asked on percentage, assume the value 100 in place of x and solve Lets try Expenditure = 300, saving = 200 Income = 500 10% increase in income new income = 550 12% increase in expenditure New expenditure = 300+12% of 300 $\qquad = 336$ New saving 214 % of saving income = $\dfrac{214 - 200}{200} \times 100$ $= \dfrac{14}{2} = 7\%$

.**Q. Rs. 555 was divided among A, B and C in the ratio of** $\dfrac{1}{4} : \dfrac{1}{5} : \dfrac{1}{6}$**. But by mistake it divided in the ratio of 4:5:6. The amount in excess received by c was.**

> **(a) 52 (b) 72 (c) 75 (d) 22**

Solution:

The ratio of A:B:C = $\dfrac{1}{4} : \dfrac{1}{5} : \dfrac{1}{6}$

LCM of 4, 5, 6 = 60

Share = A = $\dfrac{1}{4} = \dfrac{15}{4 \times 15} = \dfrac{15}{60}$

B = $\dfrac{1}{5} = \dfrac{12}{5 \times 12} = \dfrac{12}{60}$

C = $\dfrac{1}{6} = \dfrac{10}{6 \times 10} = \dfrac{10}{60}$

Share of A:B:C = 15:12:10

Original share = $\dfrac{555}{37} \times 10 = 150$

By mistake 'C' share = $\dfrac{555}{15} \times 6 = 37 \times 6 = 222$

Excess amount Received = Rs. 72.

Q. 15 men, 18 women and 12 boys working together earned Rs. 2070. If the daily wages of a man, a woman and a boys are in the ratio of 4:3:2, then daily wages of 1 man, 2 woman and 3 boys are

    (a) Rs. 135 (b) Rs.180 (c) Rs. 205 (d) Rs. 240 (e) Rs. 245

Solution:

The wages ratio of man : woman : boys = 4x : 3x : 2x

$15 \times 4x + 18 \times 3x + 12 \times 2x = 2070$

$$138x = 2070$$

$$\therefore x = \dfrac{2070}{138} = 15$$

So wages of 15 man = 60 × 15 (Note: Avoid totaling the wages)

18 woman = 54 × 15

12 boys = 24 × 15

Total wages of 1 man + 2 woman + 3 boys

$$= \dfrac{60 \times 15}{15} \times 1 + \dfrac{54 \times 15}{18} \times 2 + \dfrac{24 \times 15}{12} \times 3$$

$$= 60 + 90 + 90$$

$$= \text{Rs } 240.$$

Q. What ratio a shopkeeper shall add two type of rice, one is @ Rs. 15 and other@ Rs. 20 per Kg. get Rs. 16.50 per Kg.

   (a) 3:5 (b) 5:3 (c) 3:7 (d) 7:3 (e) 7:5

Solution:

Regular Method	Smart Technique
Let @ Rs 15 is x kg and @ Rs 20 is y kg mixed. Cost of both type are Rs. 15 × x + Rs 20 × y = Rs 16.50 × (x + y) Rs 15x + Rs 20 y = 16.50x + Rs. 16.50y The ratio of $\dfrac{A}{B}$ => 16.50x – 15x = 20y – 16.50y => 1.5x = 3.5y => $\dfrac{x}{y} = \dfrac{3.5}{1.5} = \dfrac{7}{3}$	By solving smartly using allegation method, to get the result. A B 15 20 16.50 3.5 1.5 $\dfrac{A}{B} = \dfrac{3.5}{1.5} = \dfrac{7}{3}$

Q. 300 grams of sugar solution has 40% of sugar in it. How much sugar should be added to make it 50% in the solution?

(a) 40gms (b) 80gms (c) 60gms (d) 10gms

Solution: <u>Smart Technique</u>

In solution contain 40% sugar each 10% = 30gms

$$40\% = 120\text{gms sugar}$$

$$60\% = 180\text{gms water}$$

As for question, the amount of sugar to be added to make 50 % in solution, that means water : sugar = 1:1. 60gms of sugar should be added.

Hence answer is 60gms.

Q. An alloy contains copper, zinc and nickel in the ratio of 5:3:2. The quantity of nickel in kg. that must be added to looking of this alloy to have the new ratio 5:3:3 is
(a) 3:5 (b) 5:3 (c) 3:7 (d) 7:3 (e) 7:5

Solution:

Regular Method	Smart Technique
Let x kg of nickel to be mixed according to question $$\frac{20 + x}{100 + x} = \frac{3}{11}$$ $220 + 11x = 300 + 3x$ $8x = 80$ X = 10 kg	If we calculate this simple question in our mind, to get the answer easily. Total mixture is 100 kg and the present ratio is $5x + 3x + 2x = 10x$ So each ratio is $10x = 100$ $x = 10$ 1 (single)part of nickel is required to obtain new ratio = 5:3:3 So 10 kg of nickel required.

Q. In what respective ratio, rice of verity A worth Rs 36 must be mixed with rice of verity B worth Rs 48, So that the new mixture of worth is Rs 45.

(a) 1:3 (b) 3:4 (c) 4:5 (d) 1:2 (e) None of these

Solution: <u>Smart Technique</u>

<u>A</u>   <u>B</u>

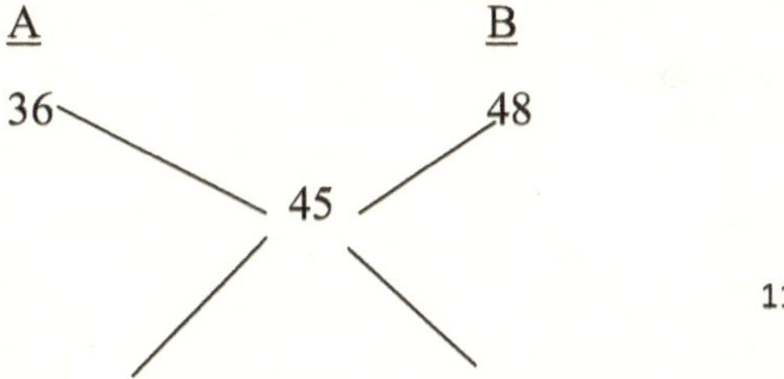

3   9

$3:9 = 1:3$

Q. The ratio of milk and water is 55 kg of in mixture is 7:4. The quantity of water that must be added to make the ratio 7:6 is

(a) 15kg (b) 10kg (c) 5kg (d) 12kg (e) 14kg

Solution:

Regular Method	Smart Technique
In 55kg of mixture Milk = $\dfrac{7}{11} \times 55 = 35kg$ Water = $\dfrac{4}{11} \times 55 = 20kg$ Let x kg of water be mixed $\dfrac{35}{20 + x} = \dfrac{7}{6}$ $=> \dfrac{5}{20 + x} = \dfrac{1}{6}$ $=> 20 + x = 30$ $=> x = 10$ kg	By simple mental calculation, we get the result Total mixture $7 + 4 = 11$ part Total Weight of mixture = 55kg So each part become = 5 kg The ratio of mixture will be $7 + 6 = 13$ part So for two parts became $2 \times 5 = 10$ kg Hence answer became 10 kg.

Q. A merchant has 100 kg sugar, part of which he sells at 8% profit and the rest at 18% profit. He gains 14% on the whole. The quantity sold at 8% profit is

(a) 640kg (b) 400kg (c) 560kg (d) 500kg (e) 600kg

Solution:

Solve the sum by allegation method

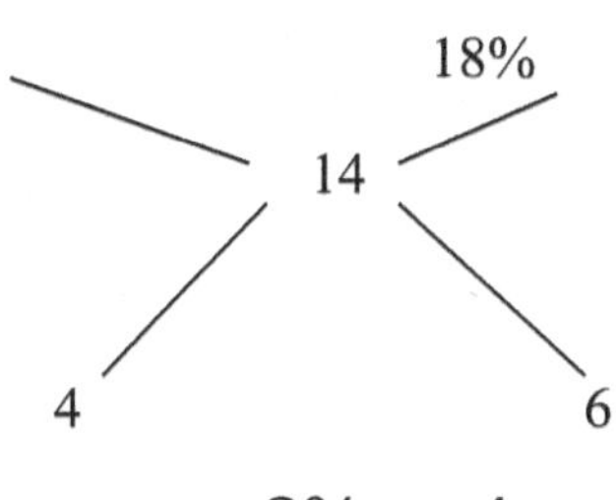

The ratio of profit of $\dfrac{8\%}{18\%}$ is $\dfrac{4}{6}$

4x + 6x = 1000kg

x = 100kg8% profit, he sells = 4 × 100 = 400kg.

Q. In what ratio should tea at Rs 350/- per kg be mixed with tea at Rs 400/- per kg in order that the mixture be worth Rs 380/- per kg.

 (a) 3:2 (b) 2:3 (c) 1:2 (d) 2:1

Solution:

Acc. To Smart Technique

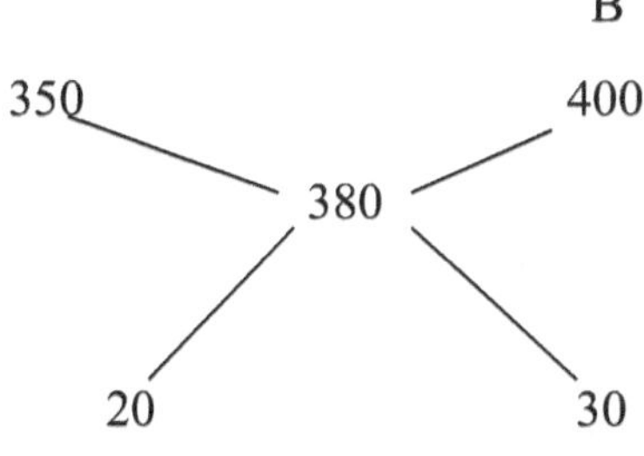

Hence the required ratio = $\dfrac{20}{30} = \dfrac{2}{3}$.

Q. The average marks scored by the students of a class is 68. The average marks of the girls in the class is 80 and that of the boys is 60. What is the percentage of the boys in the class?

(a) 40 (b) 60 (c) 65 (d) 70 (e) None of these

Solution:

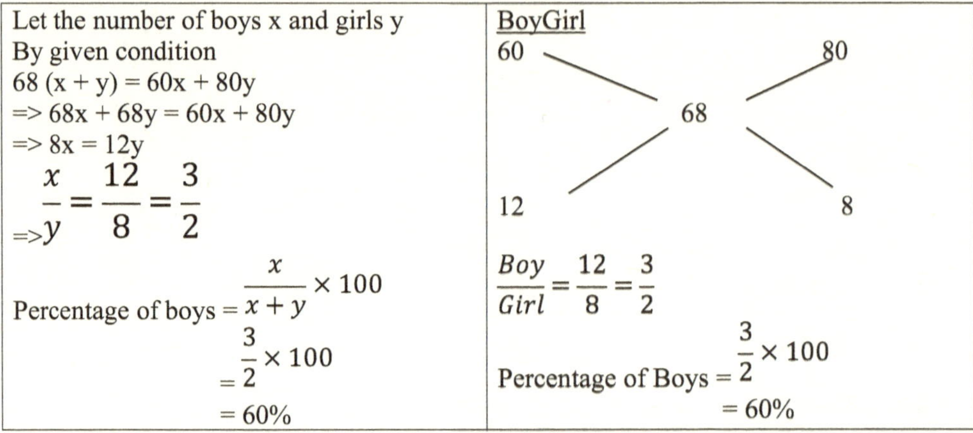

Let the number of boys x and girls y
By given condition
$68(x + y) = 60x + 80y$
$\Rightarrow 68x + 68y = 60x + 80y$
$\Rightarrow 8x = 12y$
$\Rightarrow \dfrac{x}{y} = \dfrac{12}{8} = \dfrac{3}{2}$

Percentage of boys $= \dfrac{x}{x + y} \times 100$

$= \dfrac{\dfrac{3}{2} \times 100}{2}$

$= 60\%$

$\dfrac{Boy}{Girl} = \dfrac{12}{8} = \dfrac{3}{2}$

Percentage of Boys $= \dfrac{\dfrac{3}{2} \times 100}{2}$

$= 60\%$

TECHNIQUE

RELATION BETWEEN HCF AND LCM

Q. The LCM of two numbers 2079 and their HCF is 27. If one of the numbers is 189. Find the other.

Solution: Smart Technique.

The required number $= \dfrac{LCM \times HCF}{First\ No.}$

(Note: The relation between HCF and LCM is

$$[\text{LCM of } (No_1, No_2) \times HCF (No_1, No_2) = N_1 \times N_2]$$

$= \dfrac{2079 \times 27}{189} = 297$

Q. Find the ratio between the LCM and HCF of 5, 15 and 20.

    (a) 8:1 (b) 14:3 (c) 12:1 (d) 15:3

Solution:

LCM of 5, 15, 20 is 60

HCF of 5, 12, 20 is 5

$$\frac{LCM}{HCL} = \frac{60}{5} = \frac{12}{1}.$$

Q. The HCF and LCM of two numbers are 12 and 72 respectively. If the sum of two numbers are 60. Then one of the two number will be.

    (a) 12 (b) 24 (c) 60 (d) 72

Solution:

Regular Method	Smart Technique
Let one number $N_1 = x$ $N_2 = 60 - x$ Acc. To the formula. $N_1N_2 = LCM \times HCF$ $x(60 - x) = 72 \times 12$ $\Rightarrow 60x - x^2 = 864$ $\Rightarrow x^2 - 60x + 864 = 0$ $\Rightarrow (x - 36)(x - 24) = 0$ $\Rightarrow x = 36, 24$	To get the answer by reverse technique mental option (c) and (d) rules out as the sum of $x + y = 60$ Option (a) 12, then another will not be 48. So LCM will not be there. Option (d) 24, another no is 36 Hence answer is 24 (It can be done by mental calculation also)

Q. The HCF and LCM of two number are 18 and 3780 respectively. If one of them is 540, then the second one is:

    (a) 142 (b) 126 (c) 118 (d) 112

Solution:

$$\text{The second no} = \frac{LCM \times HCL}{1st\ No}$$

$$= \frac{3780 \times 18}{540}$$

$$= 126$$

Q. The LCM of two number is 20 times their HCF and the sum of their LCM and HCF is 2520. If one number is 480, then another number will be:

(a) 300 (b) 600 (c) 1200 (d) 900

Solution:

Let HCF = x

And LCM = 20x

20x + x = 2520

$$x = \frac{2520}{21} = 120 \text{ HCF}$$

$No_1 \times No_2 = LCM \times HCF$

$$No_2 = \frac{120 \times 2400}{120}$$

$$= 600$$

Q. The HCF and LCM of two numbers are 21 and 84 respectively. If the ratio of the two numbers is 1:4, then the larger of the two numbers is.

(a) 108 (b) 48 (c) 12 (d) 84

Solution:

Let two numbers x and 4x respectively

$x \times 4x = 21 \times 84$

$4x^2 = 21 \times 84$

$x^2 = 21 \times 21$

x = 21

Larger number is 21 × 4 = 84.

Q. A and B walk around a circular field of 35 km in circumference, starting together in the same point. If they walk at the speed of 4 kmph and 5 kmph respectively in the same direction, when will they meet?

   (a) after 15 hours (b) after 35 hours (c) after 21 hours (d) after 42 hours

Solution:<u>Smart Technique</u>

The LCM of 4, 5, 35 is 140

They will meet $= \dfrac{140}{4} = 35$.

Q. LCM of $\dfrac{2}{3}, \dfrac{4}{9}, \dfrac{5}{6}$

   (a) $\dfrac{20}{3}$ (b) $\dfrac{10}{3}$ (c) $\dfrac{20}{27}$ (d) $\dfrac{8}{27}$

Solution:

LCM of $\dfrac{2}{3}, \dfrac{4}{9}, \dfrac{5}{6}$ is

$$\frac{LCM \ of \ numerator}{HCF \ of \ Denominator} = \frac{20}{3}$$

Q. The two numbers are in the ratio 2:3 and their LCM is 72. HCF of the two numbers is

   (a) 2 (b) 5 (c) 10 (d) 12 (e) 15

Solution: <u>Regular Method</u>

2x × 3x = HCF × LCM   LCM of 2x × 3x = 72

2x × 3x = HCF × 72   6x = 72   (2x × 3x = 6x as comparison)

$$HCF = \dfrac{24 \times 36}{72} = 12 \qquad\qquad x = 12$$

Q. The LCM of two numbers is 33 times of their HCF. The sum of the LCM and their HCF is 952. If one number is 42, the other number is

(a) 616 (b) 588 (c) 634 (d) 662

Solution:

Let HCF is x, LCM = 33x

LCM + HCF = 952

34x = 952

$$x = \dfrac{952}{34} = 28$$

HCF = 28, LCM = 28 × 33 = 924

$42 \times N_2 = 28 \times 924$

$$N_2 = \dfrac{28 \times 924}{42}$$

$N_2 = 616$

Q. The HCF of two numbers, each having three digits is 17 and their LCM is 714. The sum of the number will be

(a) 289 (b) 391 (c) 221 (d) 731

Solution:

Product of two number = LCM × HCF

$x \times y = 17 \times 714$ (Hint: two numbers. Each 3 digit so we consider min.
let's take 1st three digit   three digit number. Where HCF is 17 i.e. 102)
Number 102

$102 \times y = 17 \times 714$

$$y = 119$$
$$\text{Sum of the number} = 102 + 119 = 221.$$

<u>PERCENTAGE</u>

Percentage calculation is an important factor of any arithmetic solution. If we smartly calculate the percentage of any number, it will save much time to do other calculations. So it is another factor to save time and accuracy in examination. Let us calculate the percentage of any umber.

We understand that any percentage is division of 100. So it is a ratio of $\dfrac{p}{q}$ where q always become 100. There are two Smart technique to find percentage of any number.

Rule I: Convert any percentage to factor.

i.e. $\quad 50\% = \dfrac{50}{100} = \dfrac{1}{2}$

$25\% = \dfrac{25}{100} = \dfrac{1}{4}$

$75\% = \dfrac{75}{100} = \dfrac{3}{4}$

$60\% = \dfrac{60}{100} = \dfrac{3}{5}$

$40\% = \dfrac{40}{100} = \dfrac{2}{5}$ etc.

Rule II split the percentage

i.e. $\quad 40\% = 10\% \times 4$

$60\% = 50\% + 10\%$

$75\% = 50\% + 25\%$ etc.

CALCULATION OF PERCENTAGE

Ex. 75% of 600 is

Solution:

Regular Method	Smart Technique
$75\% \times 600$ $= \dfrac{75}{100} \times 600$ $= 75 \times 6$ $= 450$	75% of 600 $= \dfrac{3}{4} \times 600$ $= 450$

Ex. 260% of 450 is

Solution:

Regular Method	Smart Technique
$60\% \times 450$ $= \dfrac{60}{100} \times 450$ $= 270$	$60\% \times 40$ $= \dfrac{2}{5} \times 450$ $= 270$

Ex. 30% of 400 + 25% of 600 = ?

    (a) 250 (b) 320 (c) 370 (d) 390 (e) None of these

Solution:

Regular Method	Smart Technique

Regular Method	Smart Technique
30% of 400 + 25% of 600 $= \dfrac{30}{100} \times 400 + \dfrac{25}{100} \times 600$ $= 120 + 150$ $= 270$	30% of 400 + 25% of 600 $= \dfrac{3}{10} \times 400 + \dfrac{1}{4} \times 600$ $= 120 + 150$ $= 270$

Ex. 75% of 540 + 25% of 540

Solution:

Regular Method	Smart Technique
75% of 540 + 25% of 540 $= \dfrac{75}{100} \times 540 + \dfrac{25}{100} \times 540$ $= 15 \times 27 + \dfrac{1}{4} \times 540$ $= 405 + 135$ $= 540.$	75% of 540 + 25% of 540 $= (75\% + 25\%)$ of 540 $= 100\%$ of 540 $= 540$

Q. 45% of 2100 – 30% of 350 = 1170 - ?

(a) 230 (b) 130 (c) 330 (d) 270 (e) 170

Solution:

Regular Method	Smart Technique
45% of 2100 – 30% of 350 $= \dfrac{45}{100} \times 2100 + \dfrac{30}{100} \times 350$ $= 45 \times 21 - 3 \times 35$ $= 945 - 105$ $= 840$ $1170 - 184$ $= 330$	45% of 2100 – 30% of 350 $= (40\% + 5\%) of$ 2100 – 30% of 350 $= 840 - 105 - 105$ $= 945 - 105 = 840$ $= 1170 - 840 = 330$

Q. 45% of 360 + 288 = x% of 750, find the value of x

(a) 52 (b) 60 (c) 70 (d) 75 (e) 65

Solution:

$$\frac{45}{100} \times 360 + 288 = \frac{x}{100} \times 750$$

$$=> 36 \times 4.5 + 288 = 7.5x$$

$$=> 7.5x = 450$$

$$=> x = 60.$$

Q. 71% of a number is more than its 46% by 120. What is 30% of that number?

(a) 160 (b) 150 (c) 140 (d) 148 (e) none of these.

Solution:

Smart Technique	Alternate Method
71% - 46% = 120 => 25% = 120 => 100% = 480 => 30% = 48 × 3 　　　= 144	Let the number be x 71% of x − 46% x = 120 25% of x=120 $\frac{25}{100}x = 120$ x = 480 30% of 480 = $\frac{30}{100} \times 480$ 　　　= 144

Q. In a big garden 60% of the trees are coconut trees, 25% of the number of coconut trees are mango trees and 20% of the number of mango trees are apple trees. If the number of apple trees is 1500, then the number of trees in the garden is

    (a) 48000 (b0 50000 (c) 51000 (d) 45000

Solution:

Regular Method	Smart Technique

20% of mango trees = 1500
 	
 Mango trees = $1500 \times \dfrac{100}{20}$
 	
       = 7500
 25% coconut trees = 7500
 	
 Coconut trees = $7500 \times \dfrac{100}{25}$
 	
       = 30000
 60% of total trees = 30000
 	
 Total trees = $30000 \times \dfrac{100}{60}$
       = 50000
	Total trees in the garden
	
	 $= 1500 \times \dfrac{100}{20} \times \dfrac{100}{25} \times \dfrac{100}{60}$
	 = 50000
	 (memories the short cut technique for similar type of problem)

Q. If 50% of (x – y) = 30% of (x +y), then what percentage of x is y.

    (a) 25% (b) 30% (c) 35% (d) 40% (e) 50%

Solution: <u>Smart Technique</u>

5(x - y) = 3(x + y)

=> 2x = 8y   (do other calculation in your mind)

$$\frac{50}{100}(x - y) = \frac{30}{100}(x + y)$$

=> x = 4y

=> 25% of x = y

Q. Three – fifth of five – seventh of four – ninth of a number is 20. What is 30% of that number?

(a) 25 (b) 27 (c) 20.5 (d) 31.5

Solution:

Let the number is x

$$\frac{3}{5} \times \frac{5}{7} \times \frac{4}{9} \times x = 20$$

$$=> x = \frac{20 \times 9 \times 7 \times 5}{3 \times 5 \times 4} = 105$$

30% of x = $\frac{30}{100} \times 105 = 31.5$.   (follow 10% 105 = 10.5, 10.5 × 3 = 31.5)

Q. The ratio of zinc to copper in a mixture is 5:7. If there is 30% impurity in zinc and 35% impurity in copper. Then what is the percentage of pure metal in the mixture?

(a) 65% (b) 67.08% (c) 60.04% (d) 79.83%

Solution:

Rrgular Method	Alternate Method
Let zinc be 5x and copper 7x Pure metal = 70% of 5x + 65% of 7x $= \frac{70}{100} \times 5x + \frac{65}{100} \times 7x$ $= \frac{70x}{20} + \frac{91x}{20} = \frac{161x}{20}$ Pure metal = $\frac{161x}{20} \times \frac{1}{12x} \times 100 = 67.08\%$	Assume zinc is 50 and copper 70 Pure metal = 70% of 50 + 65% of 70 $= 35 + 45.5 = 80.5$ Purity % => 120 => 80.5 $= \frac{80.5}{120} \times 100$ $= 67.08\%$

Q. A car agency had 108 cars. He sold some of its car at 9% profit and the remaining at 36% profit and thus he earned 17% profit on the sale of all its cars. What is the number of cars that he sold at 36% profit?

(a) 28 (b) 30 (c) 32 (d) 34 (e) 40

Solution:

Regular Method	Allegation Method
Let x cars sold at 36% at 9% profit and (108-x) cars sold at 36% profit 109% of x + 136% (108 – x) = 117% of 108 => 1.09x + 1.36 (108 – x) = 1.17 × 108 => 1.09x + 1.36 × 108 – 1.36x = 1.17 × 108 => 1.36x – 1.09x = 108 (1.36 – 1.17) => 0.27x = 108 × 0.19 => x = 76 sold at 9% profit => 108 – 76 = 32 sold at 36% profit	9 36 17 19 8 Ratio of $\dfrac{9\%}{36\%} = \dfrac{19x}{8x}$ 27x = 108 x = 4 36% profit, sold = 32 cars

Q. 10% of 15% of 20% of Rs 500 is

    (a) Rs 225 (b) Rs 150 (c) Rs 67 (d) Rs 1.50

Solution:

Regular Method	Smart Technique
10% of 15% of 20% of Rs 500 $= \dfrac{10}{100} \times \dfrac{15}{100} \times \dfrac{20}{100} \times 500$ = Rs. 1.50	i.e 20% of 500 = 100 15% of 100 = 15 10% of 15 = 1.5 (It is only mental Calculation)

Q. Due to increase of 15% in the Price of milk a family reduces its consumption of milk by 15%. What is the effect in the expenditure of the family on account of milk?

    (a) 2.50% increase (b) 3.5% increase (c) 3% increase (d) 2.25% decrease

Solution:

$$\text{Net \%} = \left(+15 - 15 - \frac{15.15}{100}\right)\%$$

$$= -2.25\%$$

Q. $\dfrac{2}{5}$ **is expressed as a percentage of** $2\dfrac{6}{7}$**. The percentage is**

(a) 14% (b) 15% (c) 7% (d) 21% (e) 10%

Solution:

$$\frac{2}{5} = x\% \ of \ 2\frac{6}{7}$$

$$\frac{2}{5} = \frac{x}{100} \times \frac{20}{7} \qquad \text{then x = 14.}$$

COMPARISON OF PERCENTAGE BETWEEN THE VALUES

Split Method- Any percentage can split into 5%, 10%, 20%, 25%, 50%, 100%, 250%, 500% rather to make fraction of 100 and multiply that become quite easy and less time taking. Such Calculation can be done only by on your mind. Let us discuss

Rule-II

Ex. 75% of 600

Solution: Smart Technique

Split 75% into 50% and 25%

50% is $\dfrac{1}{2}$ of the number i.e. 300

25% is $\dfrac{1}{4}$th of the number i.e. 150

So the answer is 450.

Ex. 60% of 450

Solution: <u>Smart Technique</u>

$60\% = 50\% + 10\%$

50% is $\dfrac{1}{2}$ of 450, i.e. 225

10% is $\dfrac{1}{10}$th of 450, i.e. 45

So the answer is 270.

Q. 30% of 400 + 25% of 600

Solution:<u>Smart Technique</u>

Split $30\% = 10\% + 10\% + 10\%$ or $25\% + 5\%$

Lets Solve

10% of 400 is $\dfrac{1}{10}$th of $400 = 40$

40 in 4 times of 10 i.e. 120

Similarly 25% of 600 is $\dfrac{1}{4}$th of $600 = 150$

So the answer is $120 + 150 = 270$.

Q. 43% of 600 + 47% of 300 =?

(a) 341 (b) 399 (c) 389 (d) 409 (e) none of these

Solution:<u>Smart Technique</u>

$= (40\% + 30\%)$ of $600 + (40\% + 7\%)$ of 300

$= 240 + 18 + 120 + 21$

$= 399.$

Q. If A's salary is 25% more than B's salary, then by. What percent is B's salary less than A's salary.

Solution:

Regular Method	Smart Technique
A = B +25% of B	B's Salary = $\dfrac{100 \times x}{100 \pm x}\%$
$\Rightarrow$ A = B + $\dfrac{B}{4}$ $\Rightarrow$ A = $\dfrac{5B}{4}$	x is the % of A salary more/less than B
$\Rightarrow$ B = $\dfrac{4A}{5}$ = 80% A	$= \dfrac{100 \times 25}{125}$
$\Rightarrow$ B is only 80% A	= 20%
Therefore, B is 20% less than A.	

Q. When A's salary 40% less than B's salary, then by what percent of B's salary more than A's salary.

    (a) 66.66% (b) 33.33% (c) 20% (d) 25% (e) none of these

Solution:<u>Smart Technique</u>

B's salary $= \dfrac{100 \times 40}{100 - 40}$

$= \dfrac{100 \times 40}{60}$ = 66.66%.

Q. The Price of onions has been increased by 50%. In order to keep the expenditure on onions the same, the percentage of reduction in consumption has to be.

(a) 50% (b) $33\frac{1}{3}$ (c) 33% (d) 30% (e) **None of these**

Solution: Smart Technique

The Reduction percentage $= \dfrac{100 \times x}{100 + x} = \dfrac{100 \times 50}{100 + 50} = \dfrac{100 \times 50}{150} = 33\frac{1}{3}$.

Q. If A exceeds B by 60% and B is less that C by 20%, then A : C is,

   (a) 32:25 (b) 25:32 (c) 8:5 (d) 4:5

Solution: Smart Technique

Any percentage sum, in place of taking assumed value x, take 100 and solve the sum.

Let C = 100

 B = 80% C then B = 80

A = 160% of B then A= 128

$$\frac{A}{C} = \frac{128}{100} = \frac{32}{25}.$$

Q. A's Salary is 40% of B's salary and B's salary is 25% if C's salary. What percentage of C's salary is A's salary.

   (a) 5% (b) 10% (c) 15% (d) 20%

Solution: Smart Technique

Lets C's salary = 100

B's salary = 25% of C $= \dfrac{25}{100} \times 100$

A's Salary = 40% of B $= \dfrac{40}{100} \times 25 = 10$

Hence A's salary is 10% of C's salary.

Q. The sum of two unequal numbers is 40. If one of them is increased by 5% and the other is decreased by 5%, the numbers become equal. The difference of number is.

(a) 4 (b) 6 (c) 2 (d) 3 (e) none of these

Solution:

Let one number is x and other number $(40 - x)$

As per question

105% of x = 95% of $(40 - x)$

$105x = 95 \times 40 - 95x$

$200x = 95 \times 40$

$$x = \frac{95 \times 40}{200}$$

$x = 19$

Other number = $40 - 19 = 21$

The difference of the number $21 - 19 = 2$.

Q. A candidate who gets 20% marks in an examination fails by 30 marks. But if he gets 32% marks, he gets 42 marks more than the minimum pass marks.Find the pass percentage.

Solution:

Let full mark be x

As per given data

Pass mark is 20% of $x + 30 = 32\%$ of $x - 42$

12% of x = 72

Full mark 100% = 600

Pass mark = 20% of 600 + 30 (30 is 5% of 600)

$\qquad$ = 20% of 600 + 5% of 600

= 25%

Pass % is 25%

Alternate

20% of 600 + 30

= 120 + 30 = 150

150 be the 25% of 600.

Q. If the price of oil is increased by 25%, what will be the percentage of oil consumption that a house must reduce, so that his expenditure does not increase.

(a) 15% (b) 10% (c) 20% (d) 25% (e) none of these

Solution: <u>Smart Technique</u>

Consumption of oil reduce

$$= \frac{100 \times 25}{100 + 25}\%$$

= 20%.

TECHNIQUE

FIND THE AVERAGE IN SMART TECHNIQUE

Q. Find the average of 34, 29, 42, 35, 22, 30

(a) 25 (b) 28 (c) 30 (d) 32 (e) none of these

Solution;

Regular Method	Smart Technique
Average $= \dfrac{34 + 29 + 42 + 35 + 22 + 30}{6}$ $= \dfrac{192}{6}$ $= 32$ It is quite lengthy and possibility of error while doing the calculation.	Let us assume the average of the sum to be 30 (the value should have unit digit zero and near about middle of the given value) 34-30, 29-30, ……. +4, -1, 12, 5, -8, 0 Average Deviation $= \dfrac{+4 - 1 + 12 + 5 - 8 + 0}{6}$ $= +2$ Average $= 30 + 2 = 32$

Q. Find the average of 69, 73, 55, 71, 54 and 59

(a) 73.5 (b) 69.5 (c) 65 (d) 63.5 (e) none of these

Solution:

Consider average value is 60

Deviation = +9, 13, -5, 11, -6, -1

Average deviation $= \dfrac{9 + 13 + 11 - 5 - 6 - 1}{6} = \dfrac{21}{6} = 3.5$

Average = 60 + 3.5 = 63.5

Q. What will be the average of the following set of score?

59, 84, 44, 98, 30, 40, 58

(a) 62 (b) 66 (c) 75 (d) 52 (e) 59

Solution:

Regular Method	Smart Technique

<table>
<tr><td>

$$\frac{59 + 84 + 44 + 98 + 30 + 40 + 58}{7}$$

$$= \frac{\overline{413}}{7}$$

$$= 59$$

</td><td>

60 80 40 100 30 40 60
+1   -4   -4   +2   +2

$$\frac{59 + 84 + 44 + 98 + 30 + 40 + 58}{7}$$

$$\begin{array}{r} 410 \\ +\ 3 \\ \hline 413 \end{array}$$ (-ve sign, add the number)

$$= 413$$

Hence average $\dfrac{413}{7} = 59$

</td></tr>
</table>

Q. What is the average of 144, 153, 149, 135 and 140

   (a) 139 (b) 144.2 (c) 135 (d) 141.6 (e) none of these

Solution: <u>Smart Technique</u>

let us assume the average of the sum be 140

Average deviation +4   +13   +9   -5   0

Mean deviation = $\dfrac{+4 + 13 + 9 - 5 + 0}{5}$

$$= \frac{21}{5} = 4.2$$

Hence the Average of the sum is 144.2

Q. Find the average of the following

218, 152, 117, 207, 343, 439

   (a) 20 (b) 246 (c) 249 (d) 236 (e) 252

Solution: <u>Smart Technique</u>

218 + 152 + 117 + 207 + 343 + 439

+2   -2   +3   +3   -3   +1

$$= \frac{220 + 150 + 120 + 210 + 340 + 440 - 4}{6}$$

$$= \frac{1480 - 4}{6}$$

$$= \frac{1476}{6}$$

$$= 246.$$

Q. Find the average of the following set of scores

157, 348, 443, 221, 360, 795, 841, 101

(a) 443 (b) 368.50 (c) 408.25 (d) 348 (e) none of these

Solution: Smart Technique

$157 + 348 + 443 + 221 + 360 + 795 + 841 + 101$

$+3 \quad +2 \quad -3 \quad -1 \quad 0 \quad +5 \quad -1 \quad -1$

$$= \frac{160 + 350 + 440 + 220 + 360 + 800 + 840 + 100 - 4}{8}$$

$$= \frac{3270 - 4}{8}$$

$$= \frac{3266}{8}$$

$$= 408.25$$

Q. Find the average of the following numbers.

44, 32, 42, 51, 45, 41

(a) 44 (b) 39.5 (c) 35 (d) 42.5

Solution: Smart Technique

Let us assume the average of the above number is 40

Then 44,   32,   42,   51,   45,   41

$$+4 \quad -8 \quad +2 \quad +11 \quad +5 \quad +1 = \frac{15}{6}$$

Hence average is $40 + 2.5$

$$= 42.5.$$

TECHNIQUE

CALCULATE THE AVERAGE OF CONSECUTIVE NUMBER

Q. The sum of five consecutive even numbers is 230. What is the sum of the largest number and square of the smallest number among them?

   (a) 1684 (b) 1464 (c) 1784 (d) 1814 (e) 1614

Solution:

Regular Method	Smart Technique
Let the five consecutive even numbers are $2x$, $2x+2$, $2x+4$, $2x+6$, $2x+8$ $2x+2x+2+2x+4+2x+6+2x+8 = 230$ $10x + 20 = 230$ $10x = 210$ $x = 21$ even numbers are 42, 44, 46, 48 and 50 Acc. to question $= 50 + 42^2$ $\qquad = 50 + 1764$ $\qquad = 1814$	When consecutive even numbers are given, there must be in a sequence. Sum of 5 consecutive even no $= 230$ Average of the number $= \dfrac{230}{5} = 46$ 46 be the middle number of the given series. The number 42 44 46 48 50 Question asked $= 50 + 42^2$ $\qquad = 50 + 1764$ $\qquad = 1814$

Q. The sum of 5 consecutive odd numbers 575. What will be the sum of the next 5 consecutive odd numbers?

   (a) 625 (b) 580 (c) 600 (d) 650 € none of these

Solution: Smart Technique

Some of the consecutive odd number = 575

Average of the number = $\dfrac{575}{5}$ = 115

So numbers are =>111, 113, 115, 117, 119

The next 5 consecutive numbers are = 121, 123, 125, 127, 129

Sum of the number is 125 x 5=625.

Q. The sum of 3 consecutive odd numbers is 255. What will be the sum of the next 3 consecutive odd numbers?

   (a) 273 (b) 264 (c) 280 (d) 300 (e) 350

Solution: <u>Smart Technique</u>

The sum of 3 consecutive odd numbers = 255

The average of consecutive odd numbers = $\dfrac{255}{3}$ = 85

The numbers are 83, 85, 87

The next 3 consecutive odd numbers Unit be 89, 91, 93

The sum of the consecutive odd numbers are = 91× 3 = 273.

Q. The average of five consecutive positive integers is n.
If the next two integers are also included, the average of all these integers will be

   (a) Increase by 1 (b) remain the same (c) increase by 2 (d) increase by 1.5 (e) none of these

Solution: <u>Smart Technique</u>

If we consider any +ve value of 'n' in place of using average formula, the result will get easily and quickly. Let us assume the value of 'n' is 25.

(Note: when assume any value it should be easily divisible by the number i.e. 25 divisible by 5)

If the average of 5 consecutive integer = 25

The middle number $\dfrac{25}{5} = 5$

Hence the integers are 3, 4, $\underline{5}$, 6, 7

It include two more integer, then integers are 3, 4, 5, 6, 7, 8, 9

Hence the average = $\dfrac{3+4+5+6+7+8+9}{7}$

$= \dfrac{42}{7} = 6$

The new average will be increase by 1.

Q. The average of four consecutive odd numbers A, B, C and D respectively is 54, what is the product of A and C.

(a) 2805 (b) 2703 (c) 2915 (d) 2907 (e) none of these

Solution: Smart Technique

As per Smart Technique, any sequence of numbers, the average number is the middle number of the sequence.
Hence 54 is the middle number of the sequence.
A B 54 C D
So consecutive odd numbers are 51, 53, 55 and 57
Product of A and C = 51 × 55 = 2805.

Q. The sum of seven consecutive odd integers is 133. The least odd integer is

(a) 17 (b) 19 (c) 11 (d) 13 (e) 21

Solution:

Regular Method	Smart Technique

| Let numbers are n, n+2, n+4, n+6, n+8, n+10, n+12
n+n+2+n+4+n+6+n+8+n+10+n+12
7n = 91
n = 13
the least integer = 13 | Seven consecutive odd numbers = 133

The average of the numbers = $\dfrac{133}{7}$ = 19
The middle consecutive numbers = 19
Numbers are
13, 15, 17, <u>19</u>, 21, 23, 25
Hence least number is 13. |

Q. The average of six numbers is 32. If each of the first three numbers is increased by 2 and each of the remaining three numbers is decreased by 4, then the new average is.

    (a) 35 (b) 34 (c) 32 (d) 31 (e) 40

Solution:

Sum of the six numbers = $32 \times 6 = 192$

The new average as per the question

$$= \frac{192 + 2 \times 3 - 4 \times 3}{6}$$

$$= \frac{186}{6} = 31.$$

Q. The sum of three consecutive odd numbers s 1383. What is the largest number?

    (a) 463 (b) 459 (c) 457 (d) 461 (e) none of above

Solution: <u>Smart Technique</u>

The sum of 3 consecutive odd number = 1383

Average of 3 consecutive odd numbers = $\dfrac{1383}{3}$ = 461

The middle number is 461

Hence the numbers are 459 <u>461</u> 463

The largest number is 463.

Q. a, b, c, d and e are 5 consecutive even numbers of the sum of 'a' and 'd' is 162. Then what will the sum of all the numbers?

(a)400 (b) 380 (c) 420 (d) cannot be determined (e) none of these.

Solution: <u>Smart Technique</u>

a, b, c, d, e are five consecutive even numbers.

Let a value be x, then other number have.

x   x+2   x+4   x+6   x+8

As per question $x + x + 6 = 162$

$$2x = 156$$

$$x = 78$$

Hence numbers are 78, 80, 82, 84, 86

Sum of number is $82 \times 5 = 410$.

Q. The difference between a two digit numbers and the number obtained by interchanging the two digits of the number is 9. What is the difference between the two digits of the number?

(a) 3 (b) 2 (c) 1 (d) cannot be determined (e) none of these

Solution:

Regular Method	Smart Technique
Let the number is $10x + y$ After interchanging $10y + x$ The difference $\Rightarrow 10x + y - 10y - x = 9$ $\qquad \Rightarrow 9x - 9y = 9$ $\qquad \Rightarrow x - y = 1$	If we consider a number in our mind and calculate accordingly, we get the result within no time. Let us consider the number. Think the number 21 Interchange 12 $21 - 12 = 9$ Hence the difference is $2 - 1 = 1$

Q. The product of two successive even numbers in 6888. Which is the greater of the two numbers?

(a) 78 (b) 82 (c) 86 (d) 90 (e) none of these

Solution:

Regular Method	Smart Technique
The product of two even numbers is 6888. Let the even numbers are n, n+2 $n(n+2) = 6888$ $\Rightarrow n^2 + 2n - 6888 = 0$ $$n = \frac{-2 \pm \sqrt{4 + 27552}}{2}$$ $$= \frac{-2 \pm 166}{2}$$ $= 82, 84$ (Note: In quadratic equation $ax^2+bx+c=0$ $$\text{The value of } \alpha, \beta = \frac{-b \pm \sqrt{b^2 + 4ac}}{2a} \;)$$	Such a large sum can be solved by reverse techniques choose the option first. Option (a) 78 => numbers 76, 78 So unit digit is ….8 and the product of 76 and 78 = 5928 So not correct option Option (b) 82 =>numbers 80, 82 unit digit 0, not matched Option (c) 86 => numbers 84, 86 Unit digit 4, not matched Option (d) 90 => numbers 88, 90 Unit digit 0, not matched Hence answer is (e), because no option is matched with answer.

<u>**TECHNIQUE #**</u>

<u>**FIND THE AVERAGE WHEN A PERSON INCLUDED / EXCLUDED THE GROUP.**</u>

Q. The average age of 39 students and a teacher of a class are 11 years. If the age of teacher is excluded, the average age of class is reduced by 1. What is the age of teacher?

(a) 39 (b) 49 (c) 50 (d) 60 (e) 62

Solution:

Regular Method	Smart Technique
Average of 39 student + teacher = 11 Sum of age of 39 student + teacher = 11 × 40 = 440 If teacher is excluded, The average age of remaining 39 students = 11 − 1 = 10 Sum of ages of 39 students = 39 × 10 = 390 Teacher age = 440 − 390 = 50	It is important to calculate such solution in your mind before using pen. i.e. when Teacher leaves group, he carries his age of 11 years and also take 1 year from each student Hence Age = 11 + 39 = 50 years

Q. The average age of 30 students is 9 years. If the age of their teacher is included. It becomes 10 years. The age of teacher is

    (a) 25 (b) 30 (c) 35 (d) 40 (e) 45

Solution:

If we calculate in Smart Technique like

When teacher included, average age of 30 student increase one year each, i.e. 30 years (added to teacher age)

Now present average is 10 years

Hence teacher age is $10 + 30 = 40$ years.

Q. The average of six members in a family is 22 years. If the age of the youngest is 7 years, what was the average age of the members of the family at the time of birth of the youngest?

    (a) 15 (b) 16 (c) 17 (d) 18 (e) none of these

Solution:

The total age of six members is $22 \times 6 = 132$ years

Youngest member age is 7. At the time of birth means the youngest not included. The remaining 5 members have 7 years younger than the present time. So the total age of the member $= 132 - (7 \times 6) = 90$ years.

The average age of each members $= \dfrac{90}{5} = 18$ years.

Q. The average of four number is 72.5. The largest number is 117 and smallest is 15. The difference of other two number is 12. What is the largest number of the remaining two numbers?

    (a)70 (b) 73 (c0 84 (d) 85 (e) 93

Solution: <u>Smart Technique</u>

Average of 4 numbers 72.5

Sum of the 4 number $72.5 \times 4 = 300$

Largest + smallest = $117 + 15 = 132$

The remaining numbers $x + x - 2 = 158$

$$2x = 170$$

Largest $\qquad x = 85$

Smallest $\qquad x = 73.$

Q. The average age of 14 girls and their teacher age is 15 years. If the teacher's age is excluded, the average reduced by 1year. What is the teacher age?

(a) 32 years (b) 30 years (c) 29 years (d) 35 years (e) 36 years

Solution:

Regular Method	Smart Technique
The average age of 14 girls + teacher = 15 Total age of 14 girls + teacher = 15×15 $\qquad\qquad = 225$ If teacher age excluded, the average age reduced by 1. Total age of 14 girls = $14 \times 14 = 196$ Hence teacher age = $225 - 196 = 29$ years	Acc. to the question, The average age of 14 girls + teacher is 15 When teacher leaves, he carried his own average age, i.e. 15 and the reduced average age of 14 girls i.e. 14 years each. Hence teacher age $= 15 + 14 = 29$

Q. In a family of 5 members, the average age at present is 33 years. The youngest member is 9 years old. The average age of the family just before the birth of the youngest member was.

(a) 30years (b) 29years (c) 25 years (d) 24 years

Solution: <u>Smart Technique</u>

The average age of 5 members = 33 years

Sum of the present age of 5 members = 33x5 = 165 years

9 years ago, the sum of age of 5 members = 165 – (9 × 5) = 120 years

Just before birth of youngest member, there are 4 members in the family.

Hence the average age of the family = $\dfrac{120}{4}$ = 30 years.

Q. In a chess tournament, each of the six players will play with every player exactly once. What is the number of matches that will be played during the tournament?

    (a) 10 (b) 15 (c) 20 (d) 25

Solution: <u>Smart Technique</u>

Simple solution i.e. $\dfrac{6 \times 5}{2}$ = 15

(Note: Two players played at a time, so each player played with 5 other players)

Q. There are 20 girls and 30 boys is a class and their respective average marks are found to be 55 and 58. The average marks of the entire class are.

    (a) 56.5 (b) 56.6 (c) 56.7 (d) 56.8

Solution: <u>Smart Technique</u>

Total marks of the class = 20 × 55 + 30 × 58

$$= 1100 + 1740$$

Average marks of the class = $\dfrac{2840}{50}$ = 56.8

Q. The average age of a man and his son is 25 years. The ratio of their age is 21:4 respectively. What is the son's age?

(a) 6 years (b) 8 years (c) 12 years (d) 14 years (e) none of these

Solution: Smart Technique

The average age of man and son is 25

The total age of a man and son is 50

The ratio of F + S = 21x + 4x = 25x

25x = 50 => x = 2yeras

Son's age = 4 × 2 = 8 years.

TECHNIQUE

VERIFICATION BASED ON RATIO FOR SOLVING AGE RELATED PROBLEMS

Q. ages of Ajay and Vijay are in the ratio of 2:3 respectively. Six years hence, the ratio of their ages will become 11:15 respectively. What will be Ajay's present age?

(a) 15 (b) 24 (c) 16 (d) 35 (e) 17

Solution:

Regular Method	Smart Technique

Let the ages of Ajay and Vijay be A and V respectively A:V = 2:3 => A = 2x and V = 3x $$\frac{A+6}{V+6}=\frac{11}{15}=>\frac{2x+6}{3x+6}=\frac{11}{15}$$ => 15(2x + 6) = 11(3x + 6) => 30x + 90 = 33x + 66 => 3x = 24 => x = 8 Ajay's present age 2 × 8 = 16 years	A:V = 2:3 => Ajay's Present age must be multiple of 2. Upon verification of option (a), (d) and (e) ruled out as not multiple of 2. => Six year's hence, Ajay's age will be 11x. Again on verification of option (b) & (c) 24 + 6 = 30 not multiple of 11. 16 + 6 = 22 multiple of 11. Hence answer is 16 and option (c). (Reverse techinque be applied here)

Q. The age of father and son together was 45, 5 years back. What will be their combined age after 5 years?

(a) 65 (b) 60 (c) 55 (d) 50

Solution: <u>Smart Technique</u>

5 years back, age of F + S = 45,

Present age 45 + 10 = 55 (both have increased 5 years)

After 5 years, both have increase 5 years

Hence 55 + 10 = 65 years.

Q. The rato between the present ages of Indira and Liza is 3:8 respectively. After 8 years , Indira age will be 20 years. What was the Liza's age 5 years ago?

(a) 37 (b) 27 (c) 28 (d) 38 (e) 36

Solution:

Regular Method	Smart Technique

<table>
<tr><td>

Let present age of Indira = 3x
 Liza = 8x
After 8 years, Indira become 20 years
3x + 8 = 20
3x = 12 => x = 4
Liza age = 3x = 8 × 4 = 32
5 years Ago, the age was = 32 – 5
= 27 years

</td><td>

The present age of Indira is 12
As after 8 years, she became 20.
Present Ratio, $\dfrac{Indira}{Liza} = \dfrac{3}{8}$
So 3x = 12, x = 4
Liza age is 32
5 years ago was 32 – 5
= 27 years

</td></tr>
</table>

Q. Ages of Arun and Deepak are in the ratio of 2:1 respectively 3 years Hence, the ratio of their ages will become 5:3 respectively. What will be Arun's present age?

(a) 15 (b) 12 (c) 20 (d) 30 (e) 25

Solution: <u>Smart Technique</u>

$$\frac{A}{D} = \frac{2x}{x}$$

Arun's present age multiple of 2, So option (a) & (e) ruled out 3 years hence, the ratio will be 5:3,

So from option (b), (e), (d) if we add 3 years resultant will be multiple of 5,

12 + 3 = 15

20 + 3 = 23

30 + 3 = 33

So option (b) is the only suitable,

Hence Arun present age is 12 years.

Q. Present ages of Sameer and Anand are in the ratio of 5:4 respectively. Three years hence, the ratio of their age will be become 11:9 respectively. What is Anand's present age?

(a) 24 (b) 27 (c) 32 (d) 40 (e) 43

Solution: <u>Smart Technique</u>

The ratio $= \dfrac{S}{A} = \dfrac{5}{4}$

So Anand's present age is multiple of 4. For that option (a), (c) and (d) matched.

Again after 3 years, the ratio become $\dfrac{11}{9}$, that means if we add 3 in the option (a), (c) and (d) it should be multiple of 9.

Let us see $24 + 3 = 27$ (a)

$\qquad 32 + 3 = 35$ (c)

$\qquad 40 + 3 = 43$ (d)

So the option (a) in only matched, Hence answer is 24.

Q. The ratio of age of A and B at present is 3:1, Four years earlier the ratio was 4:1. The present age of A is.

(a) 40 years (b) 32 years (c) 36 years (d) 38 years (e) 43 years.

Solution: <u>Smart Technique</u>

i.e. A's present age must be a multiple of 3----(1)

On verification of option, only (c) 36 matched with the condition (1). So the answer is 36 years.

Again on verification of option (c), before 4 years i.e. substract from the number of (c), it should have the multiple of 4.

i.e. $36 - 4 = 32$ is the multiple of 4.

Hence answer is 36.

Q. The respective ratio of present age of Arati and Savita is Six. Arati is 9 years younger than Jahnavi. Janhavi's age after 9 years will be 33 years. The sifference between Savita and Arati age is same as present age of Jahnavi. What will come in place of x?

(a) 21 (b) 37 (c) 17 (d) 13 (e) none of these.

Solution: <u>Smart Technique</u>

Jahnavi present age = 33 – 9 = 24 years

Savita age – Arati age = 24

Arati, 9 rears younger than Jahnavi i.e. Arati age = 24 – 9 = 15 years

The age ratio of Arati : Savita = 5x : x

The age of Arati : Savita = 5 × 3 : x × 3 = 15 : 3x

3x – 15 = 24

$x = \dfrac{39}{3}$ = 13 years.

Q. The present age of the father and the son are together 46 years. 5 years ago, the father was 11 times as old as his son. The age of the son after 5 years will be.

(a) 10 years (b) 13 years (c) 14 years (d) 12 years (e) 15 years

Solution:

Regular Method	Smart Technique
F + S = 46 ....(I)	Fundamentals and mental calculation is
=> F – 5 = 11 (S – 5)	the basic of smart technique.
=> F – 11S = -50........(II)	Let's solve the math by mental
From equation (I) and (II)	calculation.

12S = 96 S = 8 and F = 38 After 5 years S = 5 + 8 = 13	Present age F + S = 46 5 years ago, both have reduce 5 years each F + S = 36 Father and son ratio = 11:1 12x = 36 => x = 3 So before 5 years, Father became = 33 + 5 =38 Son = 3 + 5 = 8 After 5 years son will 5 + 8 = 13 years (Note: the way of mental calculation only, not to be used pen)

TECHNIQUE

PROFIT AND LOSS

Profit= sold Price – cost price i.e. SP> CP

Loss = cost price – sold price   i.e CP >SP

The cost price $= \dfrac{SP}{100 + gain} \times 100 \quad = \dfrac{sp}{100 - loss} \times 100$

LEFT BLANK

TECHNIQUE #

TO FIND THE COST PRICE FROM PROFIT AND LOSS

Q. A tradesman sold an article at a loss of 20%. If the selling price had been increased by Rs.100, there would have been a gain of 5%. The cost price of the article was.

(a) 100 (b) 200 (c) 400 (d) 500 (e) 600

Solution:

Regular Method	Smart Technique
Let the cost price of article = Rs. x 1st selling price of article = $\dfrac{80x}{100}$ $= \dfrac{4x}{5}$ When selling price increase Rs.100 $\dfrac{4x}{5} + 100 = \dfrac{105x}{100}$ $\dfrac{4x}{5} + 100 = \dfrac{21x}{20}$ $=> \dfrac{21x}{20} - \dfrac{4x}{5} = 100$ $=> \dfrac{21x - 16x}{20} = 100$ $=> 5x = 2000$ $=> x = 400$ Hence the price of article is 400.	Such type of problem can be solved by simple smart formula of the cost price. i.e., **The cost price =** $\dfrac{X}{y + x} \times 100$ Where X => increased selling price x => initial loss y => final gain According this formula The unit price = $\dfrac{100}{20 + 5} \times 100$ $= \dfrac{100}{25} \times 100$ $= 400$

Q. If an article is sold at 8% profit instead of 8% loss, it would have brought Rs.12 more. Find the cost price of the article.

(a) Rs.60 (b) Rs.72 (c) Rs.70 (d) Rs.75 (e) Rs.50

Solution: <u>Smart Technique</u>

According to the cost price formula for the above sum

The cost price = $\dfrac{X}{y + x} \times 100$

$$= \dfrac{12}{8 + 8} \times 100$$

$$= \text{Rs.}75$$

Hence the cost of article is Rs.75.

Q. Mohan sold watch at 10% loss. It had sold it for Rs.45 more. He would made 5% profit. The selling price (in Rs.) of the watch was.

    (a) 300 (b) 290 (c) 110 (d) 270 (e) 900

Solution: <u>Smart Technique</u>

According to the formula for the above condition applied sum is, the cost price

$$= \dfrac{X}{y + x} \times 100$$

So the cost price of watch $= \dfrac{45}{10 + 5} \times 100 = 300$

The sold price was 10% loss. i.e. 90% of 300 = 270.

Q. A shop keeper sells an article at 15% gain. Had he sold it for Rs.18 more, he would have gained 18% the cost price of the article (in Rs.) is

    (a) 540 (b) 318 (c) 600 (d) 350

Solution: <u>Smart Technique</u>

According to the formula for the above condition applied sum is the cost price $=$

$$\dfrac{X}{y - x} \times 100$$

(Note: when both the cases have gained, there should have final gain (y) – initial (x), in place of y + x)

$$= \dfrac{18}{18 - 15} \times 100$$

$$= \frac{\frac{18}{3} \times 100}{} = 600$$

Q. An article is sold at a loss of 199. Had it been sold for Rs.120 more, then the profit would have been 21%. The cost price of the article is.

(a) Rs.300 (b) Rs.190 (c) Rs.210 (d) Rs.400

Solution:

Regular Method	Smart Technique
Article sold at a less of 19% i.e. sold at 19% less than original cost = 81% When it sold Rs.120 more i.e. 81% of cost price + 120 Profit would have 121% i.e. its price become 121% of cost price. 81% of C.P. + 120 = 121 % of C.P. 40% of C.P. = 120 $$\text{C.P.} = \frac{120}{40} \times 100 = 300$$	Simple formula for the above sum $$\text{The cost price} = \frac{X}{y+x} \times 100$$ $$\text{Cost price} = \frac{120}{19+21} \times 100$$ $$= \frac{120}{40} \times 100$$ $$= 300$$

Q. The cost price : selling price of an article is a:b. if B is 200% of a then percentage of profit on cost price is

(a) 75% (b) 125% (c) 100% (d) 200%

Solution:

$$b = 200\% \text{ of } a$$

$$\frac{a}{b} = \frac{1}{2} = \frac{CP}{SP}$$

$$\text{Profit} = \frac{SP - CP}{CP} \times 100$$

$$= \dfrac{\frac{1}{1} \times 100}{}$$

$$= 100\%.$$

Q. The reduction of Rs.12 in the selling price of an article will change 5% gain into $2\frac{1}{2}$ % loss. The cost price of the article is.

   (a) Rs.80 (b) Rs.100 (c) Rs.140 (d) Rs.160 (e) Rs.200

Solution:

$$\text{The cost price} = \dfrac{X}{y+x} \times 100$$

$$= \dfrac{12}{5+2.5} \times 100$$

$$= \dfrac{12}{7.5} \times 100$$

$$= \text{Rs.}160.$$

Q. For a certain article, if discount is 25%, the profit is 25%. If the discount is 10%, then the profit is

   (a) 50% (b) 40% (c) 30% (d) $33\frac{1}{3}$ %

Solution:

Let MP = 100

SP = 75 as discount is 25% on MP

$$\text{CP} = \dfrac{SP \times 100}{100+P} = \dfrac{75 \times 100}{125} = 60 \quad \text{as 25\% profit after discount.}$$

If discount is 10% of MP, SP = 90

$$\text{Profit \%} = \frac{SP - CP}{CP} \times 100$$

$$= \frac{90 - 60}{60} \times 100$$

$$= 50\%.$$

Q. In a certain store, the profit is 280% of the cost price. If the cost price increase by 15% and the selling price remain same, then the profit is approximately what percent of the selling price?

(a) 73.42% (b) 58.8% (c) 69.8% (d) 45%

Solution:

Let CP = 100

Profit 280%, so SP = 380

If CP increase 15%, new CP = 115

$$\text{Profit of the selling price} = \frac{380 - 115}{380} \times 100$$

$$= \frac{265}{380} \times 100$$

$$= 58.8\%$$

Q. A fan is listed at Rs.1400 and the discount offered is 10%. What additional discount must be given to bring the net selling price to Rs.1200?

(a) $16\frac{2}{3}$ (b) 5% (c) $4\frac{16}{21}\%$ (d) 6%

Solution:

Regular Method	Alternate Method

List price = Rs.1400	Let additional discount be x%
10% discount, SP = 1400 − 140 = 1260	$1400 \times \dfrac{100-10}{100} \times \dfrac{100-x}{100} = 1200$
Net selling price = 1200	
Additional discount	$\Rightarrow 1400 \times \dfrac{90}{100} \times \dfrac{100-x}{100} = 1200$
$= \dfrac{1260-1200}{1260} \times 100$	$\Rightarrow 100-x = \dfrac{1200 \times 10}{9 \times 14}$
$= \dfrac{60 \times 100}{1260}$	$\Rightarrow 100-x = \dfrac{2000}{21}$
$= \dfrac{100}{21}$	$\Rightarrow x = \dfrac{2100-2000}{21} = \dfrac{100}{21}$
$= 4\dfrac{16}{21}\%$	$\Rightarrow x = 4\dfrac{16}{21}\%$

Q. By selling a book for Rs.270, 20% profit was earned. What is the cost price of the book?

  (a) Rs.216 (b) Rs.226 (c) Rs.254 (d) Rs.225

Solution:

  SP = Rs.270

$$CP = \frac{SP \times 100}{100 + P}$$

$$CP = \frac{270 \times 100}{120}$$

  CP = Rs.225

Q. Some articles were brought at 6 for Rs.5 and sold at 5 for Rs.6 gain is

  (a) 5% (b) 36% (c) 30% (d) 44%

Solution:

$$CP \times 6 = 5 \qquad\qquad SP \times 5 = 6$$

$$CP = \frac{5}{6} \qquad\qquad SP = \frac{6}{5}$$

$$\text{Profit} = \frac{SP - CP}{CP} \times 100 \qquad \text{(Note: When CP>SP, Loss. CP<SP, gain)}$$

$$= \frac{\dfrac{6}{5} - \dfrac{5}{6}}{\dfrac{5}{6}} \times 100$$

$$= \frac{36 - 25}{30} \times \frac{6}{5} \times 100$$

$$= \frac{11}{30} \times \frac{6}{5} \times 100$$

$$= 44\%$$

Q.A man gain 20% by selling an article for a certain price. If he sells it at double the price, the percentage of profit will be.

(a) 40 (b) 100 (c) 120 (d) 140 (e) 200

Solution:

Let CP of article be Rs.100

20% profit, SP will be 120

If sells at double profits, SP = 240

$$\text{Profit \%} = \frac{240 - 100}{100} \times 100 = 140$$

Q. A trader has 25kg of pulses, part of which he sells at 9% profit and the rest at 4% profit. He gains 7% on the whole. What quantity sold at 9% profit?

Solution: <u>Smart Technique</u>

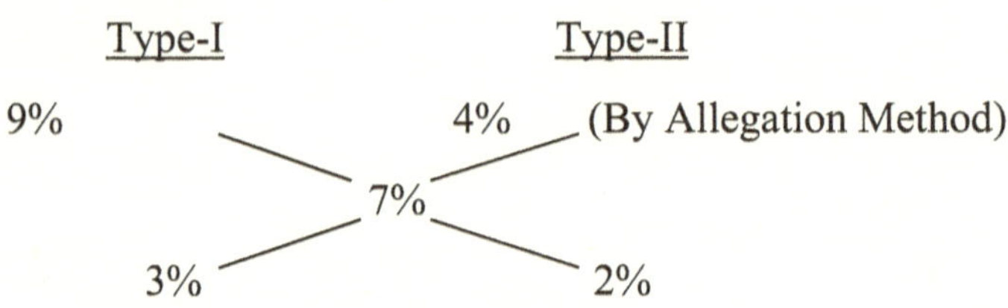

$$\frac{Type-I}{Type-II} = \frac{3}{2}$$

The quantity sold at 9% = $\dfrac{3}{5} \times 25 = 15 kg$

Q. Profit earned by selling a shirt for Rs.1200 is twice the loss occurred by selling it Rs.600. What is the CP of shirt?

(a) 1800 (b) 600 (c) 800 (d) 100 (e) none of these

Solution: <u>Smart Technique</u>

P = 2L   (Profit = Sold price – Cost Price)

=> 1200 – C = 2(C – 600)   (Loss = Cost Price – Sold Price)

=> 1200 – C = 2C – 1200

=> 3C = 2400

=> C = 800.

Q. Sold price of 16 pens is equal to the CP of 20 pens. What is the % of profit or loss?

(a) 25% profit (b) 25% loss (c) 15% profit (d) 20% profit

Solution: <u>Smart Technique</u>

SP × 16 = CP × 20

$$\frac{SP}{CP} = \frac{20}{16}$$

Note: CP > SP => loss,   CP < SP => profit

Profit = 4

$$\% \text{ of profit} = \frac{4}{16} \times 100 = 25\%$$

Q. Pravin sold an article for Rs.1170 at profit of 30%. What should be the SP, when it sold at 40% profit?

Solution:

Regular Method	Alternative Method
$SP_1 \times (100 + P_2) = SP_2(100 + P_1)$ $\Rightarrow 1170 \times 140 = SP_2 \times 130$ $\Rightarrow SP_2 = \dfrac{1170 \times 140}{130}$ $\qquad = 1260$	At 30% profit 130% = 1170 140% profit = $\dfrac{1170}{130} \times 140 = 1260$ Calculation should be done on mind i.e. 130% of 1170 = 100% of 900 140% of 900 $\Rightarrow$ 100% of 900+ 40% of 900 $\Rightarrow$ 900 + 360 = 1260

Q. The CP of a table is Rs.3200. A merchant wants to make 25% profit by selling it. At the time of sale he declares a discount of 20% on the market price. The marked price in Rs. Is

(a) 4500 (b) 5000 (c) 6000 (d) 4000

Solution: <u>Smart Technique</u>

Without using any formula, to solve the sum by mental calculation

Lets try, CP = Rs. 3200

25% profit, then SP will be 125% of 3200 = 4000 [(100% + 25%) of 3200]

Sold at 20% discount on MP

i.e. 80% of MP = 4000

$$MP = \frac{4000}{80} \times 100 = Rs.5000$$

TECHNIQUE

EFFECTIVE PERCENTAGE IN PROFIT AND LOSS

Q. A shopkeeper marks his goods in such a way that even after allowing a discount of 20%, he makes a profit of 12%. How much percentage above the cost price is the marked price?

> (a) 32% (b) 8% (c) 12% (d) 40% (e) 23%

Solution:

Regular Method	Smart Technique
$SP = \dfrac{100 - D}{100} \times MP$ $\Rightarrow SP = \dfrac{100 - 20}{100} \times MP = \dfrac{80MP}{100}$ .....(I) $\Rightarrow SP = \dfrac{100 + P}{100} \times CP$ $= \dfrac{100 + 12}{100} \times CP = \dfrac{112CP}{100}$ ......(II) From I and II we get $\dfrac{80MP}{100} = \dfrac{112CP}{100}$ $MP = \dfrac{112CP}{80} = 1.4\ CP$ MP = 140% Therefore, the marked price is 40% above the CP.	If we solve such type of problem in the given formula, itsbecome quit easy and less time taking. $P = d + m + \dfrac{d.m}{100}$ whereP = profit percentage d = discount percentage m = marked percentage $12 = -20 + m + \dfrac{(-20).m}{100}$ $\Rightarrow m - \dfrac{m}{5} = 12 + 20$ $\Rightarrow \dfrac{4m}{5} = 32$ $\Rightarrow m = 40\%$ Therefore marked price is 40% above the cost price.

Q. A shopkeeper marks his goods in such a way that after allowing a discount of 10%, he gains 17%. How much percentage above CP is the marked price?

> (a) 15% (b) 17% (c) 30% (d) 27% (e) 50%

Solution: <u>Smart Technique</u>

If we apply the suitable formula, then it became quite easy.

$$P = d + m + \dfrac{d.m}{100}$$

$$\Rightarrow 17 = -10 + m - \dfrac{10.m}{100}$$

$$\Rightarrow 17 = -10 + m - \dfrac{m}{10}$$

$$\Rightarrow m - \dfrac{m}{10} = 27$$

$$\Rightarrow \dfrac{9m}{10} = 27$$

$$\Rightarrow m = 30$$

Hence market price 30% above the cost price.

Q. A shopkeeper marks his goods in which a way that after allowing discount of 20%, he gains 28%. How much percentage above CP is the marked price?

(a) 60% (b) 56% (c) 50% (d) 48% (e) none of these

Solution: Smart Technique

If we apply the suitable formula

$$\text{Then } P = d + m + \dfrac{d.m}{100}$$

$$\Rightarrow 28 = -20 + m - \dfrac{20.m}{100}$$

$$\Rightarrow 28 = -20 + m - \dfrac{m}{5}$$

$$\Rightarrow m - \frac{m}{5} = 48$$

$$\Rightarrow \frac{4.m}{5} = 48$$

$$\Rightarrow m = \frac{48 \times 5}{4} = 60$$

Hence marked price is 60% above the cost price.

Q. The population of a town two years ago was 45000. It increased by 12% in the first year and decreased by 15% in the second year. What was the population of the town at the end of two years?

(a) 57960 (b) 42840 (c) 44820 (d) 50400 (e) none of these

Solution:

Regular Method	Smart Technique
Required population $= 45000 \times \frac{112}{100} \times \frac{85}{100}$ $= 42840$ (it required much time and chances of error)	Net % change in population $= (12 - 15 - \frac{12 \times 15}{100})\%$ $= -4.8\%$ (decrease in population) So 95.2% of 45000 $= \frac{95.2}{100} \times 45000 = 42840$

Q. An article is marked 40% above the cost price and discount of 30% is allowed. What is the gain or loss percentage?

(a) 10% gain (b) 5% gain (c) 2% loss (d) 12% loss

Solution: <u>Smart Technique</u>

If we apply the smart technique for the above sum

i.e. net effect $= (40 - 30 - \frac{40 \times 30}{100}) \%$

$$= (40 - 30 - 12)\%$$

$$= -2\%$$

Hence 2% loss.

Q. Rahim brought a gift item for Rs.510 after getting discount of 15%. He then sells it 5% above the marked price. The profit earned in this deal.

(a) Rs.150 (b) Rs.120 (c) Rs.100 (d) Rs.90 (e) none of these

Solution: <u>Smart Technique</u>

Let MP is x

85% of x = 510

$$MP = \frac{510}{85} \times 100 \qquad \text{(Avoid calculation on this step to save time)}$$

Sell it 5% above the MP

$$SP = \frac{510}{85} \times 100 \times \frac{105}{100} = 630$$

Profit = 630 – 510

= 120.

Q. Profit made by selling an article at Rs.425 is the same as the loss incurred by selling it at Rs.375. What is the CP of the article?

(a) Rs.405 (b) Rs.400 (c) Rs.410 (d) Rs.425

Solution: <u>Smart Technique</u>

When profit made by selling an article at Rs.X and loss occurred by selling it at Rs Y then the cost price of the article will be

$$\textbf{The cost price} = \frac{X + Y}{2}$$

$$= \frac{425 + 375}{2}$$

$$= \frac{800}{2} = 400.$$

Q. Profit after selling a cycle for Rs.524 is same loss after selling it for Rs.452. The cost price of the cycle is.

   (a) Rs.480 (b) Rs.500 (c) Rs.488 (d) Rs.485

Solution: <u>Smart Technique</u>

The cost price $= \dfrac{X + Y}{2}$

$$= \frac{524 + 452}{2} = \frac{976}{2} = 488.$$

Q. A trade man marks his goods 30% more than the cost price. If he allows discount of 20% on the marked price, then his gain percentage is

   (a) 15 (b) 10 (c) 6 (d) 4 (e) 5

Solution: <u>Smart Technique</u>

According to the above sum applied smart technique

$$P = (m - d - \frac{md}{100}) \%$$

$$= (30 - 20 - \frac{30 \times 20}{100}) \%$$

$$= (30 - 20 - 6) \%$$

$$= 4\%.$$

Q. Marked price of article is Rs.300. the shopkeeper gives a discount of 10% on the marked price and still gain 255. The cost price of article is.

(a) Rs.216 (b) Rs.203.50 (c) Rs.214 (d) Rs.238

Solution:

MP = Rs.300

Sells at 10% discount i.e. 90% of 300 = Rs.270

On selling Rs.270, the profit is 25%

So 125% = 270

Cost price = $\dfrac{270}{125} \times 100$

= Rs.216.

Q. A grocer mixed sugar at Rs12 per Kg with sugar at Rs.9 per Kg in a certain ratio and sold the mixture at Rs.11 per Kg to have a gain of $\dfrac{1}{8}$th of his total investment. The ratio of two type of sugar in the mixture is

(a) 7:20 (b) 9:20 (c) 1:2 (d) 3:4

Solution: <u>Regular Method</u>

Let Quantity x kg in Rs.12 and

  Quantity y Kg is Rs.9

Cost price of both sugar = 12x + 9y

Sold price of sugar = 11(x + y)

Profit = $\dfrac{1}{8}$ of (12x + 9y)

Profit = sold price – cost price

$\dfrac{1}{8}$ (12x + 9y) = 11(x + y) – (12x + 9y)

$\qquad$ = 11x + 11y -12 -9y

$12x + 9y = 8 (2y - x)$

$12x + 9y = 16y - 8x$

$20x = 7y$

$$\frac{x}{y} = 7:20$$

Q. A man sold two tables for Rs.720 each. On one he gained 20% and on the other he lost 20%. Find his total loss or gain in transaction.

  (a) loss of Rs.50 (b) loss of Rs.60 (c) gain of Rs.50 (d) gain of Rs.60

Solution:

  SP of two table = Rs.1440

$$\text{CP of two table} = \frac{720}{120} \times 100 + \frac{720}{80} \times 100$$

$$= 900 + 600 = 1500$$

$$= 1500 - 1440$$

= Rs.60 loss

Q. The price that Ravi should mark on a pair of shoes which cost him Rs.1200 to gain 12% after allowing a discount of 16% (in rupees) is

  (a) 1344 (b) 1433 (c) 1500 (d) 1600

Solution:

  CP = Rs.1200

Gain 12%, SP of 12% of 1200 = 1344 (100% of 1200 + 12% of 1200 = 1200 + 144)

After allowing discount 16%, the SP will be 1344

So 84% of MP = 1344

$$MP = \dfrac{\dfrac{1344}{84}}{} \times 100$$

$$= 1600.$$

Q. If the cost price of 10 article is equal to the selling price of 16 articles. Then the loss percentage is

(a) 30% (b) 37.5% (c) 40.6% (d) 42.5%

Solution:

Regular Method	Alternate Method
L.C.M of 10,16 is 80 CP of 10 article is 100 CP of 80 article is 80 SP of 16 article is 10 SP of 80 article is 50 Loss % = $\dfrac{CP - SP}{CP} \times 100$ $= \dfrac{30}{80} \times 100$ $= 37.5\%$	$CP \times 10 = SP \times 16$ $\dfrac{CP}{SP} = \dfrac{16}{10}$ Loss % = $\dfrac{16 - 10}{16} \times 100$ $= \dfrac{3}{8} \times 100$ $= 37.5\%$

Q. A man brought 20 dozen eggs for Rs.720. What should be the selling price of each egg, if he wants to make a profit of 20%?

(a) Rs.3.25 (b) Rs.3.40 (c) Rs.3.60 (d) Rs.3.75

Solution:

Regular Method	Alternate Method

CP of 20 dozen egg = Rs.720	CP of 20 dozen egg = Rs.720
20% profit SP = $720 \times \dfrac{120}{100}$ = Rs.864	CP of 240 egg = 720
	Cost of each egg = Rs.3.00
	20% profit, SP of each egg = Rs.3.60
SP of each egg = $\dfrac{864}{20 \times 12}$ = Rs.3.60	(Adopt this method to solve easily)

Q. List price of a book is Rs.100. A dealer sells three such books for Rs.274.50 after allowing discount at a certain rate. Find the rate of discount

    (a) 8.25% (b) 8.5% (c) 8.34% (d) 8.75%

Solution:

List price of a book Rs.100

List price of 3 books Rs.300

Sold price of 3 books Rs.274.50

$$\text{Discount \%} = \frac{300 - 274.50}{300} \times 100$$

$$= \frac{25.50}{300} \times 100$$

$$= 8.5\%.$$

TECHNIQUE

SMART TECHNIQUE TO FIND GAIN OR LOSS PERCENTAGE

Q. An article is marked 40% above the cost price and a discount of 30% is allowed. What is the gain or loss percentage?

(a) 10% gain (b) 12% gain (c) 5% loss (d) 5% gain (e) 2% loss

Solution:

Regular Method	Smart Technique
Let the cost price of article Rs.100 Marked price = Rs.140 Sold price = 70% of 140 = Rs.98 Loss percentage = $\dfrac{100-98}{100} \times 100$ $= 2\%$	This type of sum is quite easy and a small mental calculation by applying smart technique. Let's apply when these is a gain (+ve) and a loss (-ve) on same price. The net effect will be. $= \left(\text{gain}\% - \text{loss}\% - \dfrac{gain\% \times loss\%}{100}\right)\%$ $= \left(40 - 30 - \dfrac{40 \times 30}{100}\right)\%$ $= \left(40 - 30 - \dfrac{1200}{100}\right)\%$ $= (40 - 30 - 12)\%$ $= -2\%$ (-ve sign consider loss)

Q. The number of sets in an auditorium is increased by 25%. The price of ticket is also increased by 12%. Then increase in revenue collection will be .

(a) 40% (b) 20% (c) 35% (d) 45% (e) 48%

Solution: <u>Smart Technique</u>

The net effect $= (25 + 12 + \dfrac{25 \times 12}{100})\,\%$

(Note:- both % have increased so all have to be added)

$= (25 + 12 + \dfrac{300}{100}) = 40\%$ increase.

Q. Water tax is increased by 20% but its consumption is decreased by 20%. Then the increase or decrease in the expenditure of the money is

(a) no change (b) 5% decrease (c) 4% decrease (d) 4% increase

Solution: <u>Smart Technique</u>

As per the smart technique

The net effect $= (20 - 20 - \dfrac{20 \times 20}{100})\,\%$ (Note: When tax increase the sign is +ve . $= -4\%$ When decrease, the sign became –ve)

Hence result is 4% decrease.

Q. The price of an article is first decrease by 20% and then increased by 30%. If the resulting price is Rs.416. the original price of the article is.

(a) Rs.350 (b) Rs.405 (c) Rs.400 (d) Rs.450 (e) Rs.500

Solution:

Regular Method	Smart Technique
Let the original price of article Then $x \times \dfrac{80}{100} \times \dfrac{130}{100} = 416$	According to the formula The net effect $= -20 + 30 - \dfrac{20 \times 30}{100}$ $= -20 + 30 - 6$ $= 4\%$

$$\Rightarrow x = \dfrac{416 \times 100 \times 100}{80 \times 130}$$ = Rs.400 (Required much calculation)	The resulting Price 41% i.e. 104% = 416 $$100\% = \dfrac{416}{104} \times 100$$ = 400

Q. A sells an article to B at 15% profit. B sells item to C at 10% loss. If C pays Rs.517.50 for it then A purchase it at

   (a) Rs.500 (b) Rs.750 (c) Rs.100 (d) Rs.1250

Solution:

Regular Method	Smart Technique
An article sold to B at x% Profit / loss and B sells to C at y% Profit / loss, then **A's cost price** $$= \text{C's cost price} \times \dfrac{100}{100 \pm x} \times \dfrac{100}{100 \pm y}$$ According to question $$= 517.50 \times \dfrac{100}{100+15} \times \dfrac{100}{100-10}$$ $$= 517.50 \times \dfrac{100}{115} \times \dfrac{100}{90}$$ = Rs.500 (To avoid much calculation , follow the smart technique)	When same item sold purchased by two person with profit / loss **The net effect = $\left(x \pm y \pm \dfrac{100}{90}\right)$ %** According to question The net effect $$= \left(15 - 10 - \dfrac{15 \times 10}{100}\right)\%$$ $= (15 - 10 - 1.5)$ % = 3.5% profit 103.5% of CP = 517.50 $$\text{The CP} = \dfrac{517.50}{103.5} \times 100$$ = 500

Q. Ram sold two horse at the same price. In one horse he get a profit of 10% and in the other horse he gets a loss of 10%. Then Ram gets

(a) 1% loss (b) no loss no profit (c) 2% loss (d) 1% profit

Solution: Smart Technique

For this type of sum, we have a smart formula to solve without much paper work

Condition: when SP of two items is same and there is a gain of x% on one item and x% loss on other. There is a

Loss of $\left(\dfrac{x^2}{100}\right)$ % in the whole transaction.

For the above sum, the net effect = $\left(\dfrac{x^2}{100}\right)$ % loss

$$= \left(\dfrac{10^2}{100}\right) \text{ % loss } = 1\% \text{ loss}$$

Q. A sells a bicycle to B at a profit of 20%, B sells to C at a profit of 25%. If C pays Rs.225 for it, the cost price of bicycle for A is

(a) Rs.110 (b) Rs.125 (c) Rs.120 (d) Rs.150

Solution: Smart Technique

As for the smart technique for the above condition applied sum.

$$\text{The net effect} = \left(20 + 25 + \dfrac{20 \times 25}{100}\right)$$

$$= \left(20 + 25 + \dfrac{500}{100}\right)$$

$$= 50\%$$

150% of cost price = 2255

$$\text{Cost price} = \dfrac{225}{150} \times 100$$

= Rs.150.

Q. if the radio of the cost price and selling price is 5:6, the gain percentage is

(a) 20% (b) $33\dfrac{1}{3}$%(c) 25% (d) 30%

Solution:<u>Smart Technique</u>

According to question

$$\text{Gain} = \dfrac{Profit}{CP} \times 100$$

Let CP = 5x   SP = 6x

Hence profit = SP – CP = 6x – 5x = x

$$\text{Gain} = \dfrac{x}{5x} \times 100$$

= 20%.

Q. A trades man marks his goods at 20% above the cost price. He allows his customers a discount of 8% on market price. Then his profit percentage is

(a) 10.4% (b) 12.2 (c) 9.7% (d) 12%

Silution:

Regular Method	Smart Technique

Let CP = 100 MP = 120 Discount 8% on MP 92% of 120(90% of 120 + 2% of 120) = 110.4 Profit % = 10.4%	Net profit $= (20 - 8 - \dfrac{20 \times 8}{100})\,\%$ $= (20 - 8 - 1.6)\,\%$ $= 10.4\%$

Q. A businessman sells two articles at Rs.800 each on one he earns a profit of 25% and on the other he incurs loss of 25%. What will be his percentage gain or loss

    (a) 6.25% gain (b) 6.25% loss (c) 4.75% profit (d) 4.75% loss

Solution:

$$\text{Net effect on transition} = (25 - 25 - \frac{25 \times 25}{100})\,\%$$

$$= (25 - 25 - 6.25)\,\%$$

$$= -6.25\%$$

6.25% loss on whole transition.

Q. The S.P of 10 oranges is equal to the cost price of 13 oranges. Then the profit percentages is

    (a) 30% (b) 10% (c) 13% (d) 3%

Solution: <u>Smart Technique</u>

S.P × 10 = C.P × 13

$\dfrac{SP}{CP} = \dfrac{13}{10}$, Profit = 13 – 10 =3

Profit % $= \dfrac{3}{10} \times 100$

$= 30\%.$

Q. A got 30% concession on the label price of an article sold for Rs.8750 with 25% profit on the price he brought. The label price was

  (a) Rs.16000 (b) Rs. 12000 (c) Rs.10000 (d) Rs.13500

Solution:

Let label price be x.

30% concession i.e. 70% of x = 8750

Label price $x = \dfrac{8750}{70} \times 100 = 12500$

Offer selling profit on it 25% i.e. CP + 25% P.

125% of label price = 12500

Label price $= \dfrac{12500}{125} \times 100$

   $= 10000$

<u>TECHNIQUE #</u>

<u>COMPARISION OF PROFIT AND LOSS USING PROPORTIONALITY</u>

Q. Ravi sold an article Rs.460 and earned profit of 15% at what price should it have sold so as to earn a profit 20%?

     (a) 450 (b) 465 (c) 480 (d) 485 (e) 799

Solution:

Regular Method	Smart Technique
Initial selling price = Rs.460 Profit = 15% $CP = \dfrac{SP \times 100}{100 + P} = \dfrac{460 \times 100}{115}$ CP = 400 Desire profit = $\dfrac{CP \times 100 + P}{100}$ $= \dfrac{400 \times 120}{100}$ =480	To solve this problem by applying short cut method, to get result $S_1 \times (100 + P_2) = S_2 \times (100 + P_1)$ Where initial price = S_1 Initial profit = P_1 Desired price S_2 Desired price P_2 Note: if loss, in place of profit, the sign will be –Ve) $460 \times (120 + 20) = x \times (100 + 15)$ $x + 115 = 460 + 120$ $x = \dfrac{460 \times 120}{115} = 480$

Q. A merchant sold an article Rs.1200 and earned profit of 25%. At what price should it have been sold so as to earn a profit of 30%.

     (a) 1358 (b) 1428 (c) 1228 (d) 1248 (e) 1258

Solution:

By applying shortcut formula to obtain the result

$S_1 \times (100 + P_2) = S_2 \times (100 + P_1)$

$1200 \times (100 + 30) = S_2 \times (100 + 25)$

$S_2 \times 125 = 1200 \times 130$

$S_2 = \dfrac{1200 \times 130}{125}$

= Rs.1248.

Q. There would be a loss 10% if rice sold at Rs.54 per kg. to open a profit of 20%, the price of rice per kg will be.

(a) Rs.63 (b) Rs.70 (d) Rs.65 (d) Rs.72 (e) Rs.75

Solution:

Regular Method	Smart Technique
$$C.P = \dfrac{SP \times 100}{100 - L}$$ $$= \dfrac{54 \times 100}{90}$$ $$= 60$$ To earn 20% profit $$S.P = \dfrac{CP \times 100 + g}{100}$$ $$= \dfrac{60 \times 120}{100}$$ $$= Rs.72$$	If we apply the smart technique to get the answer in single step. $SP_1 \times (100 + P) = S_2 \times (100\text{-}L)$ $54 \times 120 = x \times 90$ $$x = \dfrac{54 \times 120}{90}$$ $$= Rs.72$$

Q. If a man were to sell his hand cart for Rs.720. he would loss 25%. It what price must he sell it to gain 25%

(a) Rs.1152 (b) Rs.768 (c) Rs.1200 (d) Rs.960 (e) Rs.852

Solution:

According to formula

$SP_1 \times (100 + g) = SP_2 \times (100 - loss)$

$\Rightarrow 720 \times (100 + 25) = SP_2 \times (100 - 25)$

$$\Rightarrow SP_2 = \frac{720 \times 125}{75}$$

$$= Rs.1200$$

Hence he should sell his hand craft Rs.1200 to gain 25%.

Q. A person incurs a loss of 60% buy selling a watch at Rs.423. In order to get a profit of 60%. The person should sell the watch in.

Solution: <u>Smart Technique</u>

According to Smart Technique

$$SP_1 \times (100 + P) = SP_2 \times (100 + L)$$

$$\Rightarrow 423 \times (100 + b) = x \times (100 - b)$$

$$\Rightarrow x \times 94 = 432 \times 106$$

$$\Rightarrow x = \frac{432 \times 106}{94}$$

$$\Rightarrow x = 477$$

Hence the selling prize of watch is Rs.477.

Q. After allowing a discount of 16%, there was still a gain of 5%, then the percentage of marked price over the cost price is

(a) 15% (b) 18% (c) 21% (d) 25%

Solution: <u>Smart Technique</u>

According to smart technique formula for the above condition applied sum

$$P = d + m + \frac{dm}{100}$$

According to sum

$$5 = -16 + m - \frac{16m}{100}$$

$$\frac{100m - 16m}{100} = 21$$

$$m = \frac{21 \times 100}{84}$$

$$m = 25\%$$

Q. There is a profit of 20% on the cost price of an article. The % of profit, when calculated on selling price is

(a) $16\frac{2}{3}$% (b) 20% (c) $33\frac{1}{2}$% (d) none of these

Solution:

Let CP = 100

20% profit, the SP = 120

$$\text{Profit \% on sold price} = \frac{20}{120} \times 100$$

$$= \frac{100}{6} = 16\frac{2}{3}\%$$

Q. By selling 20 meters of cloth a man gain the selling price of 4 meter of cloth. Then the gain percentage is

(a) 25 (b) 20 (c) 30 (d) 35

Solution:

Regular Method	Regular Method
Let selling price of 20 meters = Rs.100 S.P of 1mt = Rs.5 Selling Rs.100, Profit 20 The C.P will be 80 Gain % = $\dfrac{20}{80} \times 100$ $= 25\%$	On 20mt cloth selling gain 4mt. C.P of cloth = 16mt Gain % = $\dfrac{4}{16} \times 100$ $= 25\%$

Q. A person sells 36 oranges per rupees and suffers a loss of 4%. Find how many oranges should be sold per rupee to have a gain of 8%.

(a) 30 (b) 35 (c) 28 (d) 32 (e) 40

Solution:

Regular Method	Smart Technique
SP of 36 oranges = Rs.1 SP of 1 orange = $\dfrac{1}{36}$ Loss at 4% $CP = \dfrac{SP \times 100}{100 - 4} = \dfrac{1}{36} \times \dfrac{100}{96}$ SP of 1 orange = $\dfrac{CP \times (100 + 8)}{100}$ $= \dfrac{1}{36} \times \dfrac{100}{96} \times \dfrac{108}{100}$ $= \dfrac{1}{32}$ SP is 32 orange in one rupee.	For the above condition applied sum $SP_1 \times (100 + g) = SP_2 (100 - L)$ $\dfrac{1}{36} \times 108 = \dfrac{1}{x} \times 96$ $x = \dfrac{96 \times 36}{108}$ $x = 32$

TECHNIQUE

FIND THE REDUCED PRICE OR ORIGINAL PRICE AFTER THE REDUCTION OF COST

Q. A reduction of 20% in the price of apples enables a man to buy 16kg more for Rs.400. what is the reduced price per kg of apple.

(a) Rs.64 (b) Rs.60 (c) Rs.50 (d) Rs.40 (e) Rs.75

Solution:

Regular Method	Smart Technique

| Let the original price of apple = Rs.x /kg

New price = Rs.80% of x = Rs. $\frac{4}{5}$ of x

$\Rightarrow \dfrac{\frac{4000 \times 5}{4x} - \frac{4000}{x}}{4000} = 16$

$\Rightarrow \dfrac{\frac{4x}{1000}}{4000} = 16$

$\Rightarrow \dfrac{x}{1000} = 16$

$\Rightarrow x = \dfrac{1000}{16} = 62.5$

Hence reduced price = $\frac{4}{5}x$

$= \frac{4}{5} \times 62.5 = $ Rs.50 per kg | This type of sum can be solve by the application of a simple reduced formula i.e

The reduced price
$= \frac{1}{x}\left[y \times \dfrac{P}{100}\right]$ per unit

Where x = quantity of more apple buy
y = price of the article
P = percentage reduction
So the reduced price of apple

Per kg $= \dfrac{1}{16}\left[4000 \times \dfrac{20}{100}\right]$
$= \frac{1}{x} \times 800$
$= $ Rs.50 per kg |

Q. A reduction of 20% in the price of sugar enables a person to get 5.2 kg more sugar for Rs.130. the original price of sugar per kg is

(a) Rs.5 (b) Rs.7.75 (c) Rs.6.25 (d) Rs.7.50 (e) Rs.6.75

Solution:

Regular Method	Smart Technique

Let the original price of sugar = Rs.x/ kg The new price = 80% of x = Rs.$\dfrac{4}{5}x$ $\dfrac{130 \times 5}{4x} - \dfrac{130}{x} = 5.2$ $\Rightarrow \dfrac{650 - 520}{4x} = 5.2$ $\Rightarrow x = \dfrac{100}{16}$ $\Rightarrow$ original price = Rs.6.25 per kg	The original price $= \dfrac{Rx}{(100 - R)A}$ Where R = Reduction percentage A = Excess amount of item x = price of article so the original price of sugar $= \dfrac{20 \times 130}{(100 - 20) \times 5.2}$ $= \dfrac{20 \times 130}{80 \times 5.2}$ $= \dfrac{25}{4}$ $= 6.25$ per kg

Q. The price of sugar having gone down by 10%, a consumer can buy 5kg more sugar for Rs.270. the difference between the original price and reduced price per kg is

    (a) 75 paisa (b) 53 paisa (c) 62 paisa (d) 60 paisa (e) 65 paisa

Q. Solution: <u>Smart Technique</u>

The reduction price $= \dfrac{1}{x}\left[y \times \dfrac{P}{100}\right]$ Where x = 5kg

y = Rs.270

P = 10%

The original price = reduced price $\times \dfrac{100}{100 - P}$

$= 5.40 \times \dfrac{100}{90}$

$= Rs.6$

So the difference of price per kg = Rs.6 – Rs.5.40

= 60 paisa

Q. A reduction of 20% in the price of sugar enables a man to purchase 5 kg more for Rs.600. find the price of sugar per kg before reduction of price.

(a) Rs.24 (b) Rs.30 (c) Rs.32 (d) Rs.35 (e) Rs.36

Solution: <u>Smart technique</u>

According to question, the price of sugar per kg before reduction of price that means the original price of sugar per kg according to the original price per formula

i.e. to the original price $= \dfrac{Rx}{(100-R)A}$ where R = 20%

$$= \dfrac{20 \times 600}{(100-20) \times 5} \qquad A = 5$$

$$= \dfrac{20 \times 600}{80 \times 5} \qquad x = 600$$

$$= Rs.30.$$

Q. A 20% reduction in the unit of an article enables one to buy 25 items more for Rs.1000. what is the original unit of the item?

(a) Rs.10 (b0 Rs.12 (c) Rs.12.50 (d) Rs.8

Solution: <u>Smart Technique</u>

According to the formula for original price of smart technique

i.e. the original cost $= \dfrac{Rx}{(100-R)A}$ \qquad Where R = reduction cost 20

$$= \dfrac{20 \times 1000}{(100-20) \times 25} \qquad A = 25$$

$$= \dfrac{20 \times 1000}{80 \times 25} \qquad x = 1000$$

$$= Rs.10.$$

Q. A reduction in the price of apples enable a person to purchase 3 apples for Rs.1 instead of for Rs.1.25. What is the reduction of price in percentage?

(a) 20 (b) 25 (c) 30 (d) 33 (e) 35

Solution: Smart Technique

$$\text{Reduction \%} = \frac{125 \times 100}{125} \times 100$$

$$= 20\%.$$

Q. A reduction of 20% in the unit sale price of sugar enables the house wife to purchase 2kg extra in her monthly budget. How much was the earlier consumption of sugar (per month) by the family?

(a) 10kg (b) 8kg (c) 7.5kg (d0 6kg (e) 5 kg

Solution: Smart technique

According to the formula for original price of the above sum is not suitable because all the required data not given. When you solve this type of sum, it become quite easy than formula.

Let us try

Suppose earlier cost is x kg = Rs.100

Reduction of price is 20% i.e. Rs. 80 can purchase x kg Rs.100 can purchase =

$$\frac{x}{80} \times 100 = \frac{5x}{4} \text{ kg}$$

Any given condition $\dfrac{5x}{4} - x = 2$ kg

$$x = 8kg$$

Hence the earlier consumption is 8kg.

Q. A reduction in the price of petrol by 10% enables a motorist to buy 5 gallons more for Rs.180. find the original price of petrol (in Rs. Per gallon)

(a) 20 (b) 30 (c) 40 (d) 50 (e) none of these

Solution: Smart Technique

According to smart Technique

$$\text{Original price} = \frac{Rx}{(100 - R)A} \qquad \text{Where R} = 10, A = 5, x = 180$$

$$= \frac{10 \times 180}{90 \times 5}$$

$$= 4 \text{ of petrol}$$

Hence original price is Rs.4 per gallon.

Q. A reduction 20% in the price of nice enable a customer to purchase 12.5kg more for Rs.800. the original price of rice per kg is

(a) 14 (b) 16 (c) 12 (d) 15

Solution: Smart Technique

According to the formula for the above condition applied sum.

$$\text{The original price} = \frac{Rx}{(100 - R)A}$$

$$= \frac{20 \times 800}{(100 - 20) \times 12.5}$$

$$= \frac{20 \times 800 \times 10}{80 \times 125} = \text{Rs.16.}$$

Q. A person sells 36 oranges per rupees and suffers a loss of 14%. Find how many oranges should be sold per a rupee to have a gain of 8%?

Solution:

Regular Method	Smart Technique
SP of 36 oranges = Rs 1 SP of 1 orange =1/36 Loss of 4% $$CP = \dfrac{sp \times 100}{100 - 4} = 1/36 \times 100/36$$ Sold at 8% profit $$Sp \text{ of 1 orange} = \dfrac{cp \times (100 + 8)}{100}$$ $$= \dfrac{1}{36} \times \dfrac{100}{96} \times \dfrac{108}{100} = 1/32$$ Sp of 32 oranges in one rupees	For the above condition applied sum $Sp_1 \times (100+g) = sp_2 \times (100-L)$ $$\dfrac{1}{36} \times 108 = \dfrac{1}{x} \times 96$$ $$= \dfrac{96 \times 36}{108}$$ X=32

TECHNIQUE

CALCULATE R, T IN SIMPLE INTEREST SUM WHERE R = T

Q. simple interest on certain sum of 6yrs in $\dfrac{9}{25}$ of the price. The rate of interest is

   (a) 6% (b) 6.5% (c) 7% (d) 8% (e) 8.5%

Solution:

Regular Method	Smart Technique

Let principal = x $$\text{Interest} = \frac{9x}{25}$$ Rate of interest $R = \dfrac{SI \times 100}{P \times Time} = 6$ Hence Rate of interest is 6% per annum.	By smart technique, we calculate $$R = \sqrt{\frac{x}{y}}\ 10$$ Condition should be **Condition-1** principal is $\frac{x}{y}$ part of the sum **Condition II** R.I. = T $$R = \sqrt{\frac{9}{25}} \times 10$$ $$= \frac{3}{5} \times 10$$ $$= 6\%$$ Such type of sum also follow condition-2 So no calculation required.

Q. The simple interest on a sum of money is $\frac{4}{9}$ of the principal and the number of year is equal to the rate of interest per annum. The rate per annum is

(a) 5% (b) $6\frac{2}{3}$ % (c) 6% (d) $7\frac{1}{5}$ %

Solution: <u>Smart Technique</u>

According to the formula for the above condition problem is

$$R = \sqrt{\frac{x}{y}} \times 10$$

$$= \sqrt{\frac{4}{9}} \times 10 = \frac{2}{3} \times 10 = \frac{20}{30} = 6\frac{2}{3}\%$$

Q. At what time will the simple interest be $\frac{2}{5}$ of the principal at 8% per annum?

(a) 8 years (b) 7 years (c) 5 years (d) 6 years

Solution: <u>Smart Technique</u>

Let Principal x

$$\text{Interest} = \frac{2x}{5}$$

According to SI formula $\mathbf{I} = \dfrac{PTR}{100}$

$$T = \frac{I \times PTR}{PR}$$

$$= \frac{\dfrac{2x}{5} \times 100}{x \times 8}$$

$$= \frac{2 \times 100}{5 \times 8}$$

$$= 5 \text{ years.}$$

Q. At what time will Rs.500 gives Rs.50 as interest at the ratio of 5% per annum in SI.

(a) 2 years (b) 5 years (c) 3 years (d) 4 years

Solution:<u>Smart Technique</u>

According to the Question P = 500, I = 50, R = 5%

$$T = \frac{I \times 100}{P \times R}$$

$$= \frac{50 \times 100}{500 \times 5}$$

$$= 2 \text{ years.}$$

Q. At what annual payment will discharge a debt of Rs.808 due in 2 years at 2% per annum?

  (a) Rs.200 (b) Rs.300 (c) Rs.400 (d) Rs.300

Solution:

Regular Method	Smart Technique
Let 1st installment = 100 2nd installment = 102 In 2 years, total installment = 202 202 debt, annual installment 100 808 debt, annual installment $= \dfrac{100}{202} \times 808$ $= 400$	If we solve in Reverse Technique Then Annual interest is 2% Rs.8 interest will be paid on sum Rs.400 in 1 year Hence Rs.400 annual payment for the rest of 808

Q. Ankit deposited two parts of sum of Rs.25000 in different banks at the ratio of 15% per annum and 18% per annum respectively. In one year he got Rs.4050 as the total interest. What was the amount deposited at the ratio of 18% per annum?

  (a)Rs.9000 (b) Rs.12000 (c) Rs.15000 (d) none of these

Regular method	smart technique
Let Ankit Deposit Rsx in 15 % and (25000-x) in 18% $= \dfrac{x \times 1 \times 15}{100} + \dfrac{(25000 - x) \times 1 \times 18}{100} =$ 4050 $= \dfrac{15x}{100} + \dfrac{25000 \times 18}{100} - \dfrac{18x}{100} = 4050$ $\dfrac{3x}{100} = 4500 - 4050$ $= 3x = 45000$	At can be solved in two smart ways **1st by reverse technique** total interest is 4050 at we split Rs 25000 by optim $\dfrac{15000 \times 15 \times 1}{100} = 2250$ $\dfrac{10000 x 18 + 1}{100} = 1800$ Hence total interest=4050 So 15%diposit is Rs 15000 **2nd by allegation method**

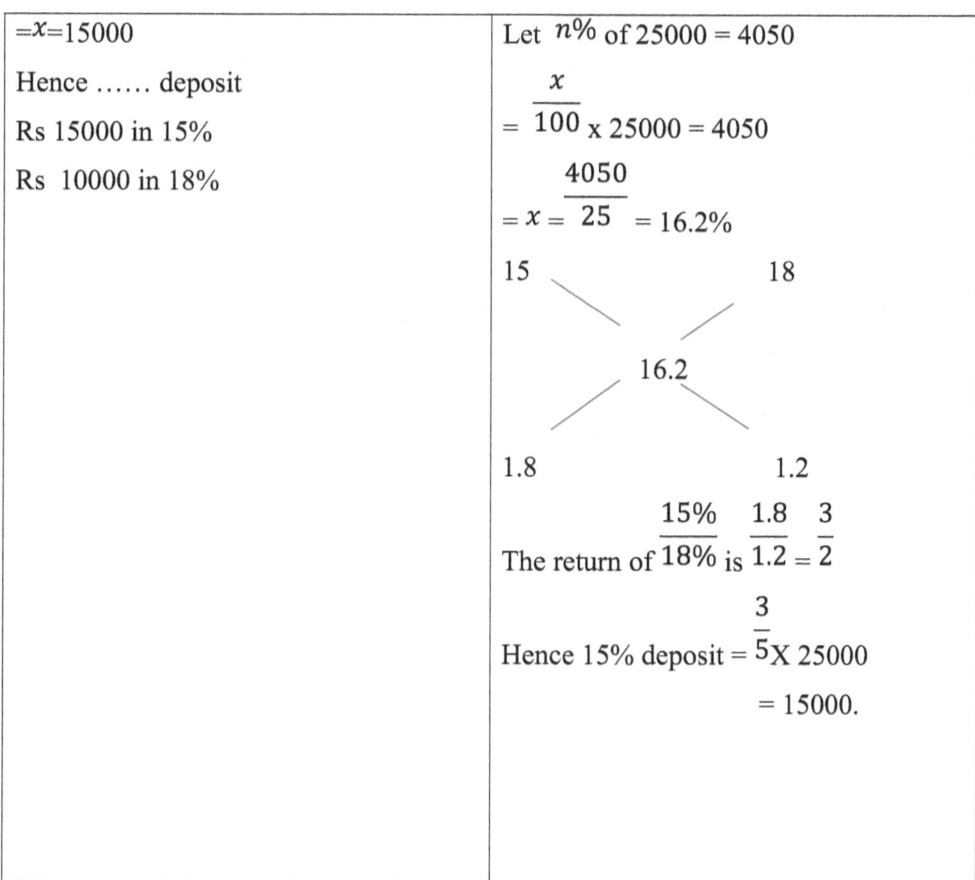

$= x = 15000$	Let $n\%$ of $25000 = 4050$
Hence …… deposit	$= \dfrac{x}{100} \times 25000 = 4050$
Rs 15000 in 15%	$= x = \dfrac{4050}{25} = 16.2\%$
Rs 10000 in 18%	15 18 16.2 1.8 1.2 The return of $\dfrac{15\%}{18\%}$ is $\dfrac{1.8}{1.2} = \dfrac{3}{2}$ Hence 15% deposit $= \dfrac{3}{5} \times 25000$ $= 15000.$

Q. The simple interest on a sum of money $is\ \dfrac{4}{9}$ of the principal and the number of year is equal to the rate of interest per annum. The rate per annum is.(a) 5% (b) $6\dfrac{2}{3}$ (c) 6% (d) $7\dfrac{1}{5}\%$

Solution: smart technique

acc. to the formula for the above condition problem is

$$R = \sqrt{\frac{x}{y}}\,10$$

$$= \sqrt{\frac{4}{9}}\cdot 10 = \frac{2}{3}\times 10 = \frac{20}{3} = 6$$

TECHNIQUE

CALCULATE THE COMPOUND INTEREST FOR 2 YEARS

Q. What will be the compound interest on 5000 of 2 years at 12% per annum

   a) **1250**   b) **1200** c) **1272** d) **2174**   e) **none of these.**

Solution.

Regular method	smart technique
$CI = p \times \left(1 + \frac{R}{100}\right)^T - p$	$CI = \left(a + a + \frac{aa}{100}\right)\% \text{ of } p$
$CI = 5000 \times \left(1 + \frac{12}{100}\right)^2 - 5000$	(where a and a are the rate of interest of two years and p is principal)
$= 5000 \times \left(\frac{112}{100}\right)\left(\frac{112}{100}\right) - 5000$	$CI = \left(12 + 12 + \frac{12.12}{100}\right)\% \text{ of } 5000$
$= 5000 \left(\frac{122 \times 122}{10000}\right) - 5000$	$= \left(24 + \frac{144}{100}\right) \times 5000$
$= 5 \times 1254.4 - 5000$	$= 25.44\ \% \times 5000$
$= 6272 - 5000$	$= 1272$
$= 1272$	

Q: What shall be the amount including compound interest of Rs 1500 invested at the interest rate of 7% in 2 years

 a) 1717.35   b) 1727.35   c) 1737.35   d) 1747

Solution.

Amount = CI +Principal

$$= \frac{(7 + 7 + \frac{7.7}{100})}{} \text{\%of } 1500 + 1500$$

= 14.49 % X 1500 + 1500

= 14.49 X 15 + 1500

= 14.49 (10+5) + 1500 (spilt the number for quick multiplication)

= 217.35+1500

= 1717.35

Q. the compound interest on a sum of Rs 7500 at 4% per annum in 2 years

 a) 618   b) 612   c) 624   e) 606   e) 621

Solution.

$$CI = \frac{4 + 4 + \frac{4.4}{100})}{} \text{\% of } 7500$$

 = 8.16 % of 7500

=0.0816X 7500

$= 612.$

Q. What will be the compound interest on a sum Rs 7500 at 4 P.C.P.A in 2 years.

a) Rs 618　　**b) Rs 612**　　**c)　Rs 624**　**d) 606**　**e) 621**

Solution.

As per the smart technique for UI for 2 years is

$$= \frac{(4 + 4 + \frac{4.4}{100})}{} \% \text{ of } 7500$$

$$= \frac{8.16}{100} + 7500$$

$$= \text{Rs } 612.$$

Q . What would be the $c.I$ accrued on an amount of Rs 9000 at the rate of 11 p.c.p.a in two years?

a) 2089.90　b)2140.90　c)2068.50　d)　2085.50　e) 2.88.90

Solution.

$$C.I = (11 + 11 + \frac{11X11}{100}) \% \text{ of } 9000$$

$$= 23.21 \% \, X \, 9000$$

=2088.90

Q. What is the compound interest on Rs 6000 at 10% per annum for one year compounded half yearly

 a) Rs 1260   b) Rs 630   c) Rs 615   d) Rs 600

Solution.

 10% per annum compounded half yearly for one year means the Rate of interest is 5% and interest counted twice a years

So for the above sim, same cond^{n}should be applied

$$CI = (5 + 5 + \frac{5.5}{100} \text{ \% of } 6000) \quad = 10.25\% \; of \; 6000$$

$$= \frac{10.25}{100} X \; 6000$$

= 615.

Q. Find the principal, If the interest rate is 10% per annum for two years is Rs 420

 a) Rs 2000   b) Rs 2200   c) Rs 1000   d) Rs 1100

Solution.

Acc. To the smart technique formula for $e.I$ is

$$eI = (10 + 10 + \frac{10.10}{100})\% \text{ of } x \quad (x \text{ the assumpnd pricipal})$$

$$= 420 = 21\% \text{ of } x$$

$$= \quad 420 = \frac{21}{100}x$$

$$= x = 2000$$

Hence principal is Rs 2000.

Q: A sum of money lent at compound interest amount to Rs 1460 in 2 years and to Rs 1606 in three years. The rate of interest per annum is

   a) 12%   b) 11% c) 10.5%   d) 10%

Sol :

Regular method	Smart Technique

Amount offer 2 years =Rs1460
Amount offere 3 years = Rs 1606
Interest on 01 years = 1606-1460
        = 146
Principal Rs 1460
Rate % = $\dfrac{100 \times 1 \times 146}{1460}$
    = 10%
	m.c.I sum, A= $(1+\dfrac{R}{100})^T$
	
	$\dfrac{(1+\dfrac{R}{100})3}{\left(1+\dfrac{R}{100}\right)2} = \dfrac{1606}{1460}$
	
	$1+\dfrac{R}{100} = \dfrac{1606}{1460}$
	
	$\dfrac{R}{100} = \dfrac{1606}{1460} - 1 = \dfrac{1606-1460}{1460}$

	$R = \dfrac{146 \times 100}{1460} = 10\%$

<u>TECHNIQUE #</u>

<u>CALCULATE THE TIME AND ROI OF COMPOUND INTEREST</u>

Q: A sum of money, deposited at some rate of interest per annum of compound interest, doubles itself in 4 years. On how many years will it become 16 times of itself at the same rate?

a) 16   b)12   c) 10   d) 8   e) 5

Sol :

Regular method	smart Technique
Let sum = 1 and rate interest = R $2 = 1(1 + \dfrac{R}{100})^4$ $2^4 = \{1(1 + \dfrac{R}{100})^4\}^4$ $16 = 1(1 + \dfrac{R}{100})^{16}$ Hence answer is 16	If the principal is compounded annually and it becomes 'n' times in t_1 years and m times in t_2 years, then $n^{\frac{1}{t1}} = m^{\frac{1}{t2}}$ According the question $n = 2 \qquad t1 = 4$ $m = 16 \qquad t2 = x$ $2^{\frac{1}{4}} = 16^{\frac{1}{x}}$ $2^{\frac{1}{4}} = 2^{\frac{4}{x}}$ $\dfrac{1}{4} = \dfrac{4}{x}$ $x = 16$ Hence time is 16 years

Q. If a sum of money compounded annually becomes 1.44 times of itself in 2 years, then the rate of interest per annum is

a) 25%   b) 22%   c) 21%   d) 20%   e) 18%

Sol: smart technique

In compound interest sum, if principal becomes 'n' times in 't' years , the rate of interest (R) is

$$R = 100\left[(n)^{\frac{1}{4}} - 1\right]\%$$

Of we apply formula in the above sum then

$$R = 100\left[(1.44)^{\frac{1}{2}} - 1\right]\%$$

$$= 100(1.2 - 1)$$

$$= 0.2 X 100$$

$$= 20\%.$$

Q: A sum of money double itself in 5 years on how many years will it become fourfold if impounded annually

a) 15   b)20   c)12   d)10

Sol: smart technique

As per the smart technique formula for the above sum

$$n^{\frac{1}{t1}} = m^{\frac{1}{t2}}$$

$$2^{\frac{1}{5}} = 4^{\frac{1}{t2}}$$

$$2^{\frac{1}{5}} = 2^{\frac{2}{t2}}$$

$$\frac{1}{5} = \frac{2}{t2}$$

$$t2 = 10 years.$$

Q: A sum of money placed at C.I double itself in 3 years on how mony years will it become 8 times of itself

   a) 6 b)9 c) 8 d) 7 e) 27

Sol: smart technique

Acc. To the smart technique for the above condition sum formula i.e

$$n^{\frac{1}{t1}} = m^{\frac{1}{t2}}$$

$$2^{\frac{1}{3}} = 8^{\frac{1}{t2}}$$

$$2^{\frac{1}{3}} = 2^{\frac{3}{t2}}$$

$$\frac{1}{3} = \frac{3}{t2}$$

$$= t2 = 9 \ years.$$

Q : A sum of money double itself at e.i in 15 years on how many years it will become sixteen times.

Sol: smart technique

Acc. To the smart technique for the above conditioned sum foumulai.e

$$n^{\frac{1}{t1}} = m^{\frac{1}{t2}}$$

$$2^{\frac{1}{15}} = 16^{\frac{1}{t2}}$$

$$2^{\frac{1}{15}} = 2^{\frac{4}{t2}}$$

$$\frac{1}{15} = \frac{4}{t2}$$

$$t2 = 60 \; years$$

Q: At what rate percent at the compound interest, does a sum of money become four fold in 2 years

    a) 150% b) 100% c) 200% d) 75% e) 50%

Sol: smart technique

Acc. To the smart technique formula for the above conditioned sum i.e

$$R = 100[(n)^{\frac{1}{t}} - 1] \, \%$$

$$= [(2)^{\frac{1}{2}} - 1]\ \%$$

$$= 100(2 - 1)\%$$

$$= 100\%.$$

Q: A sum of Rs 12000 deposited in C.I. become double after 5 years. After 20 years, it will become

 a) Rs 120000 b) Rs 192000 c) Rs 124000 d) Rs 96000

Sol: smart technique

Acc. To smart technique, for above conditioned sum

$$2^{\frac{1}{5}} = n^{\frac{1}{20}}$$

$$2^{20} = n^5$$

$$n = 2^{\frac{20}{5}} = 2^4 = 16\,times$$

$$The\ sum\ wil\ be = 12000\ X\ 16$$

$$= Rs\ 192000.$$

<u>TECHNIQUE #</u>

<u>CALCULATE THE RATE OF INTEREST IN SMART TECHNIQUE</u>

Q: At What rate of simple interest per annum, certain principal amount will be double in 8 years

   a) 8%   b) 10%   c) 12.5%   d) 12%   e) 7.5%

Sol:

Regular method	Smart technique
Let principal = interest $= x$ $\text{Rate} = \dfrac{S.I X\ 100}{Principal} = x$ $= \dfrac{x X\ 100}{x X 8}$ $= 12.5\%$	Use smart technique to solve RT=(n-1)100 Where R= Rate of interest T=number of years n = n times i.e double principle etc $R.8 = (2 - 1)100$ $R = \dfrac{100}{8} = 12.5\%$

Q: At What rate of simple interest per annum, it principal become 3 times in 20 years.

   a) 7%   b) 8%   c) 9%   d) 10%   e) 12%

Sol:

Regular method	Smart technique
Let principal $=x$, interest $=2x$ $\text{Rate} = \dfrac{S.I \times 100}{Principal \times time}$ $= \dfrac{x \times 100}{x \times 20}$ $=10\%$	Use smart technique to solve $RT=(n-1)100$ Where R= Rate of interest T=number of years n = n times i.e double principle etc $R.20 = (3-1)100$ $R = \dfrac{2 \times 100}{20}$ $= 10\%$

Q: A certain sum of money will be double in 15 years at the rate of simple interest per annum. The rate of interest is

  a) 25   b) $5\frac{1}{2}$ c) 6   d) $4\frac{1}{2}$ e) $6\frac{2}{3}$

Sol:

Regular method	Smart technique
Let principal $=x$	Acc. To smart technique

Interest also= x	$RT = (n-1)100$
Rate $=\dfrac{S.I \times 100}{Princepal \times Time}$	$R.15 = (2-1)100$
Rate $=\dfrac{x \times 100}{x \times 15}$	$R = \dfrac{100}{15} = 6\dfrac{2}{3}$
$=6\dfrac{2}{3}\%$	Hence rate of interest $= 6\dfrac{2}{3}\%$

Q: At what rate per annum will a sum double itself in 16 years?

a) **6.5%**   b) $5\dfrac{1}{4}\%$ c) $6\dfrac{1}{4}\%$ d) **none of these**

Sol: smart technique

Acc. To the formula for above condition applied sum

Is $RT = (n-1)100$

$RX16 = (2-1)100$

$R = \dfrac{100}{16}$

$= 6\dfrac{1}{4}\%.$

Q: If a sum of money double inself in 10 years. On how many years would it treble itself?

a) **15 years**   b) **20 years**   c) **12 years**   d) **none of these**

Sol : smart technique

Acc. To the formula for above condition applied sum

Is $RT = (n - 1)100$

$$R = \frac{100}{10}$$

$R = 10\%$

RT=(3-1)100

$10XT = 2X100$

$$T = \frac{200}{10}$$

$T = 20\ years.$

Q: A sum of money becomes 4 times at S.I in 10 years what is the rate of Interest.

   a) 10%   b) 20%   c)30%   d) 40%

Sol: smart technique

Acc. To the formula for the above condition applied sum is

$RT = (n - 1)100$

$R10 = (4 - 1)100$

$$R = \frac{3X100}{10}$$

$R = 30\%$.

Q: A sum of money becomes sit times at the S.I rate of 5% per annum At what rate per cent will it become twelve fold?

a)   10%   b) 12%   c) 9%   d) 11%

Sol: smart technique

Acc. To the formula for the above condition applied sum is

$RT = (n - 1)100$

$5Xt = (6 - 1)100$

$t = \dfrac{5X100}{5}$

$t = 100 \; years$

$RT = (n - 1)100$

$RX100 = (12 - 1)100$

$R = \dfrac{11X100}{100}$

$R = 11\%$

Q: At what rate of S.I at which a sum of money would double itself on 25years

a) 4%   b) 5%   c) 6 %   d) 8%

Sol: smart technique

Acc. To the formula for above condition applied sum is

$$RT = (n-1)100$$

$$R.25 = (5-1)100$$

$$R = \frac{100}{25}$$

$$R = 4 \; years$$

Q: At what time will Rs 72 become Rs 81 at $6\frac{1}{4}$% per annum is simple interest?

   a) 1 year 6 month b)2 years c)2 years 3 month   d)2years 6 months

Sol : (write approach is required to solve the sum)

Principal = 72

Interest =81-72=9

R.I = $6\frac{1}{4}$% = $\frac{25}{4}$

$$T = \frac{IX\,100}{PXR}$$

$$T = \frac{9X100}{72X\frac{20}{5}}$$

$$T = 2 \; years.$$

Q: A sum becomes Rs 2916 in 2 years at 8% per annum compound interest. The simple interest at 9% per annum for 3 years on the same amount will be

    a) Rs 675   b) Rs 650   c) Rs 625   d) Rs 660

Sol :

$$A = P(1 + \frac{R}{100})_2$$

$$2916 = p(1 + \frac{8}{100})_2$$

$$2916 = p(\frac{27}{25})_2$$

$$p = \frac{2916 X 25 X 25}{27 X 27} \quad \frac{2916 X 25 X 25}{(3X3X3X3X3X3} \text{ spilt method to simplfy})$$

P =2500

$$SI = \frac{PXTXR}{100}$$

$$SI = \frac{2500X3X9}{100}$$

=675.

Q: in what time will Rs 8000 at 3% SI per annum produce the some income as Rs 6000 does in 5 Years at 4%   SI?

(a) 3 years   b)4 years   c) 5 years   d) 6 years

Sol: smart technique

$tX8000X3 = 6000X5X4$

$t = 5\ years.$

TECHNIQUE

CALCULATE THE DIFFERENCE OF C.I & S.I. FOR THE PERIOD OF 2 YEARS

Q: Calculate the difference between the C.I. and S.I on sum of Rs 20000 at 15% per annum for a period of two years.

a) 350   b) 400   c) 450   d)550   e)none of these

Sol:

Regular method	smart technique

$SI = \dfrac{PTR}{100}$ $= \dfrac{20000 \times 2 \times 15}{100}$ $= Rs\ 6000$ $CI = (a + a + \dfrac{a^2}{100}\% \ of\ 20000$ (smart technique formula) $= (15 + 15 + \dfrac{15^2}{100})\%\ of\ 20000$ $\dfrac{32.25}{100} \times 20000$ $= 6450$ The difference $= 6450 - 6000$ $= 450$	If we apply a smart formula for the above sum, it will solve the sum in quickest as well as error free. **condition** When the diff (D) of CI and SI for the period of two year, P the principal and R the rate of interest $D = p(\dfrac{R}{100})_2$ For the above sum D$= 20000(\dfrac{15}{100})^2$ $=20000\ X\dfrac{15}{100}X\dfrac{15}{100}$ $=2X225$ $=450$

Q; The difference between simple and compound interest on a certain sum of money for 2 years at 4% per annum isRs 1. The sum is

    a) 650   b) 630   c)625   d)640

Sol: smart technique

Acc. To the formula for the above condition applied sum is

$D = p(\dfrac{R}{100})_2$

$$1 = p(\frac{4}{100})_2$$

$$1 = p(\frac{1}{25})_2$$

p=625.

Q: the difference between C.I and S.I on a sum Rs 400 for 2 years is Rs 4 find the rate of interest

    a) 5%   b)10%   c)12%   d)15%

Sol: smart technique

Acc. To the formula for the above eondition applied sum is

$$D = P(\frac{R}{100})_2$$

$$4 = 400(\frac{R}{100})_2$$

$$4 = 400 X \frac{R2}{100 X 100}$$

$$R = \frac{4 X 100 X 100}{400}$$

$$R = \sqrt{100}$$

$$R = 10\%.$$

Q: The difference between the compound and simple interest on a certain sum of money 12% per annum for 2 years Rs 72. Find the sum when the interest compounded annually.

a) **Rs 5200**   b) **Rs 4400**   c) **Rs 5000**   d) **none of these**

Sol: smart technique

Acc. To the formula for the above condition applied sum is

$$D = R(\frac{R}{100})_2$$

$$72 = P(\frac{12}{100})_2$$

$$72 = PX\frac{12X12}{100X100})$$

$$P = \frac{72X100X100}{12X12}$$

$$P = 500$$

TECHNIQUE

CALCULATE THE DIFFERENCE OF C.I & S.I. FOR THE PERIOD OF 3 YEARS

Q: Find difference between the compound and simple interest on principal amount of Rs 375 at 20% per annum for 3 years.

   a) 52   b) 48   c) 42   d) 37

Sol:

Regular method	Smart technique
$S.I = \dfrac{PTR}{100}$	When the diff. between C.I and S.I is given for 3 years with same principal and same R.I then the difference will be
$\dfrac{375 X 3 X 20}{100}$	
$= 225$	$$D = P\left(\dfrac{R}{100}\right)_2 \left(\dfrac{300 + R}{100}\right)$$
$C.I = P(1 + \dfrac{R}{100})_3 - P$	We apply this formula to the above some
$= 375[(1 + \dfrac{20}{100})_3 - 1]$	$D = 375\left(\dfrac{20}{100}\right)_2 \left(\dfrac{300 + 20}{100}\right)$
$= 375\left[\dfrac{6X6X6}{5X5X5} - 1\right]$	$D = 375 X \dfrac{20X20}{100X100} X \dfrac{320}{100}$
$= 375\left(\dfrac{216 - 125}{125}\right)$	$= 48$

$$= 375 X \frac{91}{125}$$

$$= 273$$

Hence difference $= 273 - 225$

$$= 48$$

Q: on what sum will the difference between SI and e.I for 3 years at 4% per annum amount to Rs3.04?

   a) Rs. 1250   b) Rs. 625   c) Rs. 650   d) Rs 675

Sol: Smarts technique

Acc. to the formula for the above condition applied sum is

$$D = p\left(\frac{R}{100}\right)_2 \left(\frac{R + 300}{100}\right)$$

$$3.04 = P\left(\frac{4}{100}\right)_2 \left(\frac{4 + 300}{100}\right)$$

$$3.04 = P\left(\frac{1}{25}\right)_2 \left(\frac{304}{100}\right)$$

$$\frac{304}{100} = P \frac{1}{625} X \frac{304}{100}$$

$P = 625$

Q: The difference between e.I and S.I on a usm of money for 3 years at 5% per annum is Rs 6% find the sum.

   a) Rs 7000   b) Rs 8000   c) Rs 9000   d) Rs 10000

Sol: Smart technique

Acc. To the formula for the above condition applied sum is

$$D = P(\frac{R}{100})_2 (\frac{R + 300}{100})$$

$$61 = P(\frac{5}{100})_2 (\frac{300 + 5}{100})$$

$$61 = p(\frac{1}{20})_2 (\frac{305}{100})$$

$$61 = pX\frac{1}{400}X\frac{305}{100}$$

$$P = \frac{61X400X100}{605} = 8000.$$

Q. The C.I. for 2 years on a capital is Rs 2 more than the S.I. If the rate of interest is 5% per year, then the capital would be

   a) Rs 800   b) Rs 840   c) Rs 880   d) Rs 882

Sol: Smart Technique

Acc. to the formula for the above and applied sum is

$$D = P\left(\frac{R}{100}\right)^2$$

$$2 = P(5/100)^2$$

$$2 = P\frac{1}{400}$$

$$p = 800.$$

TECHNIQUE

RELATION BETWEEN C.I & S.I.

Q: The simple interest on a certain sum of money for 2 years at 6% per annum is 300. The compound interest at the same rate for the same period will be

    a) Rs 310   b) Rs 308   c) Rs 307   d) Rs 309

Sol

Regular method	Smart technique

Let principal is p	Acc. To smart technique for the above
Acc. To the question on S.I	condition applied sum
$$p = \dfrac{I \times 100}{TR}$$	Condition:- When the S.I on the principal 'P' at R% of interest for 'T' year is given. Then the c.I on the same condition is
$$p = \dfrac{300 \times 100}{2 \times 6}$$	
$= 2500$	$$C.I = S.I\left(1 + \dfrac{R}{200}\right)$$
$$cI = \left(a + a + \dfrac{a^2}{100}\right)\% \text{ of } 2500$$	Let me apply this formula to the above sum
$$= \left(6 + 6 + \dfrac{36}{100}\right)\% \text{ of } 2500$$	$$c.I = 300\left(1 + \dfrac{6}{200}\right)$$
$= 12.36\ \% \text{ of } 2500$	
$$\dfrac{12.36}{100} \times 2500$$	$$c.I = 300 \times \dfrac{206}{200}$$
$= 309$	$= 309$
Hence the c.I is 309 at the same rate and same period	Hence c.I is 309

Q: get the compound interest on a certain sum at 10 % per annum for 2 year is Rs 21 what would be the simple interest?

   a) **Rs20**   b) **Rs 16**   c) **Rs 18**   d) **Rs 20.50**

Sol: Smart technique

Acc. To the formula for the above condition applied sum is

$$C.I = S.I\left(1 + \dfrac{R}{200}\right)$$

$$21 = S.I\left(1 + \frac{10}{200}\right)$$

$$21 = SI \; \frac{21}{20}$$

$$S.I = \frac{21 X 20}{21}$$

$$= 20.$$

Q: compound interest on a certain sum of money for 2 years at 6 % be Rs 25.75 what be the S.I

    a) Rs 25   **b) Rs 24**   **c) Rs 20**   **d) Rs 15**   **e) none of the above**

Sol: smart technique

Acc. to the formula for the above condition applied sum is

$$c.I = S.I\left(1 + \frac{R}{200}\right)$$

$$25.75 = SI\left(1 + \frac{6}{200}\right)$$

$$25.75 = SI \; X \; \frac{206}{200}$$

$$SI = \frac{25.75 \; X \; 100}{103}$$

$$SI = 15.$$

Q: The ratio of eI and SI on certain sum of 10% per annum for 2 years is

    a) 7:5   **b) 21:20**   **c) 8:5**   **d) 20:19**

Sol: smart technique

As per smart technique, the relation between c.I and SI for certain sum in same period and same rate of interest is

$$c.I = SI\left(1 + \frac{R}{200}\right)$$

$$c.I = SI\left(1 + \frac{10}{200}\right)$$

$$cI = SI \; X \; \frac{210}{200}$$

$$\frac{cI}{SI} = \frac{210}{200}$$

$$\frac{cI}{SI} = \frac{21}{20}$$

Q. compound interest on a certain sum for two years is Rs 618, whereas the simple interest on the same sum at the same rate for two year is Rs 600. The rate of interest per annum is:

    a) 18%   **b) 9%**   **c) 6%**   **d) 3%**

Sol: Smart technique

Acc. To the formula the above condition applied sum is

$$cI = SI\left(1 + \frac{R}{200}\right)$$

$$618 = 600\left(1 + \frac{R}{200}\right)$$

$$618 = 600 + \frac{600 X R}{200}$$

$$\frac{R}{200} = \frac{18}{600}$$

$$R = 6\%.$$

Q. What sum will give Rs 244 as the difference between S.I and C.I at 10% in $1\frac{1}{2}$ years compounded half yearly

a) 28000   b) 32000   c) 36000   d) 40000   e) 45000

Sol.

Regular method	Smart technique

e.I as 10% in $1\frac{1}{2}$ years compounded $\frac{1}{2}$ year	$D = P\left(\dfrac{r}{100}\right)_2\left(\dfrac{R+300}{100}\right)$

e.I as 10% in $1\frac{1}{2}$ years compounded $\frac{1}{2}$ year

i.e $R.I = 5\%\ period = 3$

$$e.I = p[(1 + \frac{5}{100})_3 - 1]$$

$$= p[(1 + \frac{1}{20})_3 - 1]$$

$$= P[(\frac{21}{20})_3 - 1]$$

$$= P\left[\frac{9261}{8000} - 1\right]$$

$$= P \times \frac{1261}{8000}$$

$$e.I = 0.157625P$$

$$S.I = \frac{P \times 3 \times 5}{100} = 0.15P$$

$$0.157625P - 0.15P = 244$$

$$0.007625P = 244$$

$$= p = Rs.\ 32000$$

$D = P\left(\dfrac{r}{100}\right)_2\left(\dfrac{R+300}{100}\right)$

Acc. To question 10 % compounded $\frac{1}{2}$ yearly i.e R.I is 5%

$$244 = P\left(\frac{5}{100}\right)_2\left(\frac{5+300}{100}\right)$$

$$244 = P \times \frac{1}{20 \times 20} \times \frac{305}{100}$$

$$P = 32000$$

Q: The simple and compound interest on a sum of money for 2 years are Rs 8400 and Rs 8652 respectively. The Rate of interest per annum is

a) 6%   b) 7.5%   c) 9%   d) 4.5%

Sol:

Regular method	Alternate method
Amount for 1st year $= \dfrac{8400}{2} = Rs\ 4200$ Amount for 2nd years $= 8652 - 4200$ $= Rs.\ 4452$ *intereat on peincipal of Rs 4200* *for one year* $4452 - 4200$ $= Rs\ 252$ *Rate of interest* $= \dfrac{IX100}{PXT}$ $= \dfrac{252X100}{4200}$ $= 6\%$	Right approach required to some the sum $eI = SI\left(1 + \dfrac{R}{200}\right)$ $8652 = 8400\left(1 + \dfrac{R}{200}\right)$ $\dfrac{8652}{8400} - 1 = \dfrac{R}{200}$ $\dfrac{R}{200} = \dfrac{252}{8400}$ $R = 6\%$

TECHNIQUE

TIME AND WORK PROBLEM SOLVED BY SMART TECHINQUE

Q: A can do a work in 15 days, B can do the work In 30 days both A and B con do the work in how many days?

a) 10   b) 12   c) 15   d) 25   e) 14

Sol:

Regular method	smart technique
A can do a work in = 15 days	Let's A complete in X days
A can work in 1 day $=\dfrac{1}{15}$ of work	B complete in Y days
B can do the work = 30 days	Both A & B complete in $\dfrac{XY}{X+Y}days$
B can work in 1 day $=\dfrac{1}{30}$ of work	$=\dfrac{15X30}{15+30}=\dfrac{15X30}{45}=10\ days$
Both A & B can do in	
1 day $=\dfrac{1}{15}+\dfrac{1}{30}$	Hence result is 10 days
$=\dfrac{3}{30}=\dfrac{1}{10}th\ of\ work$	
So both A & B con do the work in 10 days	

Q. Pipe A and B can fill the tank in 3 and 4 hours respectively. If both pipe open, the tank will fill in ?

a) $1\frac{1}{2}$ hourse

b) $1\frac{3}{4}$ hourse

c) $1\frac{5}{7}$ hourse

d) 2 hourse

Sol:

Regular method	smart technique
A can fill the tank = 3 hours	*let's A tank can fill in x hours*
A can fill in 1 hour = $\frac{1}{3}$ *of thorth*	*B tank can full in y hours*
B can fill the tank = *4 hours*	*Both A & B can fill* $= \dfrac{xy}{x+y}$ *hours*
B can fill in 1 hour = $\frac{1}{4}$ *per tank*	$= \dfrac{3X4}{3+4}$
Both *A & B can fill in*	$= \dfrac{3X4}{4}$
$1\ hour = \dfrac{1}{3} + \dfrac{1}{4}$	$= \dfrac{12}{7}$
$\dfrac{7}{12}$ *of the tank*	$= 1\frac{5}{7}$ *hours*
Both A & B can fill the tank in	
$\dfrac{12}{7} = 1\frac{5}{7}$ *hours*	

Q. A can complete a work in 12 days . 'A' and 'B' together can complete the same work in 8 days . in how many days can 'B ' alone complete the some work

a) 15   b) 18   c) 24   d) 28   e) none of these

Sol: Smart technique

'B' work =(A+B) work − A work

Acc. To the formula

$$= \frac{xy}{x-y}$$ Where $x = work\ completed\ by\ A\ X\ B$

$$y = work\ completed\ by\ A$$

$$= \frac{12X8}{12-8}$$

$$= \frac{12X8}{4}$$

$$= 24\ days.$$

Q. A and B can do a job together in 7 days . B is $1\frac{3}{4}$ times as efficient as A .the same job can be done by B alone in

a) $\frac{49}{4}days$
b) $\frac{49}{3}days$
c) $11\ days$
d) $\frac{28}{3}days$

Sol: smart technique

For the above sum there will be a smart formula to apply i.e

cond^n 1. Both have to complete the work in n days

2. A is more efficient than A

Then A and B can separately do the work

$$A = \left(\frac{n+1}{n}\right)n\ days \qquad B = (n+1)day$$

Acc. to this formula for the above sum

$$B = \left(\frac{n+1}{n}\right)x\ days\ where\ \ n = 1\frac{3}{4} = \frac{7}{4}days$$

and x=7 day

$$= \frac{\dfrac{7}{4}+1}{\dfrac{7}{4}}\ X\ 7$$

$$= \frac{11}{4}\ X\ \frac{4}{7}\ X\ 7$$

$$= 11\ days.$$

Q: A,B,C can complete a work in 10 days , 12 days and 15 days respectively. A and B together commence the work and they leave it after 4 days. What is the time taken by C to complete the remaining work.

Sol:

Regular method	Smart technique

A complete a work = 10 days A work in 1 days $=\dfrac{1}{10}$ B complete a work = 12 dyas B complete in 1 days $=\dfrac{1}{12}$ Both A & B can work in 1 days $\dfrac{11}{60}X4 = \dfrac{11}{15}$ $work\ left = 1 - \dfrac{11}{15} = \dfrac{4}{15}$ $C\ complete\ 1\ work = 15\ days$ $C\ complete\ \dfrac{4}{15}\ work = 15X\dfrac{4}{15}$ $= 4\ days$	L.c.m of 10,12,15,is 60 consider eating 60 tafeess is a work **eatstotal tafeessEat in 1 day** A 10 days 60 6 B 12 days 60 5 C 15 days 60 4 Both A and B eat in 1 day 6+5=11 Both A & B eat in 4 days = 44 Let's left 60-40=16 C eats in $\dfrac{16}{4} = 4\ days$

Q : A and B can do a work in 12 and 20 days respectively. If after they work at it together for some days. C who can do the whole work in 10 days . finishes it in 2 days . how long did A and B work together.

   a) 4 days   b) 6 days   c) 8 days   d) 10 days   e) none of these

Sol:

Regular method	Smart technique		
Work done by C = $2X\dfrac{1}{10} = \dfrac{1}{5}$	Eats total ladues Eat in aday		
	A 12	60	5
	B 20	60	3

$Remaining\ work = 1 - \dfrac{1}{5} = \dfrac{4}{5}$	C 10 60 6
$A\ and\ B\ in\ 1\ day = \dfrac{1}{12} + \dfrac{1}{20}$	$C's\ eat\ in\ 2\ days = 2X6 = 12$
$= \dfrac{5+3}{60} = \dfrac{8}{60}$	$Ladies\ left = 60 - 12 = 48$
$A\ and\ B\ do\ \dfrac{8}{60}\ in = 1\ days$	$A + B\ eats\ 8\ ladues\ in\ 1\ day$
$A\ and\ B\ can\ do\ work = \dfrac{60}{8}$	$for\ 48\ days\ we\ tame\ \dfrac{48}{8} = 6\ days$
$A\ and\ B\ can\ do\ \dfrac{4}{5}\ work = \dfrac{60}{8}X\dfrac{4}{5}$	
$= 6\ days$	

Q. A can do a work in 9 days .get 'B ' is 50% more efficient to A , then how many days can B do the same work?

    a) 13.5   b) 4.5   c) 6   d) 3   e) 6.5

Sol:

Regular method	Alternate method
$100\%\ of\ A = 150\ \%\ AB$	$B\ can\ do\ the\ work = \dfrac{100Xx}{100 + y}$
$\dfrac{A}{B} = \dfrac{150}{100} = \dfrac{3}{2}$	$= \dfrac{100X9}{100 + 50}$
$3x = 9$	$= \dfrac{100X9}{150}$
$x = 3$	$= 6\ days$
$2x = 3.2 = 6\ days$	

Q . 40 men can finish a work in 15 days get the work is to live completed 3 days earlier , how many more people should live employed?

    a) 15   b) 10   c) 8   d) 3   e) none of these

Sol:

$$\frac{D1M1}{W1} = \frac{D2M2}{W2}$$

$$\frac{15X40}{1} = \frac{xX12}{1}$$

$$x = \frac{15X40}{12}$$

$$x = 50$$

$10 \; more man required.$

Q. some carpenters promised to do a work in 9 days but 5 of them were absent and the remaining men did the job in 12 days .the original number of carpenter was

    a) 24   b) 20   c) 16   d) 18   e) 15

Sol:

$let \; original \; number \; a \; carpenter \; is \; x$

$$xX9 = (x - 5)X12$$

$$9x = 12x - 60$$

$$3x = 60$$

$$x = 20$$

Q. 56 workers can complete a work in 14 days .If the work is to be completed in 8 days . then how many extra workers are required

a) 36   b) 48   c) 44   d) 42   e) 46

Regular method	Smart technique
56 worker comleted in 14 days	*such type of problem can be solved*
1 worker completed in 14X15 days	*by simple formula and used it*
get it is completed in 8 days	*efficiently to get the result*
worker to beneeded $= \dfrac{14X56}{8}$	$\dfrac{M1D1}{W1} = \dfrac{M2D2}{W2}$
$= 98$	*where M1, M2 = number of worker*
extra worker $= 98 - 56 = 42$	*D1, D2 = number of day*
	W1,W2 = number of work
	$\dfrac{56X14}{1} = \dfrac{8Xx}{1}$
	$= x = 98$
	entra worker reguned $= 98 - 56 = 42$

Q. 250 men can finish a work in 20 days working 5 hours day to finish the work within 10 days working 8 hours a day .the minimum number of men required.

a) 310   b) 300   c) 313   d) 312   e) 315

Sol: Smart technique

If we apply the above formula

$$\frac{M1 D1 H1}{W1} = \frac{M2 D2 H2}{W2}$$

where m1, m2 = number of worker

D1, D2 = number of days

$H1, H2 = number\ of\ hour$

$W1, W2 = number\ of\ work$

$$\frac{250\ X\ 20\ X\ 5}{1} = \frac{M2\ X\ 10\ X\ 8}{1}$$

$$= M2 = \frac{250\ X\ 20\ X\ 5}{8 X 10} = 312.5$$

As the question ask for minimum number of men, so the required answer is 313

.

Q. If 90 men can do a certain job in 16 day, working 12 hours a day, then the part of that work which can be completed by 70 men in 24 days , working 8 hours a day is

a) $\dfrac{5}{8}$ b) $\dfrac{1}{3}$ c) $\dfrac{7}{9}$ d) $\dfrac{2}{3}$

Sol: Smart technique

get we apply the formula , then

$$\frac{M1 D1 H1}{W1} = \frac{M2 D2 H2}{W2}$$

$M1 = 90\ men$

$D1 = 16\ daus$

$W1 = 1\ work$

$H1 = 12\ hours$

$M2 = 70\ men$

$D2 = 24\ days$

$H2 = 8\ hours$

$W2 = X$

23

$$\frac{90X16X12}{1} = \frac{70X24X8}{x}$$

$$x = \frac{70X24X8}{90X16X12}$$

$$= \frac{7}{9}\ parts.$$

Q. 12 monkeys can eat 12 bananas in 12 minutes .on how many minutes can 4 monkeys eat 4 bananas

    a) 12   b)10   c)4   d)8   e)6

Sol: Smart technique

If such type of sum is solved in time and work met ... *asy.*

lets apply formula to solve.

$$\frac{M1D1H1}{W1} = \frac{M2D2H2}{W2}$$

$$\frac{12X12}{12} = \frac{4Xx}{4}$$

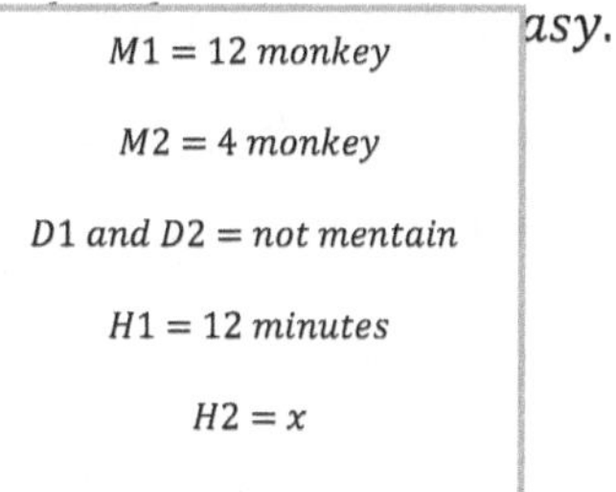

$x = 12\ minutes$

Q. Three men can complete a price of work in 6 days .two days after they started the work , 3 more men joined them how many days will they take to complete The remaining works

    a) 1 day   b) 2 days   c) 3 days   d) 4 days

Sol: Smart technique

Apply smart technique for the above condition sum

$$\frac{M1D1}{W1} = \frac{M2D2}{W2}$$

As per the question, work after two days, $2/3^{rd}$ will be left and 3 more men have joined

$$\frac{3X2}{1/3} = \frac{6XD2}{2/3}$$

$$D2 = \frac{3X2X2}{6}$$

$D2 = 2 \; days$

Q. A certain number of men can do a work in 60 days. If there were 8 more joined, it would be completed 10 days earlier. Then how many men were there to start the work.

(a) 70 (b) 55 (c) 45 (d) 40

Sol.

Acc. to the formula for above condition applied sum is

$$\frac{M1D1}{W1} = \frac{M2D2}{W2}$$

$xX60 = (n + 8)(60 - 10)$

$60x = 50x + 400$

$10x = 400$

$x = 40.$

So 40 men were started the work.

Q. 12 men construct 1.5 km of road in 7 days. 28 men will construct 12 km of road in

a) 20 days   b) 24 days   c) 28 days   d) 38 days e) none of these

Sol: Smart technique

Apply smart technique for the above condition sum

$$\frac{M1D1}{W1} = \frac{M2D2}{W2}$$

$$\frac{12 X 7}{1.5} = \frac{28 X x}{12}$$

$$x = \frac{12 X 12 X 7 X 10}{15 X 28}$$

$x = 24\ days$

Q: a garrison of 1800 men has provisions for 6 weeks at 5 kg per man per day. How many weeks can the same provision last for 1200 men at 3 kg per man per day?

a) 12   b) 18   c) 15   d) 9   e) 4

Sol:

Acc. to smart technique for the above condition applied formula

$$\frac{M1D1H1}{W1} = \frac{M2D2H2}{W2}$$

$Where \ M1, M2 = provisim \ for \ men$

$D1, D2 = privision \ for \ week$

$H1, H2 = capacity \ to \ cper \ day$

$W1, W2 \ = not \ mentioned \ i.e \ 1$

$1800X6X5 = 1200XxX3$

$$= x = \frac{1800X6X5}{1200X3}$$

$x = 15$

Q: A can do $\frac{1}{4}$ of work in 10 days. B can do $\frac{1}{3}$rd 0f the work in 20 days. In how many days can both A and B together do the work?

a) 25 days   b) 30 days   c) 32 days   d) 24 days

Sol: smart technique

$'A' can \ do \ a \ work \ 40 \ days$ $(note{:}other \ calulation \ do \ of \ on \ your \ mind)$

$'B' can \ do \ a \ work \ 60 \ days$

$$both \ A + B \ con \ do = \frac{60 \ X \ 40}{60 + 40}$$

$$= 24 \ days$$

Q. A and B together on together finish a work in 30 days .they worked at in for 20 days and then B left . theremaing work was done by A done in 20 more days. A alone con finish the work in.

   a) 50 days   b) 60 days   c) 54 days   d) 48 days

Sol: Smart technique

this type of sum required correct approach to solve quickly

$A + B \text{ in } 1 \text{ days can do} = \dfrac{1}{30} \text{the work}$

$A + B \text{ in } 20 \text{ days con do} = \dfrac{20}{30} = \dfrac{2}{3} \text{work}$

$\text{work left } 1 - \dfrac{2}{3} = \dfrac{1}{3}$

$A \text{ alone do} \dfrac{1}{3} \text{work in } 20 \text{ days}$

$A \text{ con do te work in } 60 \text{ days}.$

Q. A can complete a piece of work in 12 days. B is 60% more efficient than A. the number of days. That B will take to complete the some work is.

   a) 6   b) $7\dfrac{1}{2}$ c) 8   d) $8\dfrac{1}{2}$

Sol:

Regular method	smart technique
$100\% \text{ of } A = 160\% \text{ of } B$	*when A can do a work in x days*
$\dfrac{A}{B} = \dfrac{160}{100} = \dfrac{8x}{5x}$	*and B is y%more or less efficient*
	that A then B can do the work

<table>
<tr><td>

A can do the work in 12 days

$8x = 12$

$x = \dfrac{12}{8}$

$5x = \dfrac{12}{8} X\,5 = \dfrac{15}{2} = 7\dfrac{1}{2}$

B can do it in $7\dfrac{1}{2}$ *days*

</td><td>

$\dfrac{x\,X\,100}{100 + y}$

let me put the value in the above fomula

it become quite easy and time saving

$\dfrac{12\,X\,100}{100 + 60} = \dfrac{12\,X\,100}{160}$

$= 7\dfrac{1}{2}$

</td></tr>
</table>

Q. If 5 men earn Rs 540 in 4 days, and then earning of 7 men in 6 days is

    a) Rs 1440   b) Rs 1134   c) Rs 1270   d) Rs 1468

Sol:

Regular method	Smart technique
5 *men 4 days earn Rs* 540 5 *men 1 day earn Rs* 135 1 *men 1 day earn Rs* 27 7 *men 1 day earn Rs* 189 7 *men 6 days earn Rs* 1134	*the above condition applied sum ,* *Related formula* $\dfrac{m1D1}{Wa1} = \dfrac{m2D2}{Wa2}$ Wa = wages m= men D= days $\dfrac{5\,X\,4}{540} = \dfrac{7X6}{x}$ $x = \dfrac{7X6X540}{5\,X\,4}$ $x = 1134$

Q. A does 20 % less work than B. If A can complete a piece of work in $7\dfrac{1}{2}$ days then B can do it in

a) 4 days   b) 6 days   c) 8 days   d) 10 days

Sol:

$80\%\ of\ A = 100\%\ of\ B$

$Ratio\ of\ \dfrac{A}{B} = \dfrac{5}{4}$

$5x = \dfrac{15}{2}$

$x = \dfrac{15}{2 \times 5} = \dfrac{3}{2}$

$B\ can\ do = \dfrac{3}{2} \times 4 = 6\ days.$

<u>TECHNIQUE #</u>

<u>**TIME AND DISTANCE RELATFD SUM SOLVED BY SMART TECHINQUE**</u>

Q. A train moves past a telegraph post and a bridge 264 metre long in 8 seconds and 20 seconds respectively. What is the speed of train?

Sol.

Regular method	Smart technique
let the length of train be x meters *speed fo train when passeds telegraph* $pole = \dfrac{x\ m}{8 sec}$ *speed of train when passes the bridge* $\dfrac{x+264}{20} sec$ $now\ \dfrac{x}{8} = \dfrac{x+264}{20}$ $20x = 8x + 264 \times 8$ $12x = 264 \times 8$ $x = \dfrac{264 \times 8}{12} = 176m$ $speed\ of\ train = \dfrac{176}{8} = 22\dfrac{m}{sec}$ $= 22 \times \dfrac{18}{5}\ km/hr$ $= 79.2\ km/hr$ $\left(note{:}x\dfrac{m}{sec} = x\dfrac{18km}{5\ hr} \right)$	Train passes (a) A telegraph post i.e its own length. (b) A bridge i.e its own length + bridge length Time taken to cross the bridge length 264 mtrs= 20 sec. − 8sec. =12 sec. So the speed of the train in 12sec=264 mtrs 1 sec =264/12 =22 m/sec Speed of the train in km/hr =22x18/5 = 79.2 km/hr.

Q. A train running at a speed of 72km/hr and crosses a 260m long platform in 23sec. what is the length of the train in meters?

 (a) 200   (b) 240   (c) 220   (d) 160

Sol.

Train moves in 23 sec= 23X 20 =460m.

Train length =total distance cover – plat form length

Train length =460- 260 =200m.

Q. A car travel from city A to city B at an average speed of 60km/hr and reaches in time. If the car reduces its speed to 50km/hr, it takes 16min more to reach.what is the distance between the cities.(in km)

(a) 60   (b) 80   (c) 85   (d) 86

Sol.

Let the distance be x

Acc. to question $\dfrac{x}{50} - \dfrac{x}{60} = \dfrac{16}{60}$

$$\dfrac{x}{300} = \dfrac{16}{60}$$

$$X=80km.$$

Q.A and B travel the same distance at speed of 9 km/hr and 1okm/hr respectively. If A takes 36min more than B, then the distance travel by each is

(a) 48km   (b) 54km   (c) 60km   (d) 66km

Sol.

Acc. to the formula for above $cond^n$ applied sum

$$\frac{x}{9} - \frac{x}{10} = \frac{\frac{1}{36}}{60}$$

$$\frac{x}{90} = \frac{36}{60}$$

$$x = \frac{36 \times 90}{60}$$

X=54km

Hence the distance travel by each is 54km.

Q.150m long train passes a telegraph pole in 10sec and a bridge in 40sec. Find the ratio of the length to that of bridge length.

(a) 1:2   (b) 2:3   (c) 1:4   (d) 4:1

Sol.

Cross the telephone pole i.e. the length of the train

Train travel in 10 sec =150m

$$1sec =15m$$

$$40sec =15 \times 40 \text{ return} =600m \text{ (bridge length + train length)}$$

Bridge length =600 -150 =450m

The ratio of the length to that of bridge length =150 :450

$$=1:3$$

Q. A train travel from Dehradun to Delhi at a speed of 40km/hr and returns at 0kn/hr. Find the average speed of whole journey.

(a) 60km/hr   (b) 48km/hr   (c) 40km/hr   (d) 50km/hr

Sol.   Smart Technique

The average speed= $\dfrac{2XY}{X+Y}$ Where X as Forward speed & Y as return speed

Acc to question the average speed $=\dfrac{2X40X60}{40+60}$

$$=\dfrac{2X40X60}{100}$$

=48km/hr

TECHNIQUE

CALCULATE THE USUAL TIMR IN TIME AND DISTANCE RELATFD SUM

Q.A man driving at $\dfrac{3}{4}$ th of his original speed reaches his destination 20 minutes later than the usual time. Then the usual time is.

   (a) 45minute(B) 60minutes (c)75minutes   (D) 120minutes

Sol.

Regular method	smart technique

As you know, the speed and time are inversely proportional for a fixed distance i.e. $d = \dfrac{s}{t}$ $\dfrac{4}{3}$ usual time- usual Time = 20 minutes $= \dfrac{1}{3}$X usual time = 20 minutes usual time = 60 minutes	As per smart technique , when person change his speed to $\left(\dfrac{x}{y}\right)$ of usual speed and get , **late by Z minute then** **The usual time** $= \dfrac{Z}{\dfrac{y}{x} - 1}$ According to question The usual speed $= \dfrac{20}{\dfrac{4}{3} - 1}$ $= \dfrac{20}{\dfrac{1}{3}}$ = 60 minutes **Note: get early by Z minutes** the usual time $= \dfrac{Z}{1 - \dfrac{y}{x}}$

Q. **If a person decreases his speed to $\dfrac{5}{8}$ th of original speed , he is 12 minutes late how many minutes does he take at his original speed**

   (a) 20   (b) 30   (c) 15   (d) 12   (e) 10

Sol. Smart technique

Speed is $\dfrac{5}{8}$ th of original speed i.e $\dfrac{x}{y}$

Late by 12 minutes i.e Z= 12

So the usual time = $\dfrac{12}{\dfrac{8}{5}-1}$

$=\dfrac{12}{\dfrac{8-5}{5}}$

$=\dfrac{12}{\dfrac{3}{5}}$

$=\dfrac{12X5}{3}$

= 20 minutes.

Q: Walking at three fourth of his usual speed a man covers a certain distance in two hours more than the time he takes to cover the distance at his usual speed . the time taken by him to cover the distance with his usual speed is

   (a) 4.5 hr   (b) 5.5 hr (c) 6 hr   (d) 6.5 hr (e) 5 hr

Sol. Smart technique

Usual time= $\dfrac{Z}{\dfrac{y}{x}-1}$

$$= \frac{\frac{2}{4}}{\frac{3}{3} - 1} = 6 \text{ hrs}$$

Q. Walking at $\frac{3}{4}$ of his normal speed , a man take $2\frac{1}{2}$ hours more than the normal time . find the normal time

(a) 7.5 hr   (b) 6 hr   (c) 8 hr   (d) 805 hr   (e) 12hr

Sol. Smart technique

Usual time $= \dfrac{Z}{\frac{y}{x} - 1}$

When $Z = 2\frac{1}{2}$ hr $= \frac{5}{2}$ hr

$$= \frac{\frac{5}{2}}{\frac{4}{3} - 1}$$

$$= \frac{\frac{5}{2}}{\frac{1}{3}}$$

$$= \frac{5 \times 3}{2}$$

$$= 7.5 \text{ hr.}$$

Q: walking $\dfrac{3}{4}$ is his normal speed, raju is 16 minutes late in reaching his school . the usual time taken by him to cover the distance between his home and school is

   (a) 48 min   **(b) 45 min**   **(c) 60 min**   **(d) 42 min**

Ssol. mart technique

According to the formala

The usual time = $\dfrac{Z}{\dfrac{y}{x} - 1}$

$$= \dfrac{\dfrac{16}{\dfrac{4}{3} - 1}}{} = 48 \text{ min.}$$

Q: walking at $\dfrac{6}{7}$ th of his usual speed a man is late by 25 minutes . his usual to cover the distance is

   (a) 2:30   **(b) 2:15**   **(c) 2:10**   **(d) 2:00**

Sol. Smart technique

Acc. To the smart technique

The usual time = $\dfrac{Z}{\dfrac{y}{x} - 1}$

$$= \dfrac{\dfrac{25}{7}}{\dfrac{7}{6} - 1}$$

$$= 150 \text{ min}$$

$$= 2{:}30 \text{ min}$$

Q: Walking at $\dfrac{4}{3}$ of his usual speed a man reaches his office 20 minutes fast what is the time taken by him to reach his offce at his usual speed

   (a) 50 min   **(b) 60 min**   **(c) 70 min**   **(d) 80 min**

Sol. Smart technique

Acc. To smart technique

The usual speed $= \dfrac{Z}{1 - \dfrac{y}{x}}$ (reached his office early by Z minutes)

$$= \dfrac{20}{1 - \dfrac{3}{4}}$$

$$= \dfrac{20}{\dfrac{1}{4}}$$

$$= 80 \text{ minutes}$$

Hence his usual speed in 80 minutes

<u>TECHNIQUE #</u>

DISTANCE BETWEEN THE TRAIN BASED ON PROPOSIONALITY

Q. When two train starts at the same time form two station and proceed towards each other at the rate of 20 km/hr and 25 km / hr . When they meet , one train travel 80 kms more than the other. The distance between the station

   (a) 750 km   (b) 720km   (c) 700 km   (d) 650km   (e) 640km

Sol.

Regular method	Smart technique
Let distance between two station **d** and when they meet , the distance of foastor train $x+80$ and slower train x $x+x+80=d$ At reaching point , both train travel equal time , so $\dfrac{x}{20}=\dfrac{x+80}{25}$ $25x=20x+1600$ $5x=1600$ $x=320$ Total distance $d=320+320+80$ $\quad =720kms$	If we remember a simple technique , the above problem can be solved in a single line **Total Distance =** $\dfrac{d(x+y)}{x-y}$ Where d= diff. of distance between the train $x=speed\ of\ faster\ train$ $y=speed\ of\ slower\ train$ Distance between the station = $\dfrac{80(25+20)}{25-20}$ $=\dfrac{80X45}{5}$ $=720\ kms$

Q. Two trains start at the same time form A and B, proceed towards each other at the speed of 75 km/hr and 50 km/hr respectively. When both meet at a point in between , one train found to be travelled 175 km more than the other . fine the distance between A and B.

   (a) 758 km   (b) 857 km   (c) 875 km   (d) 785km   (e) 758 km

Sol. Smart technique

According to formula

$$\text{The distance between A and B} = \frac{d(x+y)}{x-y}$$

$$= \frac{175(75+50)}{75-50}$$

Where $d = diff.\ of\ distance\ between\ the\ train$

$$= \frac{175 \times 125}{25}$$

$$x = Speed\ of\ faster\ train\ i.e\ 75\frac{km}{hr}$$

$$y = speed\ of\ slower\ train\ i.e\ 50\frac{km}{hr}$$

$=875km$

Q. Two train of equal length are running on paraller lines in the same direction at the rate of 46 km/hr and 36 km/hr. The faster train passes the slower train in 36 seconds . the length of each train is

(a) 50m   (b) 72m   (c) 80m   (d) 82m

Sol:

Let length of train is x

Acc. To question

$$\frac{2x}{(46-36)\frac{5}{15}} = 36$$

$$\frac{2x \times 18}{10 \times 5} = 36$$

$$x = 50m.$$

Q: Two trains start at the same time from A and B and proceed towards B and A at 36 km /ph and 42 km/hr respectively. when then meet, it is found that one train has moved 48 km more than the other. What is the distance between A and B

   (a) 624 km   (b) 636km   (c) 544km   (d) 460km   (e) none of these

Sol.

Regular method	Smart Technique
Let distance between A and B be 'd'	On distance covered by first train in 1 hrs is 36 km and second train is 42 km
Let the distance between A and meeting point be X and that between B and meeting point be $x + 48$	$= diff.\ of\ distance\ is\ 1\ housr = 43 - 3($
$x + (x + 48) = d$	Total diff. of distance covered by two train it meeting point = 48 km
Since the two train start at the same time , the time taken	Total time for which two train travel = $\dfrac{48}{6} = 8\ hrs$
By each train to reach the meeting point is equal	
$T1 = T2 => \dfrac{D1}{S1} = \dfrac{D2}{S2} \quad (T = \dfrac{D}{S})$	Distance covered by two trains in 1 hr $= 36 + 42 = 78$
$=> \dfrac{X}{36} = \dfrac{x + 48}{42}$	Distance covered Train in
$= 7x = 6x + 288$	$8\ hr = 78 X 8 = 624\ km$
$x = 288$	
$required\ answer, d = x + (x + 48)$	
$= d = 288 + 288 + 48 = 624\ km$	

Q. A train leaves station A at the speed of 30 km ph . At the same time , another train deprrts from station 'B' at the speed of 45 kmp. When they meet , it is found that one train has travelled 60 km more than the other what the distance between A and B

   (a) 150 km   (b) 300 km   (c) 360km   (d) 420 km (e) 540

Sol. Smart technique

The distance covered by 1st train 30 kmph and 2nd train 45 kmph. The diff. of distance between two trains in 1 hr

45-30= 15km

Total diff. of distance between two train when they meet is 60 km

So the time for which two train travel = $\dfrac{60}{15} = 4\ hr$

Both train travel in 1 hr $= 30 + 45 = 75$

Total distance travel both train in 4 hr = 75 X 4

$$= 300\ kms$$

Hence Answer is 300 kms.

Q. Two trains , each of length 125 meter are running in parallel tracks in opposite direction. One train is running at a speed 65 km / hr and they cross each other in 6 seconds . the speed of other train is

    (a) 75 km/hr   **(b) 85 km/hr**   **(c) 95 km / hr**   **(d) 105 km/hr**

Sol.

Regular method	Alternate method
Total distance to becovered $= 125 + 125 = 250$ Time = 6 seconds Relative speed = $\dfrac{250}{6} X \dfrac{3600}{1000}$ $= 150\ km/hr$ Speed of other train $150 - 65 = 85\ km/hr$	Train moving in opposite direction $Time = \dfrac{l1 + l2}{(S1 + S2)\dfrac{5}{18}}$ l1&l2 length of train $6 = \dfrac{125 + 125}{(65 + x)\dfrac{5}{18}}$ **train** s1 &s2 speed of $6 = \dfrac{250X18}{(65 + x)5}$ $65 + x = 150$

	$x = 85 km$/hr

Q. How long(times in second)will a 450m long train take to cross a girl walking with a speed of 5km/hr in the direction of the moving train. The speed of the train is 65 km/hr

(a) 27 (b) 28 (c) 29 (d) 30

Sol.

When object moving in same direction

$$Time = \frac{l1 + l2}{(S1 - S2)\frac{5}{18}}$$

l1&l2 length of train

s1 &s2 speed of train

$$T = \frac{450}{(65 - 5)\frac{5}{18}}$$

$$Time = \frac{450 X 18}{60 X 5}$$

=27 sec.

Q. A train 280m long is moving at a speed of 60kmph. What is the time taken by the train to cross a platform 220m of long?

(a) 45sec (b) 40sec (c) 35sec (d) 30sec

Sol.

Train speed = 60kmph = $60 \times \dfrac{5}{18}$ m/sec   i.e. train cross in 1 sec

$\dfrac{60 \times 5}{18}$ Metre distance cross in 1 sec

500m (280+220) cross in = $\dfrac{500 \times 18}{60 \times 5}$

= 30 sec.

Q.Two train length of 250m and 200 m are running in same direction. If the train cross each other in 45sec and the speed of first train is 27km/hr, the speed of the second train is

(a) 36km/hr   (b) 72km/hr   (c) 54km/hr   (d) 63km/hr

Sol.

When object moving in same direction, time to cross each other

$$Time = \dfrac{l1 + l2}{(S1 - S2)\dfrac{5}{18}}$$

l1&l2 length of train

s1 &s2 speed of train

$$45 = \dfrac{200 + 250}{(x - 27)\dfrac{5}{18}}$$

$$45 = \dfrac{450 \times 18}{(x - 27)5}$$

90x18 = 45x (x-27)

X= 63 km/hr.

Q. Two train 100m and 95m long passes each other in 27seconds when run in the same direction and in 9seconds when it run in opposite direction. Speed of the trains is (km/hr).

(a) 52, 26 (b) 36, 18 (c) 40, 20 (d) 44, 22

Sol.

Let the speed of the train be x & y km/hr

When object moving in same direction, time to cross each other

$$Time = \frac{l1 + l2}{(S1 - S2)\frac{5}{18}}$$

$$27 = \frac{100 + 95}{(x - y)\frac{5}{18}}$$

$$27 = \frac{195X18}{(x - y)5}$$

$(x - y)$ =26.-----------(1)

When Train moving in opposite direction

$$Time = \frac{l1 + l2}{(S1 + S2)\frac{5}{18}}$$

$$9 = \frac{100 + 95}{(x + y)\frac{5}{18}}$$

$$9 = \frac{195 X 18}{(x+y)5}$$

$(x+y)$ =78--------------(2)

From equation (1) & (2)

X=52km/hr   y=26km/hr.

Q. Two train 70m and 80m length running on parallel track at speed of 68km/hr and 40km/hr respectively in opposite direction. In how many seconds will they pass each other?

(a) 10sec (b) 8sec (c) 5sec (d) 6sec

Sol.

When Train moving in opposite direction

$$Time = \frac{l1 + l2}{(S1+S2)\dfrac{5}{18}}$$

$$t = \frac{70+80}{(68+40)\dfrac{5}{18}}$$

$$t = \frac{150 X 18}{108 X 5} \quad T = 5sec.$$

TECHNIQUE

THE PROBLEM RELATED TO $BOAT$ AND STREAM

The problem related to Boat and Stream can be solved by some simple formula based on smart technique. Related formulas are

(a)Speed of Boat= $\dfrac{S1 + S2}{2}$ km/hr   where S1 Up stream speed of the boat
                                S2 Downstream speed of boat

(b)Speed of stream/Current= $\dfrac{S1 - S2}{2}$ km/hr

(c)Upstream Speed=(U-V)km/hr   Where U Speed of the Boat
V Speed of current/stream
(d)Downstream speed=(U+V) km/hr

Q: A boat travel 36 km up stream in 9 hr and 42 km downstream in 7 hrs. Find the speed of boat in still water

   (a) 3 km/hr   (b) 4 km / hr   (c) 5 km / hr   (d) none of these

Sol.

Upstream speed of boat = $\dfrac{36}{9} = 4 \ km$ /hr

Downstream speed of boat = $\dfrac{42}{7} = 6 \ km$ /hr

Speed of boat = $\dfrac{S1 + S2}{2} = \dfrac{4 + 6}{2} = 5 \ km$ /hr

Q: A man can row at 10 km/hr, if it takes total 5 hr for him to go to a place of 24 kms and return, then find the speed of the water in current.

    (a) 5 km / hr   (b)4 km / hr   (c) 2 km /hr   (d) 12 km/hr

Sol.

Let speed of current =x km/hr

Speed of boat =$10\ kmph$

$$\frac{24}{10+x}+\frac{24}{10-x}=5$$

$$24(10-x)+24(10+x)=5(10^2{-}x^2)$$

$$480=500-5x^2$$

$$5x^2=20$$

$$x^2=4$$

$$x=2km/hr$$

Q: the speed of the current is 5 km/h . A motor boat goes 10 km upstream and back again to the starting point in 50 min. the speed of the motor boat in still water is.

    (a) 20 km/h   (b) 24 kmph   (c) 25 kmph   (d) 28 kmph

Sol.

Regular method	Alternate method
Let speed of boat x $=\dfrac{10}{x+5}+\dfrac{10}{x-5}=\dfrac{50}{60}$ $=\dfrac{10(x-5+x+5)}{x^2-5^2}=\dfrac{5}{6}$	$\dfrac{10}{x+5}+\dfrac{10}{x-5}=\dfrac{50}{60}=\dfrac{5}{6}$ if you think smartly and follow the reverse technique (from the option) you get the answer i.e

$= 12X2x = x^2 - 25$	$\dfrac{10}{25+5} + \dfrac{10}{25-5} = \dfrac{10}{30} + \dfrac{10}{20} = \dfrac{1}{2} + \dfrac{1}{3}$
$x^2 - 25x + x - 25 = 0$	
$= x(x-25) + 1(x-25) = 0$	$= \dfrac{5}{6}$
$= x = 25, -1$	
Speed of boat = 25 km/hr	Hence the option (e) 25 is correct

Q: A boat can travel 10.2 km up stream in 50 minutes . of the speed of the water current is $\dfrac{1}{5}$ th of the speed of the boat in still water , then how much distance the boat can travel diunstream in 48 minutes.

    (a)14.8 km   (b) 15.6 km   (c) 15.2 km (d) 17.4 km(e) 14.4km

Sol.

Up stream $= \dfrac{10.2}{x - \dfrac{x}{5}}$ let x be the speed n the boat in still water

$= \dfrac{10.2}{x - \dfrac{x}{5}} = \dfrac{51}{60}$

$5x - x = \dfrac{10.2X60X5}{51}$

$5x - x = 12X5$

$= x = 15km$

Speed of stream $= \dfrac{1}{5}X15 = 3\ km$

Both travel in downstream in 48 min $(15+3)\ X\dfrac{48}{60}$

$= 18X\dfrac{48}{60}$

$= 14.4 \; km$

Q: the speed of a boat in still water in 6 km/hr and the speed of the stream 1.5 km/hr. A man row to a place at a distance of 22.5 km and come back to the starting point. The total time taken by him is

(a)10 hr (b) 6:10 hr   (c) 6: 20 minute   (d) 8 hours

Sol.

Acc. To the question

$$= \frac{22.5}{6 + 1.5} + \frac{22.5}{6 - 1.5}$$

up stream speed x+v, down stream u-v

$$= \frac{22.5}{7.5} + \frac{22.5}{4.5}$$ (use smart technique to calculate)

$= 3 + 5$

$= 8 \; hr$

Q: A boat moves down stream at the rate of 1 km in $7\frac{1}{2}$ minuutes and up stream at the rate of 5 km an hour what is the speed of the boat in still water ?

(a) $3\frac{1}{2}kmph$ **(b) 8kmph   (c)** $6\frac{1}{2}kmph$ **(d) 4 kmph**

Sol.

Down stream speed = 8 kmph $(7\frac{1}{2}\text{min } in \; move \; 1 \; km \; 60\text{min} . move \; 8 \; km)$

Up stream speed = 5 kmph

Speed of boat = $\dfrac{8+5}{2} = 6\dfrac{1}{2} kmph$

Q: A motor boat can travel at 10 kmph in still water. If travelled 91 km downstream and returned to the same place, taking altogether 20 hrs. Find the rate of flow of river

  (a) 2 kmph   **(b) 4 kmph**   **(c) 3 kmph**   **(d) 5 kmph**

Sol.

Regular method	alternate method
Speed of stream = x $= \dfrac{91}{10+x} + \dfrac{91}{10-x} = 20$ $91(10-x+10+x)$ $20(10-x)(10+x)$ $91 X 20 = 100 X 20 - 20 X\, x^2$ $20x^2 = 20(100-91)$ $x^2 = 9$ $x = 3$	Let speed of stream $=x$ $\dfrac{91}{10+x} + \dfrac{91}{10-x} = 20$ If we consider the value from the option and Apply in L.H.S of eqution Option (a) $= \dfrac{91}{10+2} + \dfrac{91}{10-2}\ not\ divisible$ $option\ (b) = \dfrac{91}{10+4} + \dfrac{91}{10-4}\ not\ divisible$ $option\ (c) = \dfrac{91}{10+3} + \dfrac{91}{10-3} = 7 + 13 = 20\ R.H$ Hence answer is 3 Note: while considering number , see the R.H.S answer also . whether it is divisible or any fractional numbers

Q: A boy can swim in still water at speed of 10 kmph. If the speed of the current would have been 5 kmph, then the boy could swim 60 km in how much time

  (a) Upstream in 4 hours   **(b) downstream in 12 hours**

  (c) upstream in 6 hours   **(d) down stream in 4 hours**

Sol.

in upstream direction $= \dfrac{60}{10-5} = 12hrs$

in down stream direction $= \dfrac{60}{10+5} = 4\ hrs$

Though direction is not given,then answer obtained from the given choise, hence answer (d)

Q: A man can row 30 km downstream and return in a total of 8 hours. If the speed of the boat in still water is four times the speed of current, then speed of current is (in kmph)

(a) 1   (b) 2   (c) 3   (d) 4   (e) 5

Sol.

Let speed of current $=x$

Speed of boat $=4x$

$$\dfrac{30}{4x+x} + \dfrac{30}{4x-x} = 8$$

$$\dfrac{30}{5x} + \dfrac{30}{3x} = 8$$

$$\dfrac{6}{x} + \dfrac{10}{x} = 8$$

$$8x = 16$$

$$x = 2.$$

Q: A boat running in downstream covers a distance of 30 km in 2 hrs while coming back the boat takes 6 hrs to cover the same distance . What is the speed of boat in km/hr

   (a) 15kmph   (b) 10kmpm   (c) 12kmph   (d) 5kmph

Sol.

Let speed of boat x and speed of current y

$$= \frac{30}{x+y} = 2$$

$$x + y = 15$$

$$\frac{30}{x-y} = 6$$

$$x - y = 5$$

$$2x = 20$$

$$x = 10 kmph \ speed \ of \ boat$$

Q: The speed of boat in still water is 16 kmph and speed of current in 2 kmph . If takes total of 6.5 hrs to row upstream form point A to point B and downstream form point B to point C . If the distance from point A to B is two third the distance between B and C. what is the total distance travelled by the boat

   (a) 112 km   (b) 98km   (c) 90 km   (d) 105km

SOl.

Let the distance B to C $=x$

Then distance A to B$=\dfrac{2}{3}x$

Acc. to the question

$$\frac{\frac{2}{3}x}{16-2} + \frac{x}{16+2} = 6.5$$

$$\frac{2x}{3 X 14} + \frac{x}{18} = \frac{13}{2}$$

$$\frac{x}{21} + \frac{x}{18} = \frac{13}{2}$$

$$\frac{6x + 7x}{126} = \frac{13}{2}$$

$$x = \frac{126}{2} = 63$$

$$total\ distance = 63 + \frac{2}{3} X 63$$

$$= 63 + 42$$

$$105 km$$

Q: A man rows a boat 18 km in 4 hours downstream and returns upstream in 12 hrs, then the speed of stream km/h is

(a) 1   (b) 1.5   (c) 2   (d) 1.7

Sol.

Downstream speed $= \frac{18}{4} = 4.5 kmph$

$$upstream\ speed = \frac{18}{12} = 1.5 kmph$$

$$speed\ in\ steram = \frac{4.5 - 1.5}{2}$$

$$= 1.5 \, kmph$$

Q: A moter boat whose speed in still water is 15 km/hr goes 30 km downstream and come back in total 4 hours 30 minutes. Determine the speed of stream.

(a) 2kmph   (b) 3kmph   (c) 4kmph   (d) 5kmph

Sol.

Regular method	Alternate method
Let speed in stream $x \, kmph$ Acc. To question $= \dfrac{30}{15+x} + \dfrac{30}{15-x} = 4\dfrac{1}{2}$ $= \dfrac{30}{15+x} + \dfrac{30}{15-x} = \dfrac{9}{2}$ $= 30\{(15-x)+(15+x)\} = \dfrac{9}{2}(15x^2 - x^2)$ $= 900 \times 2 = 9(225 - x^2)$ $= x^2 = 25$ $= x = 5$	$\dfrac{30}{15+x} + \dfrac{30}{15-x} = \dfrac{9}{2}$ If we find a value from the given option and put in the L.H.S of the above equation then solution become quite easy and less time lets think 5 as the answer L.H.S $\dfrac{30}{15+5} + \dfrac{30}{15-5} = \dfrac{30}{20} + \dfrac{30}{10}$ $= \dfrac{3}{2} + 3 = \dfrac{9}{2} = R.H.S$ Hence Answer in 5 kmph

TECHNIQUE

USE REVERSE TECHNIQUE TO FIND UNKNOWN VALUE

Q: The product of two number is 70 and their sum 17. what is the difference between the two ?

(a) 3   (b) 4   (c) 5   (d) 6   (e)7

Sol.

Regular method	smart technique
$let\ x + y = 17$ $xy = 70$ $(x - y)^2 = (x + y)^2 - 4XY$ $(x + y)^2 = 289 - 4 \times 70$ $x - y = \sqrt{9} = 3$ $x + y = 17$ $x - y = 3$ $2x = \ \ 20$ $x = 10$ $y = 7$	Sum of two number is 17 **cond^n I** Many combination are their like 10+7, 9+8,12+5,etc…. Product of the number is 70 **cond^n II** If we observe the two condition One set i.e 10,7 only can match both condition Their difference will be 3

Q: If x be the least number , which when divided by 5,6,7 and 8 leaves reminder 3 in each case but when divided by 9 leaves no reminder, then the digit is

    (a) 18   **(b) 21**   **(c) 24**   **(d) 22**   **(e) 27**

Smart technique

Get we use the reverse technique to solve the sum, it becomes easy and quick, let us try in the given 5 option, option (a) 18 and (e) 27 are dividible3 by 9 hence other three i.e b, c,d are ruled out

Again when the number divided by 5,

Leaves reminder 3

So the number is 18 , after div. by 5 leave 3 asreminder

The number 27 , after div. by 5 leave 2 as reminder

Hence answer is 18

Q: Rahim reared some hen and goats.If the heads of both are 90 and their leg are 248 . How many goats are their

(a) 32   (b) 34   (c) 36   (d) 40   (e) 38

Sol.

Regular method	Smart technique
Let hen be x and goat y $x + y = 90$____________ 1 $2x + 4y = 248$ _______2 *multiply 2 on equetion* $2x + 2y = 180$ $2x + 4y = 248$ $\underline{-\quad-\qquad-}$ $\qquad 2y = 68$ $y = 34$	Total leg 248---------1 Total head is 90 ---------2 If we choose the answer from the option , then If 32 goat , then hen becomes =58 Leg become (32 X4)+(58x2)=244 if 34 goats , then hen becoms 56 Leg become (34 X4)+(56X2) 136+112 = 248match No other option match like this , so answer us 34 *note:you can choose the option by seleting unit digit also*

Q: sum of the two number is 15. Addition of their square is 113. What are the two number.

(a) 4,11   (b) 5,10   (c) 6,9   (d) 7,8   (e) 3,12

Sol.

Regular method	smart technique

Let bar number be x *and* y
$x + y = 15$__________1
$X^2 + y^2 = 113$---------2
$(x + y)^2 = x^2+y^2+2xy$
$225 = 113 + 2xy$
$2xy = 112$
$xy = 56$
$(x - y)^2 = x^2+y^2 - 2xy$
$= 113 - 2X56$
	$x + y = 15$ *condn* 1
	$x^2+y^2=113$ **condn** 2
	
	Option (a) $4^2+11^2 = 16+121=137$(wrong)
	   (b) $5^2+10^2 = 25+100= 125$(wrong)
	   (c) $6^2+9^2=36+31 = 117$(wrong)
	   (d) $7^2+8^2 = 49+64= 113$(right)
	   (e) $3^2+12^2 = 9+144$(wrong)

	Note : *All such calucalation do it on your mind and reject by seling by unit value . It will more quick than this method . It con do only after some practices*
$= 113 - 112$ $(x - y)^2 = 1$ $x - y = 1$ -----------3 $x + y = 15$ $x - y = 1$ $2x = 16$ $x = 8, y = 7$	

Q: A number x is divisible by 7, when this number is divided by 8, 12 and 16, it leaves a reminder 3 in each case. The least value of x is:

   (a) 150   (b) 147   (c) 148   (d) 149   (e) 230

Smart technique

out of 5 given options, any number is divisible by 7

only option (b) 147 is divisible by 7 , so other option are ruled out

The other condition, when divided by 8, the reminder is 3 also fulfilled by option (b)

Hence answer is 147

Q: The sum of the digits of a three digit number is 17 and the sum of the squarers of its digits is 109. If we substract 495 from that number , we shall get a number consisting of the same digits writhen in reverse order . find the number

   (a) 773   (b) 863   (c) 683   (d) 944

Smart technique

By using reverse technique to get the answer easily and quickly

Condition 1:- all option have sum of digit is 17

Condition 2:- sum of square number in 109 = only option (b) & (e)

Condition 3 :- option (b) i.e substract 495 , we get 368

Hence option (b) is the answer

Q: In a race the first four winners are to be awarded points. Each winner's point must be 5 more than that of the next position winner. The total sum of the points to be3 awarded is 50 . what will be the points for the 3rd position winner

   (a) 30   (b) 20   (c) 10   (d) 5

Smart technique

Form the option

	1st	2nd	3rd	4th	
Let us take option(d) 5	15	10	5	0	$\neq 50$
10	20	15	10	5	= 50

Hence the 3rd winnerhave 10 points.

Q: At a dinner party, every two guests used a bowl of rice between them , every three guests used a bowl of dal among them and every four guests used a bowl of curd used among them. There are altogether 65 bowls. What is the number of guests present at the party.

   (a) 90   (b) 80   (c) 70   (d) 60

Smarts technique

Acc. To reverse Technique, we follow certain rule

i.e

    2 guest = 1 bowl rice

    3 guest = 1 bowl dal

4 guest = 1 bowl curd

On the above option 60 is the only common multiple of 2,3 and 4 for further verification total bowl should be 65 .

Hence answer is 60.

Q: The sum of the cubes of two numbers is 793. The sum of the numbers is 13. Then the difference of the two number is

   (a) 7   (b) 8   (c) 5   (d) 6

Regular method	Smart technique
Let a and b be the two numbers $a^3+b^3=$ 793 $(a+b)^3-3ab(a+b) = 793$ $(13)^3-3ab(13) = 793$ $ab = \dfrac{1404}{39} = 36$ $(a-b)^2=(a+b)^2 - 4ab$ $(a-b)^2= (13)^2 - 4 \times 36$ $= 169 - 144$ $(a-b)^2= 25$ a-b = 5	(Note: Always a+b and a-b should be same i.e either both should have odd or even) so on the above condition option (b) and(d) ruled out option (a) a-b=7 a+b = 13 a= 10 then b= 3 so unit digit 10^3+3^3=............7 option (c) a- b= 5 a+b=13 a= 9, b= 4 so unit digit 9^3+4^3= **9+*4= **3 Hence option (c) a-b=5 is correct

Q: When an integer k is divided by 3, the reminder is 1, and when k+1 is divided by 5, the reminder is 0. From the following , the possible value of k is

   (a) 62   (b) 63   (c) 64   (d) 65

Follow the reverse technique to get the answer

Option (a) $62 \div 3 = reminder\ 2 \neq cond\ 1\ (reminder\ 1)$

   (b) $63 \div 3 = Reminder\ 0 \neq code\ 1$
   (c) $64 \div 3 = reminder\ 1\quad when\quad 64 + 1 = 65$

$divided\ 5, reminder\ is\ 0\ matched\ both\ condition$

   (d) $65 \div 3 = remind\ 2 \neq condn\ 1$

Hence 64 be the answer

Q: $\dfrac{1}{x^3+x^3}=18,$ *then the value of* $\left(x+\dfrac{1}{x}\right)$ *is*

(a) 0   (b) 1   (c) 2   (d) 3

$$\left(x+\frac{1}{x}\right)^3 = x^3+x^3 + \frac{1}{x^3} + 3.x.\frac{1}{x}\left(x+\frac{1}{x}\right)$$

$$\left(x+\frac{1}{x}\right)^3 = 18 + 3.(3). (by\ option)$$

$$\left(x+\frac{1}{x}\right)^3 = 27$$

$$\left(x+\frac{1}{x}\right) = 3$$

Q: The difference of the cube of the two number is 61, their sum is 9. What is the difference of the two number

(a) 1   (b) 2   (c) 4   (d) 8

Sol.

$x^3 - y^3 = 61$

$x + y = 9$
$x - y = 1$
$2x = 10$

$x = 5$

$y = 4$

Put the value $5^3 - 4^3 = 61$

Hence $x - y = 1$

Q:A and B have money in the ratio 2:1 get A gives Rs. 2 to B the money will be in the ration 1:1 what were the initial amount they had

  (a) Rs 12 and Rs. 6   (b) Rs 16 and Rs. 8   (c) Rs. 8 and Rs. 4

  (d)Rs. 6 and Rs. 3

Smart technique

Lets solve from option all option fulfil the cond^n i.e $\dfrac{x}{y} = \dfrac{2}{1}$

Cond^n . 2 after giving Rs. 2 to B, ration $\dfrac{A}{B} : \dfrac{1}{1}$

  (a) 10:8 $\neq$ 1:1
  (b) 14:10 $\neq$ 1:1
  (c) 6:6 $=$ 1:1
  (d) 4:5 $\neq$ 1:1

Hence option (c) will be the correct answer.

TECHNIQUE

FIND THE VALUE OF UNKNOWN DIGIT FROM GIVEN DATA

Q: the difference between a two digit number and the number obtained by inter changing, the two digit of the number is 9. If the sum of the two digits number is 15, Then what is the original number

(a) **89**   (b) **67**   (c) **87**   (d) **96**   (e) cannot be determined

SOl.

Regular method	smart technique
Let the number be $10x + y$ The number get by interchanging the digit= $10y + x$ $10x + y - (10y + x) = 9$ $9x - 9y = 9$ $x - y = 1$ $x + y = 15$ $2x = 16$ X=8 $x + y = 15$ $y = 7$	Two gidit no – interchange no = 9 Sum of digit=15 If we look for the option , two options are follow the cond^n 1 & 2 i.e c, d So only 87 is the correct answer to write

Q: When 'n' is divisible by 5, the reminder is 2 , what is the reminder when n^2 is devided by 5.

(a) **2**   (b)**3**   (c) **4**   (d) **5**   (e) **6**

Sol.

Regular method	smart technique
$n = 5q + 2$	For such type of problem,

By square both side	we assume a number that have remainder 2 after divisible by 5
$n^2 = (5q + 2)^2$ $= 25q^2 + 10q + 4$ $n^2 = 5(5q^2 + 2q) + 4$ So the reminder is 4	such number are = 7,12,17,22 etc let us take 7 the remainder is 2 after divisible by 5 the square of 7 is 49, the remainder will be 4 after divisible of 5 (so without any calculate we get the result)

Q: To find the value of x is $\sqrt{x + 2\sqrt{x + 2\sqrt{x + 2\sqrt{3x}}}} = x$

   (a) 1   (b) 3   (c) 6   (d) 12

Smart technique

If we compare the value of x with the option.

Let $x = 1$, $2\sqrt{3x} = 2\sqrt{3}$ never become 1 in L.H.S.

$x = 3$ $\sqrt{x + 2\sqrt{x + 2\sqrt{x + 2\sqrt{3x}}}}$

$= \sqrt{3 + 2\sqrt{3 + 2\sqrt{3 + 6}}}$

$= \sqrt{3 + 2\sqrt{3 + 6}}$

$= \sqrt{3 + 2.3}$

$= \sqrt{9} = 3$

Hence L.H.S = R.H.S of putting the value is $x = 3$

Q: Get $4x + 5y = 83$ **and** $3x:2y = 21:22$ *then* $y - x$ *equal to*

(a) **3**   (b) **4**   (c) **7**   (d) **11**

Smart technique

Lets first take $\dfrac{3x}{2y} = \dfrac{21}{22}$

$$= \dfrac{x}{y} = \dfrac{7}{11}$$

$x = 7, y = 11$ *put this value for conformation in* $4x + 5y = 28 + 55 = 83$

Hence $y - x = 4$

Q: *get* $3^{2x-y} = 3^{x+y} = \sqrt{27}$ *then the value of* 3^{x-y} *will be*

(a) $\dfrac{1}{\sqrt{3}}$ (b) $\dfrac{1}{\sqrt{27}}$ (c) $\sqrt{3}$ (d) **3**

Smart technique

$$3^{2x-y} = 3^{x+y} = 3^{\frac{3}{2}}$$

$$= 2x - y = \frac{3}{2}$$

$$= x + y = \frac{3}{2}$$

$$3x = 3$$

$$x = 1$$

$$y = \frac{3}{2} - 1 = \frac{1}{2}$$

hence $3^{x-y} = 3^{1-\frac{1}{2}} = \sqrt{3}$

Q: *get $x(x-3) = -1$ then the value of $x^3(x^3-18)$ is*

   (a) 0   (b) -1   (c) 2   (d) 1

Smart technique

$$x(x-3) = -1$$

$$(x-3) = -\frac{1}{x} \qquad\qquad apply\ formula$$

$$(x-3)^3 = \left(-\frac{1}{3}\right)^3 \quad (a-b)^3 = a^3 - b^3 - 3ab(a-b)$$

$$x^3 - 27 - 3.x.3(x-3) = \frac{-1}{x^3}$$

$$x^3 - 27 - 9x\left(-\frac{1}{x}\right) = -\frac{1}{x^3}$$

$$x^3 - 18 = -\frac{1}{x^3}$$

$$x^3(x^3 - 18) = -1$$

Q: *If $(x^3 - y^3):(x^2 + xy + y^2) = 5:1$ and $(x^2 - y^2):(x-y) = 7:1$, then the ratio of $2x:3x$ equals*

   (a) 3:2   (b) 2:3   (c) 4:1   (d) 4:3

$$\frac{x^3 - y^3}{x^2 + xy + y^2} = \frac{5x^2 - y^2}{1\ x-y} = \frac{7}{1}$$

$$\frac{(x+y)(x^2 + xy + y^2)}{x^2 + xy + y^2} = \frac{5(x+y)(x-y)}{1\quad xy} = \frac{7}{1}$$

$x - y = 5$ ....1 $\qquad\qquad$ $x + y = 7$.............2

from equ. 1 *and* 2

$x = 6$ *and* $y = 1$

$$\frac{2x}{3y} = \frac{2.6}{3.1} = \frac{4}{1}$$

TECHNIQUE

SUBSTITUTION METHOD USED IN ALGEBRA

Q:- If a+b+c=0 then the value of $\left(\dfrac{a^2}{bc} + \dfrac{b^2}{ca} + \dfrac{c^2}{ab}\right)^2$ **is**

    (a) 1 $\qquad$ (b) 2 $\qquad$ (c) 3 $\qquad$ (d) 4 $\qquad$ (e) 5

Sol:

Regular Method	Smart Technique

a+b+c=0 a+b= -c $(a+b)^3 = (-c)^3$ $a^3 + b^3 + 3ab(a+b) = -c^3$ $a^3 + b^3 + c^3 + 3ab(-c) = 0$ $a^3 + b^3 + c^3 = 3abc$ Then $\dfrac{a^2}{bc} + \dfrac{b^2}{ca} + \dfrac{c^2}{ab}$ $\dfrac{a.a^2}{abc} + \dfrac{b.b^2}{bca} + \dfrac{c.c^2}{bca}$ $\dfrac{a^3}{abc} + \dfrac{b^3}{abc} + \dfrac{c^3}{abc}$ $\dfrac{a^3 + b^3 + c^3}{abc}$ $\dfrac{3abc}{abc} = 3$	Substitution method in the method to put assumed value in place of using formula and get the result. Let us put assumed value of a,b,c As a=2, b=-1 and c=-1 So a+b+c =2-1-1=0 If we put the value of a,b,c in $\dfrac{a^2}{bc} + \dfrac{b^2}{ca} + \dfrac{c^2}{ab} = \dfrac{2^2}{(-1)(-1)} + \dfrac{(-1)^2}{(-1)^2} + \dfrac{(-1)^2}{(2)(1)}$ $\dfrac{4}{1} + \left(\dfrac{-1}{2}\right) + (\dfrac{-1}{2})$ $4 - \dfrac{1}{2} - \dfrac{1}{2} = \dfrac{8-1-1}{2} = \dfrac{6}{2} = 3$ Hece answer is 3 it is quite easy and less time taking

Q:If $\dfrac{a}{b} = \dfrac{c}{d} = \dfrac{e}{f} = 3$, the $\dfrac{2a^2 + 3c^2 + 4e^2}{2b^2 + 3d^2 + 4f^2}$ = ?

(a) 2   (b) 3   (c) 4   (d) 9   (e) 15

Sol:-

Regular Method	Smart Technique
$\dfrac{a}{b} = \dfrac{c}{d} = \dfrac{e}{f} = 3$ so a= 3b, c= 3d , e= 3f $\dfrac{2(3b)^2 + 3.(3d)^2 + 4(3f)^2}{2b^2 + 3d^2 + 4f^2}$ $\dfrac{2.9b^2 + 3.9d^2 + 4.9f^2}{2b^2 + 3d^2 + 4f^2}$	$\dfrac{a}{b} = \dfrac{c}{d} = \dfrac{e}{f} = 3$ get we assumed a=c=e=3 b=d=f=1 and put the value in the give question $\dfrac{2(3)^2 + 3.(3)^2 + 4(3)^2}{2.1 + 3.1 + 4.1}$ $\dfrac{2.9 + 3.9 + 4.9}{2 + 3 + 4}$ (note : to calculate it in mind and get

$\dfrac{9(2b^2 + 3d^2 + 4f^2)}{2b^2 + 3d^2 + 4f^2}$	the result) $\dfrac{9(2 + 3 + 4)}{2 + 3 + 4}$
Ans : 9	=9

Q: If $3(a^2 + b^2 + c^2) = (a + b + c)^2$ **then the relation between a, b and c is**

(a) A=b=c   (b) a $\neq$ b=c   (c) a $\neq$ b $\neq$ c   (d) a=b $\neq$ c

Sol:

Instead of using formula, if we put any value of a,b and e, we get the result quickly and easily .
let us if a=b=c=1 , then the value of

L.H.S $= 3(1^2 + 1^2 + 1^2) = 9$ a=b=c

R.H.S $= (1 + 1 + 1)^2 = 3^2 = 9$

Similarly get we put a=b=c=2, then the value of

L.H.S $= 3(2^2 + 2^2 + 2^2) = 3.12 = 36$

R.H.S $= (2 + 2 + 2)^2 = 6^2 = 36$

 L.H.S = R.H.S get a=b=c

Hence answer is a=b=c

Q: the value of $\dfrac{(0.67 X 0.67 X 0.67) - (0.33 X 0.33 X 0.33)}{(0.67 X 0.67) + (0.67 X 0.33) + (0.33 X 0.33)}$

(a) 3.4   (b)1.1   (c)11   (d) 0.34   (e) none of these

Sol:

Regular Method	Smart Technique

	Get we observe the question, it follow some standard formula. So we put it in smart way. Let us apply the formula let
$\dfrac{(0.67X0.67X0.67) - (0.33X0.33X0.33)}{(0.67X0.67) + (0.67X0.33) + (0.33X0.33)}$	a=0.67 b=0.33 then

$$\frac{0.30076 - 0.03594}{0.4489 + 0.2211 + 0.1089}$$

$$\frac{0.26482}{0.7789}$$

= 0.33999

=0.34

Get we observe the question, it follow some standard formula. So we put it in smart way. Let us apply the formula let

a=0.67

b=0.33

then

$$\frac{(0.67X0.67X0.67) - (0.33X0.33X0.33)}{(0.67X0.67) + (0.67X0.33) + (0.33X0.33)}$$

$$\frac{a^3 - b^3}{a^2 + ab + b^2}$$

$$= \frac{(a - b)(a^2 + ab + b^2)}{a^2 + ab + b^2}$$

= a-b

= 0.67-0.33

= 0.34

Hence the answer is 0.34

Q: If a,b,c are positive and a+b+c = 1 , then the least value of $\frac{1}{a} + \frac{1}{b} + \frac{1}{c}$ is

   (a) 1   (b) 9   (c) 5   (3) 3   (e) 0

Sol:

Smart technique

Instead of doing calculation to obtain result, we put the value of a,b, c , is become easy and less time taking, let us try.

a+b+c =1 , we consider such a value that the addition of a,b,c is 1

i.e a=b=c=$\frac{1}{3}$ so $\frac{1}{3} + \frac{1}{3} + \frac{1}{3} = \frac{3}{3} = 1$

then the least value of $\frac{1}{a} + \frac{1}{b} + \frac{1}{c}$

= 3+3+3

$$= 9$$

Q: If $x^2 + y^2 + z^2 = 2(x - y - z) - 3$, **then the value of 2x-3y+4z is [assume that x,y,z are all real number]**

   (a) 9   (b) 1   (c) 10   (d) 3   (e) 0

Sol:

Regular Method	Smart Technique

$x^2 + y^2 + z^2 = 2(x - y - z) - 3$
 $x^2 + y^2 + z^2 = 2x - 2y - 2z - 3x^2 - 2x + 1y^2$
 $(x - 1)^2 + (y - 1)^2 + (z - 1)^2 = 0$
 $(x - 1)^2 = 0$, $(y - 1)^2 = 0$, $(z - 1)^2 = 0$
 x=1 , y=-1 , z=-1
 The value of 2x-3y+4z
 = 2.1-3(-1)+4(-1)
 = 2+3+4
 =1
	if we smartly consider the value if x,y and z in such a way that both L.H.S and R.H.S should be equal , we can solve it easily . let us
	 if we take x=1 , y =-1 and z=-1
	 L.H.S = $(1)^2 + (-1)^2 + (-1)^2 = 3$
	 R.H.S = 2(1-(-1)-(-1)-3
	   = 2X3-3= 3
	 So L.H.S= R.H.S
	 So we ensure that x=1 , y=-1 , z= -1
	 Get we put the value in
	 2x-3y + 4z
	 = 2.1-3(-1)+4(-1)
	   = 2+3-4
	 =1

Q: If a+b+c=0 then the value of $\left(\dfrac{a+b}{c} + \dfrac{b+c}{a} + \dfrac{c+a}{b}\right)\left(\dfrac{a}{b+c} + \dfrac{b}{c+a} + \dfrac{c}{a+b}\right)$ **is**

   (a) 8   (b) -3   (c) 9   (d) 0   (e) 4

Sol: Smart technique

For the above sum, the value of a,b,c need not be assumed but smartly apply such a formula that it can solve in memory only let us try

if a+b+c= 0 so a+b=-c , b+c=-a , c+a=-b then we put for the above value

$$= \left(\frac{a+b}{c} + \frac{b+c}{a} + \frac{c+a}{b}\right)\left(\frac{a}{b+c} + \frac{b}{c+a} + \frac{c}{a+b}\right)$$

$$\left(\frac{-c}{c} + \frac{-a}{a} + \frac{-b}{b}\right)\left(\frac{a}{-a} + \frac{b}{-b} + \frac{c}{-c}\right)$$

= (-1-1-1) (-1-1-1)

= (-3)(-3)=9

Q: get x+y+z=6 , then the value of $(x-1)^2 + (y-2)^2 + (z-3)^2$ **is**

(a) $3(x-1)(y-2)(z-3)$　　(b) $(x-1)(y-2)(z-3)$　(c) $2(x-1)(y-2)(z-3)$　(d) $3xyz$

Sol:

Split the data as per asked question

$(x-1)(y-2)(z-3) = 0$

As year know when a+b+c =0, a³+b³+c³=3abc

Hence answer $3(x-1)(y-2)(z-3)$

Q: get bc+ab+ca= abc , then the value of $\dfrac{b+c}{bc(a-1)} + \dfrac{a+c}{ac(b-1)} + \dfrac{a+b}{ab(c-1)}$

(a) 0　　(b) 1　　(c) $-\dfrac{3}{2}$　　(d) $-\dfrac{1}{2}$

Sol:

Correct approach in algebric sum can save much time and help to do in mental calculataion, though a sum can solve in many ways.

Regular Method	Smart Technique
$\dfrac{b+c}{bc(a-1)} + \dfrac{a+c}{ac(b-1)} + \dfrac{a+b}{ab(c-1)}$ $= \dfrac{b+c}{abc-bc} + \dfrac{a+c}{abc-ac} + \dfrac{a+b}{abc-ab}$ $= \dfrac{b+c}{ab+bc+ca-bc} + \dfrac{a+c}{ab+bc+ca-ac} + \dfrac{a+b}{ab+bc+ca-ac}$ $= \dfrac{b+c}{a(b+c)} + \dfrac{a+c}{a(b+c)} + \dfrac{a+b}{a(b+c)}$	if we do a single portion out of the three portion and match all to get result more quick than earlier $\dfrac{a+b}{bc(a-1)} = \dfrac{a+b}{abc}$ $\dfrac{a+b}{ab+bc+ca-bc} = \dfrac{a+b}{a(a+b)} = \dfrac{1}{a}$ So other two have $\dfrac{1}{b}$ and $\dfrac{1}{c}$ Add all $\dfrac{1}{a} + \dfrac{1}{b} + \dfrac{1}{c}$

$\dfrac{1}{a}+\dfrac{1}{b}+\dfrac{1}{c}$ $=\dfrac{\dfrac{ab+bc+ca}{abc}}{}$ $\quad or\ \dfrac{abc}{abc}$ $\dfrac{ab+bc+ca}{ab+bc+ca}=1$	$\dfrac{ab+bc+ca}{abc}=\dfrac{abc}{abc}=1$

Q; get a= 25 b= 15, c=-10 then the value of $\dfrac{a^3+b^3+c^3-3abc}{(a-b)^2+(b-c)^2+(c-a)^2}$ is

(a) 30　　　　(b) -15　　　　　　(c)-30　　　　(d) 15

Sol:

Regular Method	Smart Technique
$\dfrac{a^3+b^3+c^3-3abc}{(a-b)^2+(b-c)^2+(c-a)^2}$ $=\dfrac{25^3+15^3+(-10)^3-3.25.15.-10}{(10)^2+(25)^2+(-35)^2}$ $=\dfrac{15625+3375-1000-11250}{100+625+1225}$ $\dfrac{29250}{1950}=15$	$\dfrac{a^3+b^3+c^3-3abc}{(a-b)^2+(b-c)^2+(c-a)^2}$ $=\dfrac{\frac{1}{2}(a+b+c)\{(a-b)^2+(b-c)^2+(c-a)^2}{(a-b)^2+(b-c)^2+(c-a)^2}$ $=\dfrac{1}{2}(a+b+c)$ $=\dfrac{1}{2}(25+15-10)$ $=15$

Q: get $a^2+b^2+c^2=ab+bc+ca$, then $\dfrac{a+c}{b}$ is equal to

(a) 1　　　(b) 2　　　(c) 3　　　(d) 4

Sol:

Regular Method	Smart Technique

$a^2 + b^2 + c^2 = ab + bc + ca$ $a^2 + b^2 + c^2 - ab - bc - ca = 0$ Multiply 2 in both site $2a^2 + 2b^2 + 2c^2 - 2ab - 2bc - 2ca = 0$ $a^2 - 2ab + b^2 - 2bc + a^2 - 2ac + c^2 = 0$ $(a-b)^2 + (b-c)^2 + (c-a)^2 = 0$ a=b , b=c , c=a a=b=c the value of $\dfrac{a+c}{b}$ $\dfrac{2a}{=a} = 2$	If $a^2 + b^2 + c^2 = ab + bc + ca$ assume the value of a,b,c lets a=b=c=1 then $a^2 + b^2 + c^2 = 3$ L.H.S $ab + bc + ca = 3$ R.H.S So we consider a=b=c=1 The value of $\dfrac{a+b}{b}$ $\dfrac{2}{=1}$ =2

Q: If $x^3 + y^3 = 72$, $xy = 8$, **then the value of** $x - y$.

    (a) 8   (b) 4   (c) 2   (d) 5

Sol: **smart technique**

If we see the two equation i.e $x^3 + y^3$ **=72**

$$xy = 8$$

Assume value 4 and 2 i.e 4.2 = 8

$$= 4^3 + 2^3 = 64 + 8 = 72$$

so we can obtained the result without much calculation

Hence the result 4-2=2

Q: If $x^2 + y^2 + \dfrac{1}{x^2} + \dfrac{1}{y^2} = 4$ **then the value of** $x^2 + y^2$ **is**

    (a) 2   (b) 4   (c) 8   (d) 16

Sol:

Regular Method	Smart Technique

$x^2 + y^2 + \dfrac{1}{x^2} + \dfrac{1}{y^2} = 4$ $= (x - \dfrac{1}{x})^2 + (y - \dfrac{1}{y})^2 = 0$ $x - \dfrac{1}{x} = 0 \qquad y - \dfrac{1}{y} = 0$ $x^2 - 1 = 0 \quad y^2 - 1 = 0$ $x^2 = 1 \quad y^2 = 1$ $x^2 + y^2 = 2$	It can be solved by a small mental calculation assume the value of $x = y = 1$ Then L.H.s = $1^2 + 1^2 + \dfrac{1}{1^2} + \dfrac{1}{1^2} = 4$ Hence $x = y = 1$ $x^2 + y^2 = 1^2 + 1^2 = 2$

Q: get $x^2 - y^2 = 80$ **and** $x - y = 8$**, the average of x and y is**

   (a) **2**   (b) **3**   (c) **4**   (d) **5**

Sol:

Regular Method	Smart Technique
$x^2 - y^2 = 80$ $(x - y)(x + y) = 80$ $x + y = \dfrac{80}{8}$ $x - y = 8$ $x + y = 10$ $2x = 18$ $x = 9$ $y = 10 - 9 = 1$ Average x,y = $\dfrac{x + y}{2}$ =5	If we do a little mental calculation for this sum we con obtain the result without using paper and pen . Let's try, we think such a numbers which $x^2 - y^2 = 80$ and $x - y = 8$ lets think over 9 and 1 L.H.s $= 9^2 - 1^2 = 80 - 1 = 80$ $9 - 1 = 8$ Hence nos. are 9 and 1 Av of the number $\dfrac{9 + 1}{2} = 5$

Q: get $x + \dfrac{1}{x} = \sqrt{3}$ **then the value of** $x^{18} + x^{12} + x^6 + 1$ **is**

   (a) **0**   (b) **1**   (c) **2**   (d) **3**

Sol:

$$x + \dfrac{1}{x} = \sqrt{3}$$

(Note : before solving the sum see the required power of the x for solving . Here x^6 is the common for all given x Power Hence we Change the power of x accordingly)

$$\left(x + \frac{1}{x}\right)3 = (\sqrt{3})^3$$

$$x + \frac{1}{x} + 3.x.\frac{1}{x}\left(x + \frac{1}{x}\right) = (\sqrt{3})^3$$

$$x^3 + \frac{1}{x^3} + 3.\sqrt{3} = 3\sqrt{3}$$

$$= \quad x^3 + \frac{1}{x^3} = 0$$

$$= x^6 + 1 = 0 \ = x^6 = -1$$

$$= x^{18} + x^{12} + x^6 + 1$$

$$= (x^6)^3 + (x^6)^2 + (-1) + 1$$

$$= (-1)^3 + (-1)^2 + (-1) + 1$$

$$= -1 + 1 - 1 + 1$$

$$= 0$$

Q: If $x^2 + 2 = 2x$, then the value of $x^4 - x^3 + x^2 + 2$ is

   (a) 0   (b) 1   (c) -1   (d) $\sqrt{2}$

Sol:

$$= x^4 - x^3 + x^2 + 2$$

$$= x^2(x^2 - x) + x^2 + 2 \quad \text{(put value of } x^2 + 2 = 2x, x^2 = 2x - 2)$$

$$= (2x - 2)(2x - 2 - x) + 2x$$

$$= (2x - 2)(x - 2) + 2x$$

$$= 2x^2 - 4x - 2x + 4 + 2x \qquad \text{(multiply 2 in both side} 2x^2 = 2(2x - 2) = 2x^2 = 4x - 4)$$

$$= 4x - 4 - 4x - 2x + 4 + 2x$$

$$= 0$$

Q: If $\dfrac{x}{y} = \dfrac{a+2}{a-2}$, then the value of $\dfrac{x^2-y^2}{x^2+y^2}$ is

(a) $\dfrac{4a}{a^2+4}$ (b) $\dfrac{2a}{a^2+4}$ (c) $\dfrac{4a}{a^2+2}$ (d) $\dfrac{2a}{a^2+2}$

Sol:

Regular Method	Smart Technique
$\dfrac{x}{y} = \dfrac{(a+2)}{(a-2)}$ $\dfrac{x^2}{y^2} = \dfrac{(a+2)^2}{(a+2)^2}$ $\dfrac{x^2-y^2}{x^2+y^2} = \dfrac{(a+2)^2-(a-2)^2}{(a+2)^2+(a-2)^2}$ $= \dfrac{a^2+4+4a-(a^2+4-4a)}{a^2+4+4a+a^2+4-4a}$ $= \dfrac{a^2+4+4a-a^2-4+4a}{a^2+4+4a+a^2+4-4a}$ $= \dfrac{8a}{2a^2+8}$ $= \dfrac{4a}{a^2+4}$	Such method of solving can not the fruitful in competitive exam . apply smart technique to solve such type of sum, lets try Assume any value of "a" which is most convenientassume a=6 $\dfrac{x}{y} = \dfrac{6+2}{6-2} = \dfrac{8}{4} = \dfrac{2}{1}$ $\therefore x = 2 \quad y = 1$ $\dfrac{x^2-y^2}{x^2+y^2} = \dfrac{4-1}{4+1} = \dfrac{3}{5}$ Then which option become $\dfrac{3}{5}$ do it on mental calculation (a) $\dfrac{4a}{a^2+4} = \dfrac{4.6}{36+4} = \dfrac{24}{40} = \dfrac{3}{5}$ true (b) $\dfrac{2a}{a^2+4} = \dfrac{2.6}{36+4} = \dfrac{12}{40} = \dfrac{3}{10}$ false Like this we solve in shortest possible time

TECHNIQUE

HIGHEST COMMON FACTOR (H.C.F.) IN ALGEBRA

Q: Find the H.C.F of $x^2 + 5x + 4$ and $x^2 + 7x + 6$

Sol:

Regular Method	Smart Technique
Fractional method $x^2 + 5x + 4 = x^2 + 4x + x + 4$ $= x(x + 4) + 1(x + 4)$ $= (x + 4)(x + 1)$	$x^2 + 5x + 4$ $x^2 + 7x + 6$ $-\quad-\quad-$ $\qquad -2x - 2$

294

$x^2 + 7x + 6 = x^2 + 6x + x + 6$ $= x(x + 6) + 1(x + 6)$ $=(x + 6)(x + 1)$ Hence H.C.F $= (x + 1)$	$= -2(x + 1)$ Hence H.C.F $= (x + 1)$

Q: Find H.C.F of $(2x^2 - x - 3)$ **and** $(2x^2 + x - 6)$

  (a) $(2x + 3)$ **(b)** $(2x - 3)$ **(c)** $(x + 2)$ **(d)** $(x + 2)(2x + 3)$

Sol:

Regular Method	Smart Technique
$2x^2 - x - 3 = 2x^2 - 3x + 2x - 3$ $= x(2x - 3) + x(2x - 3)$ $= (2x - 3)(x + 1)$ $2x^2 + x - 6 = 2x^2 + 4x - 3x - 6$ $= 2x(x + 2) - 3(x + 2)$ $= (x + 2)(2x - 3)$ Hence H.C.F $= (2x - 3)$	$2x^2 - x - 3$ $2x^2 + x - 6$ $-\quad\ -\quad +$ $\quad\ -2x + 3$ $-1(2x - 3)$ Hence H.C.F $= 2x - 3$

Q: Find H.C.F of $x^3 - 7x - 6$ **and** $x^3 + 8x^2 + 17x + 10$

Sol :

Smart technique

$x^3 - 7x - 6$

$x^3 + 8x^2 + 17x + 10$

$-\quad\ -\quad\ -\quad\quad\ -$

$-8x^2 - 24x - 16$

$-8(x^2 + 3x + 2)$

Hence H.C.F of the equation is $x^2 + 3x + 2$

Q: $x^3 + 6x^2 + 5x - 12$ **and** $x^3 + 8x^2 + 19x + 12$ **, find H.C.F of the above equation**

Sol: Smart technique

$x^3 + 6x^2 + 5x - 12$

$x^3 + 8x^2 + 19x + 12$

$\quad - \quad - \quad\quad - \quad\quad -$

$- 2x^2 - 12x - 24$

$- 2(x^2 - 6x + 12)$

H.C. F is $x^2 - 6x + 12$

Q: The H.C.F of $x^3 - 6x^2 + 11x - 6$, $x^3 + x^2 - 9x - 9$ **and** $x^3 + 6x^2 + 5x + 12$ **is**

    (a) $x^2 - x + 1$ **(b)** $x - 2$ **(c)** $x - 3$ **(d)** $x^2 - 2x + 3$

Sol: smart technique

$x^3 + 6x^2 + 11x - 6$

$x^3 + x^2 - 9x - 9$

$\quad - \quad - \quad\quad + \quad\quad +$

$\quad\quad - 7x^2 + 20x + 3$

$x^3 + x^2 - 9x - 9$

$x^3 + 6x^2 + 5x + 12$

$\quad - \quad\quad + \quad\quad - \quad\quad -$

$7x^2 - 14x - 21$

$- 7x^2 + 20x + 3$

$7x^2 - 14x - 21$

$6x - 18$

$6(x - 3)$

Hence H.C.F is $x - 3$

Q: Find the H.C.F of the $x^3 - 3x^2 - 4x + 12$ **and** $x^3 - 7x^2 + 16x - 12$

(a) $(x - 6)$　　　　**(b)** $(x - 3)$　　**(c)** $x^2 - 5x + 6$　　　　**(d)** $x^2 + 5x + 6$

Sol : Smart Technique

$x^3 - 3x^2 - 4x + 12$

$x^3 - 7x^2 + 16x - 12$

$\quad - \quad + \quad - \quad\quad +$

$4x^2 - 20x + 24$

$+ 4(x^2 - 5x + 6)$

H.C.F of the equation is $(x^2 - 5x + 6)$

Q: H.C.F of $6x^4 - 11x^3 + 16x^2 + 22x + 8$ **and** $6x^4 - 11x^3 - 8x^2 + 22x - 8$

Sol : smart technique

$6x^4 - 11x^3 + 16x^2 + 22x + 8$

$6x^4 - 11x^3 - 8x^2 + 22x - 8$

$\quad - \quad + \quad\quad + \quad - \quad\quad +$

$\qquad\qquad 24x^2 - 44x + 16$

$\qquad\qquad 4(6x^2 - 11x + 4)$

H.C.F of the Equation $6x^2 - 11x + 4$

<u>TECHNIQUE #</u>

<u>AREA AND PERIMETER</u>

Q: A circular copper wire of radius 35cms is bent to from a rectangle. If the length of rectangle is 26 cms more than the breath of rectangle, then what is the length is rectangle

(a) 72   (b) 64   (c) 62   (d) 68

Sol: Perimeter of rectangle = Perimeter of circle

$$= 2X\frac{22}{7}X35 \quad (R = 35)$$

$$= 220 \quad (use\ methed\ 22X10)$$

Breath $= x$

Length $= 26 + x$

$2(x + 26 + x) = 220$

$2x = 110 - 26 = 84$

$x = 42\ length$

Breath = 26+42 = 68

Q: the ratio between the length and breadth of a rectangular field is 5:4. If the breadth is 20m less than length, the perimeter of the field is

(a) 260m   (b) 280m   (c) 360m   (d) None

Sol:

$$\frac{Length}{breath} = \frac{5x}{4x}$$

The difference is 20

So $x = 20$ so length is 5x =100

      Breath is 4x=80

Perimeter $= 2(L + B) = 2X180 = 360$

Q: The length of rectangle is 1.5 times width. If the area is 1350 sq meter. what is its perimeter

(a) 120m (b) 130m   (c) 140m   (d) 150m

Sol:

If width is x , length 1.5x

Area = 1350

$1.5x \ X \ x = 1350$

$x^2 = \dfrac{1350}{1.5} = 900$

$x = 30$

Width = $30(x)$

Length = $45(1.5x)$

$Perimeterr = 2(45 + 30) = 150mt$

On smart technique, find the length & width of the rectangle

$15.xXx = 1350$

$15x^2 = 13500 = 900$ **(calculation in single line)**

$x = \sqrt{900} = 30$

Q: The length of Rectangle is increased by 20% and width is decreased by 20%, the area decreased by

  (a) 8%   (b) 0.8%   (c) 1.2%   (d) 4%

Sol: Let length be 100m & breath be 50m

Area = LXb =100 X 50 =5000 sqm

Length increase 20% so L =120

Width decrease 20% so W = 40

Charged area = 120 X 40 = 4800

Area decrease = 5000-4800=200

% is area decrease = $\dfrac{200}{5000} X100$

=4%

Use the smart technique with suitable formula, like

= 20% -20%- $\dfrac{20X20}{100}$

= - 4%(-ve sing indicate decrease)

When no particular value is

Q: The perimeter of a rectangular plot is 48m and area is 108 m². The dimension of the plot is

  (a) 36 m and 3m   (b) 12m and 9m   (c) 27m and 4m   (d) 18m and 6m

Sol : Smart technique

Perimeter = 48

$2(L + B) = 48$

L+B=24

L X B =108

Use reverse technique to get answer quickly on cond^n-I ,

only option (d) is followed i.e 18+6 = 24 cond^{n}II , 18X6=108

Hence answer is 18m and 6m

Aiternate $(L-B)^2 = (L+B)^2 - 4LB$

$$= (24)^2 - 4.108$$

$$= 576 - 432$$

$$= 144$$

L – B = 12

L + B = 24
L – B =12
2L=36

L=18

B=6

Q: The are of a rectangle is thrice that of a square. The lenth of rectangle is 20cm and the breath of rectangle in $\dfrac{3}{2}$ times that side of square. The side square in cm is

 (a) 10   (b) 15   (c) 20   (d) 30   (e) 60

Sol: Smart technique

In a single step formula can help to solve such a long type of sum.

Let side of square is a

Breath $= \dfrac{3}{2}a$

Area of rectangle = 3Xarea of square

$$20 \times \frac{3}{2} a = 3 \times a^2$$

a = 10cm

Q: the ratio of the length and breath of a rectangular plot is 6:5 respectively. If breath of the plot is 34m less than the length , what is the perimeter of rectangular plot ?

 (a) 374m   (B) 408m   (c) 814m   (d) 748m   (e) none of these

Sol : Smart technique

The diff of ratio of L and B is one

Length is 6x and breath is 5x, diff is 34 so length is 6X34

$$=204$$

Breath is 5X34

    = 170

Perimeter = 2(L+b)

      = 2(204+170)

    = 2X374

    =748 m

Q: A rectangular garden is to be twice as long as its width. If 360m of fencing including gate will totally enclose this garden. What is the length of the garden.

 (a) 120m   (b) 130m   (c) 140m   (d) 150m

Sol : Smart technique

Perimeter = 360

2(L +W) =360

 (L+W) =180

Let W=x then L= 2x

3x=180

X= 60

So length of the garden is 2x=120m

Q: the length and breadth of a rectangular field are 25m and 15m. Two roads each of width 20m parallel to length and breadth exactly in the centre of field cut each other and reaming area has grass. The area of grass section is

$$\text{(a) } 295 \text{ m}^2 \quad \text{(b) } 299 \text{ m}^2 \quad \text{(c) } 300 \text{ m}^2 \quad \text{(d) } 375\text{m}^2 \quad \text{(e) } 410 \text{ m}^2$$

Sol: area of field $= (25 \times 15) \text{ m}^2$

Area of road $= (2 \times 25 + 2 \times 15) - 2 \times 2$

Area of grass $= (25 \times 15) - (80-4)$

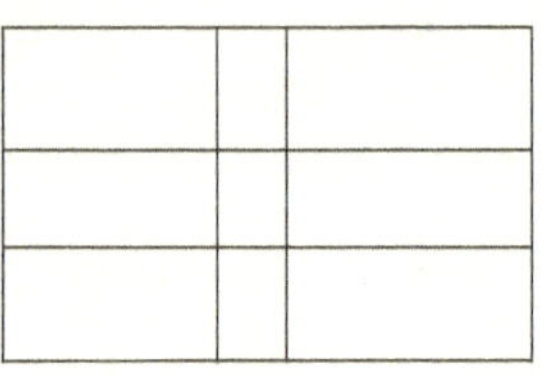

$= 375 - 76$ (use smart technique for calculation $(20+5)15$)

$= 299 \text{ m}^2$

Q: the area of a rectangle whose length is five more than twice its width is 75 sq unit. The length is

(a) 5 unit   (b) 10 unit   (c) 15 unit   (d) 20 unit

Sol:

Let width of rectangle $=x$

Length $= 2x+5$

$x(2x+5) = 75$ (use substitution method , to get result x= 5

L.H.S $= 5(2 \times 5+5) = 75$ R.H.S

$2x^2 + 5x - 75 = 0$

$2x^2 + 15x - 10x - 75 = 0$

$x(2x+15) - 5(2x+15) = 0$

$x = 5 \ , x = -\dfrac{15}{2}$

Length $= 2x + 5 = 2 \times 5 + 5 = 15 \, m$

Q: sides of a parallelogram are in the ratio 5:4. Its area is 1000 sq meter. Altitude in the greater side is 20 meter. Altitude in the smaller side is (in metre)

(a) 30   (b) 25   (c)15   (d)10   (e) 5

Sol : area of the parallelogram = side x altitude

$5x \times 20 = 1000$

$x = 10 \, m$

Sides are 50 and 40 meter

$40 \times h = 1000$

$h = 25 \, metre$

Altitude of smaller side is 25 meter.

Q: If the length fo each side of a regular tetrahedron Is 12cm, then the volume of tetrahedron

(a) $112\sqrt{2}cucm$ **(b)** $144\sqrt{2}cucm$ **(c)** $72\sqrt{2}cucm$ **(d)** $12\sqrt{2}cucm$

Sol: Smart technique

Vol. of tetrahedron = $\dfrac{a^3}{6\sqrt{2}}$

$$= \dfrac{12 \times 12 \times 12}{6 \times \sqrt{2}}$$

$$= 144\sqrt{2} \, cu \, cm$$

Q: A room is 18 m long and 15 m wide. It is to be covered by square tiles of maximum area, find the number of square tiles required to cover the floor

(a)30   **(b) 45**   **(c) 20**   **(d) 15**

Sol:

The H.C.F of 18 and 15 is 3

No of square tiles required$= \dfrac{area \ of \ rectangle}{(HCF)^2}$

$$\frac{18X15}{3X3} = 30$$

Q: If the perimeters of a rectangle and a square are equal, the ratio of two adjacent sides of the rectangle is 1:2, then the ratio of area of rectangle and that of the square is

  (a) 1:1   (b) 1:2   (c) 4:5   (d) 8:9

Sol: Let side of square be a and rectangle length be x &2xperimeter

$4a = 2(x + 2x)$

$$4a = 6x$$

Perimeter ratio of $\dfrac{rectangel}{square} = \dfrac{2}{3}$

Area ratio = $\dfrac{2X4}{3^2} = \dfrac{8}{9}$

Q: The area of the rectangle is 4 times the area of a square. The length of rectangle is 90cms and breadth of the rectangle is $\dfrac{2}{3}$ rd of the side of the square. What is the length of the side of the square?

  (a) 10m   (b) 20cm   (c) 9cm   (d) 15cm

Sol: let side of square be a cm

Breadth of rectangle = $\dfrac{2}{3}acm$

Length   = 90 cm

Acc. To question $90X\dfrac{2}{3}a = 4.a^2$

$$a = 15 \; cms$$

Q: the breadth of a rectangular hall is three Fourth of its length. If the area of the floor is 768 sqm. Then the difference between length and breadth of the hall is

(a) 8m **(b) 12m** **(c) 24m** **(d) 36m**

Sol: Let length of hall xm

Breadth of hall $\dfrac{3}{4}x$

Area = 768

$$xX\dfrac{3}{4}x = 768$$

$$x^2 = 768\,X\,\dfrac{4}{3}$$

$$x = \sqrt{256\,X4}$$

$$x = 32$$

Length = 32, breadth = $32\,X\,\dfrac{3}{4} = 24\,m$

Difference = 8m

Q: The perimeter of a rectangle is 160m and difference of two sides is 48m. Find the side of a square whose area is equal to the area of this rectangle.

(a) 32m **(b) 8m** **(c) 4m** **(d) 16m**

Sol: $2(L + b) = 260$

$L + b = 80$

$L - b = 48$

$2L = 128 = L = 64$

$b = 16$

Area of rectangle = $64\,X\,16$

$a^2 = 64X16$ (abroad totaling in this step)

$a = \sqrt{64X16}$

$= 8\,X\,4$

$= 32$

Q: the length of a longest rod that can be placed on a room which is 12 cm long , 9m broad and 8m high is.

  (a) **27m**   (b) **19m**   (c) **17m**   (d) **13m**

Sol: longest rod can be placed

$$= \sqrt{12^2 + 9^2 + 8^2} = \sqrt{144 + 81 + 64} = \sqrt{289} = 17\,m$$

TECHNIQUE

PERCENTAGE CHANGE IN AREA OF A QUADRILATERAL

Q: the length of a rectangle increased by 40% and its breadth increased by 20%. What will be the percentage increase in the area of the rectangle .

  (a) **50%**   (b) **10%**   (c) **60%**   (c) **65%**   (e) **68%**

Sol:

Regular Method	Smart Technique
Let the original length L And breadth B Area = L X B New length = LX 40% of L = 1.4 L New Breadth = B X 20% of B = 1.2 B New area = 1.4LX1.2B=1.68LB New area increase=1.68LB-LB % of area changes = $\dfrac{0.68}{100} = 68\%$	The percentage change in area of the rectangle can be measured by using effective formula i.e $\left(a + b + \dfrac{ab}{100}\right)\%$ Where $a = 40$, $b = 20$ So percentage change in area $= 40 + 20 + \dfrac{40.20}{100}$ $= 68\%$ (Note : When % decreases , the sing became –ve)

Q: If the side of a square is increased by 25% then how much percentage does its area get increased?

  (a) **50**   (b) **56.25**   (c) **156.25**   (d) **36.25**   (e) **12.25**

Sol:

Regular Method	Smart Technique
Let side of a square be 20 units Area = (20)²=400 25% increase on side , i.e side = 25 units New area = (25)²=625	When side increase 25% net area increased % $= \left(25 + 25 + \dfrac{25.25}{100}\right)\%$

Increased % = $\dfrac{625 - 400}{400} \times 100$

$= \dfrac{225}{400} \times 100$

$= 56.25\%$

	$= 56.25\%$

Q: If the length and breadth of a rectangular field are increased, the area increases 50%. If the length was increased by 20%, by what percentage was breadth increased.

(a) 30%   (b) 25%   (c) 20%   (d) 10%   (e) none of these

Sol:

Regular Method	Smart Technique
Data given in percentage , so assume value in 10's multiple Let's length be 10units Breadth be 20 units L X b= area of rectangular 10 X 20= 200 L increase 20% = new length 12 B increase $x\%= ((100 + x)\%\ of\ 20$ Area increase 50% = new area 300 $12X(100 + x)\%of\ 20 = 300$ $\dfrac{100 + x}{100}X20 = 25$ $x = 125 - 100 = 25\%$	Let x% of breadth increased $\left(20 + x + \dfrac{20.x}{100}\right)\% = 50\%$ $20 + x + \dfrac{x}{5} = 50$ $\dfrac{6x}{5} = 30$ $x = 25\%$

Q: the length of a rectangle increase by 20% and its breadth is decrease by 10%, what be the percentage change in area

(a) 5% increase (b) 8% increase   (c) 10% decrease (d) 10% increase   (e) no change

Sol:

Regular Method	Smart Technique
Let the original length rectangle be 10 unit and breadth 20 unit Area of rectangle = 10X20=200 sq unit new length = 12 and breadth =18 New area of rectangle =	$\left(a - b - \dfrac{ab}{100}\right)\%\ where\ a = 20, b = 10$ $= \left(20 - 10 - \dfrac{20X10}{100}\right)\%$ $= 8\%\ increase$

$12 \, X18 = 216 \, sq \, unit$ Change in area =216-200=16 sq mt $\dfrac{16}{200}X100 = 8\% \, increase$ % change	

Q: If the length of a rectangle is increased by 10% and its breadth is decreased by 10% the change in it area will be

  (a) 1% decrease (b) 1% increase   (c) 10% increase (d) no change

Sol: Smart technique

Acc. To the formula for the above condition applied sum

The change in area $= \left(10 - 10 - \dfrac{10.10}{100}\right)\%$

$$= (10 - 10 - 1)\%$$

$$= -1\%$$

-1% i.e 1% decrease in area

Q: If the length of a rectangular plot of land is increased by 5% and the breadth is decreased by 10%. How much will its area increase or decrease.

  (a) 6.5 % increase(b) 5.5 % decrease   (c) 5.5%increase(d) 6.5% increase

Sol: Smart technique

The net change in area $= (5 - 10 - \dfrac{5.10}{100})\%$

$$= (5 - 10 - .5)\%$$

$$= -5.5\%$$

Hence net decrease in area 5.5%

Q: If the length of a rectangular field is increased by 20% and the breadth is reduced by 20%, the area of rectangle will be 192 m². What is the area of original rectangle?

  (a) 184m² (b) 196m² (c) 204m² (d) 225m² (e) 200m²

Sol: Smart technique

The net changes in area $= \left(20 - 20 - \dfrac{20.20}{100}\right)\%$

$$= -4\%$$

After change the area = 192

i.e 96 % of original area = 192

original area $= \dfrac{192}{96} X100$

$$= 200m^2$$

Q: the length of a rectangle is halved, while its breadth is tripled. What is the percentage change in area?

(a) 50% increase (b) 50% decrease (c) 25% increase (d) 75% decrease

Sol: Smart technique

Length of rectangle is halved i.e reduce by 50%

Breadth is tripled   i.e increase by 200%

So % changes in area $= \left(-50 + 200 - \dfrac{50.200}{100}\right)\%$

$$= (-50 + 200 - 100)\%$$

$$= (200 - 150)\%$$

$$= 50\%$$

Hence area increases 50%

Q: the breadth of a rectangular plot is decreased by 20%, by what %should the length be increased to keep the area same?

(a) 20   (b) 30   (c) 25   (d) 50

Sol:

Smart technique	Alternate method
Required changed $= \dfrac{100.x}{100 - x}\%$	Let length of rectangle 10 units Breadth 20 units Area = 200 sq units Acc. To question

$= \dfrac{100.20}{80}\%$	$(10 + x\% \, of \, 10)X16 = 200$
	$x\% \, of \, 10 = \dfrac{200}{16} - 10$
$= 25\%$	$= \dfrac{x}{10} = \dfrac{40}{16}$
	$x = 25$

Q: The maximum length of a pencil that can be kept in a rectangular box dimensions 8 cm X 6cm X 2cm is(in cm)

(a) $2\sqrt{13}$ (b) $2\sqrt{14}$ (c) $2\sqrt{26}$ (d) $10\sqrt{2}$

Sol:

The max. Length of pencil can be placed in

$\sqrt{8^2 + 6^2 + 2^2}$

$\sqrt{64 + 36 + 4}$

$\sqrt{104}$

$2\sqrt{26} \ cm$

TECHNIQUE

AREA AND PERIMETER OF CIRCLE

Q: If the perimeter of a circle is decreased by 50%, then the percentage of decrease in area is

(a) 20   (b) 50   (c) 80 (d) 75

Regular method	Smart technique
Perimeter of circle = $2\pi r$ Let radius of circle 14 units (in place of r, use a suitable digit) Perimeter = $2X\dfrac{22}{7}X14$ =88 Reduced to 50% , the new perimeter =44 And radius will be y unit Area of old circle = $\pi X14^2$ $= \dfrac{22}{7}X14X14$ = 616 sq unit Area of new circle = $\pi X7^2$ $= \dfrac{22}{7}X7X7$ = 154 sq unit Decrease % = $\dfrac{616-154}{616}X100$	Perimeter decrease 50% i.e radius decrease 50% net effect in area $\left(-50-50+\dfrac{50.50}{100}\right)\%$ $(-100+25)\%$ $= 75\%$

$\dfrac{46200}{616}$	
=	
= 75%	

Q: A wire in the form of a circle of radius 98 cm is cut and bent in the form of a square. The side of the squiare thus formed is

(a) 146 cm (b) 152 cm (c) 154cm (d) 156 cm

Sol :

Perimeter of circle $2\pi r$ is bent to form a square

$2X\dfrac{22}{7}X98 = 4a$ where a is the side of the square

$a = 2X\dfrac{22}{7}X\dfrac{98}{4}$

$= 156 \; cm$

Q: If area of an equilateral triangle is $36\sqrt{3}$ cm² then the area of the inscribed circle is:

(a) $48\pi cm^2$ (b) $36\pi cm^2$ (c) $24\pi cm^2$ (d) $12\pi cm^2$

Sol:

$\dfrac{\sqrt{3}}{4}a^2 = 36\sqrt{3}$ $a = 12cm$

Readies of inscribed circle $= \dfrac{a}{2\sqrt{3}} = \dfrac{12}{2\sqrt{3}} = 2\sqrt{3} \; cm$

Area of the circle $= \pi(2\sqrt{3})^2$

$= 12\pi$ cm²

Q: The diameter of $<$ a circle circumscribing a square is $15\sqrt{2}$m . what is the length of the side fo square

(a) 15cm (b) 12cm (c) 10cm (d) 15cm

Sol:

Diameter of the circumscribing

Circle = diameter of square= $15\sqrt{2}$

Area of the square = $\dfrac{1}{2}d^2 = \dfrac{1}{2}(15\sqrt{2})^2$

$= \dfrac{1}{2}X15X15X2$

$a^2 = 15x15$

$a = 15\ cm$

Q: the area of two circles is in the ratio 1:2 if the two circles are bent in the form of squares. What is the ratio of their areas?

(a) 1:2   **(b) 1:3**   **(c) 1:4**   **(d) 1:$\sqrt{2}$**

Sol:

$$\dfrac{\pi r1^2}{\pi r_2^{\,2}} = \dfrac{1^{r_1}}{2r_2} = \dfrac{1}{\sqrt{2}}$$

Perimeter = $\dfrac{2\pi r_1}{2\pi r_2} = \dfrac{4a_1}{4a_2}$ (4a is perimeter % squ)

$$\dfrac{a_1}{a_2} = \dfrac{1}{\sqrt{2}}$$

The ratio of area of the square $\dfrac{a_1^2}{a_2^2} = \dfrac{(1)^2}{\sqrt{2}^2}$

$= \dfrac{1}{2}$

Q: If the circumferenceand area of a circle are numerically equal , then the diameter is equal to

(a) Area of the circle   (b) 4   (c) $\dfrac{\pi}{2}$ (d) 2π

Sol: circumference of circle = area of circle

$2\pi r = \pi r^2$

$r = 2$

Diameter = $2r = 4$

Q: If a wire is bent in to the shape of a square , the area of the square is 81cm² . when the were is bent into a semi circular shape , the area of the some circular is

    (a) 154 cm²   **(b) 77 cm²**   **(c) 44 cm²**   **(d) 22cm²**

Sol.

$a^2 = 81$

$a = 9\ for\ each\ side\ fo\ a\ square$

Perimeter of circle = perimeter of square

$$= 4 \times 9 = 36$$

Hence length of the were = 36 cm

Perimeter of semicircle = $\pi r + d = 36$

$$= \frac{22}{7}r + 2r = 36$$

$$r = 36 \times \frac{7}{36} \times 7$$

Area ofsemicircle $= \frac{1}{2}\pi r^2 = \frac{1}{2} \times \frac{22}{7} \times 7 \times 7$ =77 cm²

Q: the number of revolution, a wheel of diameter 40 cm makes in traveling a distance of 176 m is

    (a) 140   (b) 150   (c) 160   (d) 166   (e) 180

Sol: the radius of wheel = $\frac{40}{2} = 20cm = 0.2m$

Wheel travel distance in 1 recirculation = perimeter of wheel

$$2 \times \frac{22}{7} \times 0.2 = \frac{8.8}{7}m$$

$$\frac{8.8}{7}m = 1\ rev$$

$$176m = \frac{70}{88} \times 176$$

$= 140$

TECHNIQUE

TRIANGLE BASED FORMULA AND ITS APPLICATION

Related terms and formula

CircumCenters: the point of intersection of perpendicular bisectors of the side of a triangle circumcentre is equidistance from all vertices of a triangle .

Incenter: the point of intersection of angle bisectors of a triangle. Incentre is equidistance form all side of a triangle.

Orthocenter: The Point of intersection of all the altitudes of a triangle. In a right angled triangle the othocenter lies at the largest vertex contain right angle

Centroid: The point of intersection of all the medians of a triangle. centroid divided each median in the ratio 2:1

In a triangle, if the bisectors of any two angles meet at a point, then the angle formed by them is 90^0 more than the half of the third angle

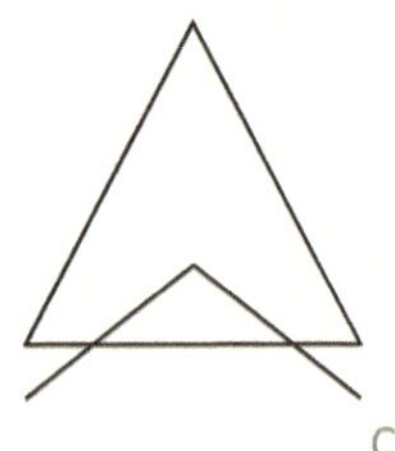

$$BOC = 90 + \frac{1}{2} BAC$$

iF bisector of any two extensor angle

$$BOC = 90 - \frac{1}{2} BAC$$

Area of equilateral triangel whose side 'a' is $\frac{\sqrt{3}}{4} a2$

Height of an equilateral triangle = $\frac{\sqrt{3}}{2} a$

Radius of circumcircle = R= $\frac{a}{\sqrt{3}}$

Radius of in circle = r = $\frac{a}{2\sqrt{3}}$

radius of circle = $\dfrac{area\ of\ triangle}{semi\ perimetor\ of\ triangle}$

Q: O is the incenter of ΔPQR and if QPR = 50^0, then the measure of QOR is

  (a) 125^0 (b) 115^0 (c) 100^0 (d) 130^0

Sol:

As per the question

The angle of internal bisector

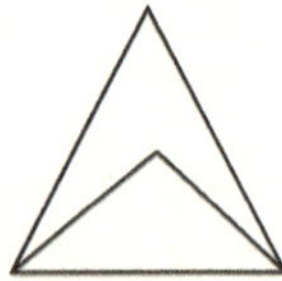

QOR= $90 + \frac{p}{2}$

$$= \dfrac{90 + \dfrac{50}{2}}{}$$

$$=115^0$$

Q: the side of an equilateral triangle is $20\sqrt{3}cm$**.the numerical value of the radius of the circle circum scribing the triangle is.**

(a) 20cm   (b) $20\sqrt{3}$ (c) $20\pi\ cm$ (d) $\dfrac{20}{\pi}\ cm$

Sol: radius of circum circle $R = \dfrac{a}{\sqrt{3}}$

$$R = \dfrac{20\sqrt{3}}{\sqrt{3}}\ cm$$

$$R = 20\ cm$$

Q: If ABC is a right angle triangle with A = 90^0 AN is perpendicular to BC, BC = 12 cm and AC =

6 cm then the ratio of $\dfrac{area\ \Delta\ ANC}{area\ \Delta\ ABC}$

(a) 1:3   (b) 1:2   (c) 1:4   (d) 1:6

Sol:

In two similar Δ

$$\dfrac{area\ of\ \Delta\ ANC}{area\ of\ \Delta\ ABC} = (\dfrac{P_1}{P_2})^2$$

$$= (\dfrac{6}{12})^2$$

$$= \dfrac{1}{4}$$

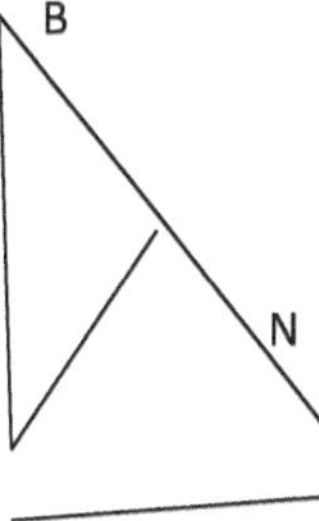

Q: the area of an equilateral triangle is $9\sqrt{3}$**m² the length (in meter) of the median is**

(a) $2\sqrt{3}$ (b) $3\sqrt{3}$ (c) $3\sqrt{2}$ (d) $2\sqrt{2}$

Sol:

Equilateral $\Delta\ area = 9\sqrt{3}$

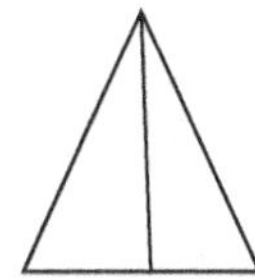

$$\frac{\sqrt{3}}{4}a^2 = 9\sqrt{3}$$

$a = 6 \; cm$

Length of median (height) = h

Side = a

(in equilateral Δ, $median$ devided the base into two equal part)

$$h^2 = 6^2 - 3^2$$

$$h = \sqrt{36 - 9}$$

$$h = 3\sqrt{3} \; cm$$

ALTERNATE METHOD

Area of $\Delta = 9\sqrt{3}$

$$\frac{\sqrt{3}}{4}a^2 = 9\sqrt{3}$$

$a = 6$

Height of equilateral Δ

$$h = \frac{\sqrt{3}}{4}a$$

$$= \frac{\sqrt{3}}{2} X \, 6$$

$$= 3\sqrt{3}$$

Q: O is the in center of the $\Delta \, ABC$, $if \; BOC = 116^0$ then BAC is

   (a) 42^0 (b) 62^0 (c) 58^0 (d) 52^0

Sol:

The point of intersection of angle inside the Δ is called incentre

$$BOC = 90 + \frac{A}{2}$$

$$116^0 = 90 + \frac{A}{2}$$

A= 52⁰

Q: the area of on isoscles triangle is 4 cm². Get the length of the third side is 2cm, the length of each equal side is (in cm)

(a) 4   (b) $2\sqrt{3}$ (c) $3\sqrt{2}$ (d) $\sqrt{17}$

Sol: AD is the height of the $\triangle ABC$

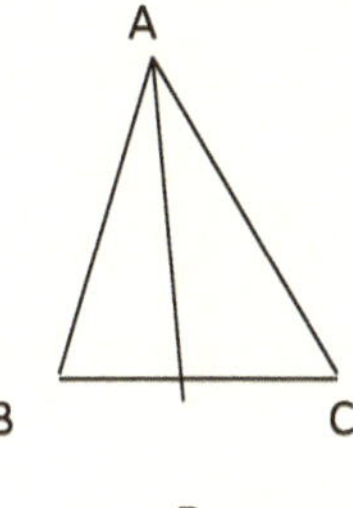

Hence BD = CD = 1cm

Area of$\triangle$

$$\frac{1}{2} X\, 2\, X\, h = 4$$

h = 4 cm

Then the value of x

AB² = AD²+BD²

$x^2 = 4^2 + 1^2$

$X = \sqrt{16+1} = \sqrt{17}$

Q: In a $\triangle\, ABC$ **,** $ABC = 5\, ACB$ **and BAC = 3 ACB , then ABC=**

(a) 80⁰   (b) 100⁰   (c) 120⁰   (d) 130⁰

Sol:

On a $\triangle, A + B + C = 180^0$

B= 5 c,   A= 3 c

3 C + 5 C + C = 180⁰

9 C = 180⁰

C= 20⁰

B = 5 C = 5X20 = 100⁰

Q: If area of an equilateral triangle is a and height b, then the value of $\dfrac{b^2}{a}$ is

(a) 3   (b) $\dfrac{1}{3}$ (c) $\sqrt{3}$ (d) $\dfrac{1}{\sqrt{3}}$

Sol:

Let the side be x

Area a = $\dfrac{\sqrt{3}}{4}x^2$

Height b= $\dfrac{\sqrt{3}}{2}x$

The value of $\dfrac{b^2}{a} = \dfrac{\left(\dfrac{\sqrt{3}}{2}x\right)^2}{\dfrac{\sqrt{3}}{2}x^2} = \dfrac{\dfrac{3}{4}x^2}{\dfrac{\sqrt{3}}{4}x^2} = \dfrac{3\sqrt{3}}{\sqrt{3}X\sqrt{3}}$

$= \sqrt{3}$

Q: in an equilateral triangle, the length of its in radius be 4 cm, then the area of the triangle is

(a) $54\sqrt{3}$sq cm $\qquad$ (b) $56\sqrt{3}\ sq\ cm$ $\qquad$ (c) $36\sqrt{3}\ sq\ cm$ $\qquad$ (d) $48\sqrt{3}\ sq\ cm$

Sol:

Radius of in circle r = $\dfrac{a}{2\sqrt{3}}$

$4=\dfrac{a}{2\sqrt{3}}$

$a = 8\sqrt{3}$

Area of equilateral $\Delta = \dfrac{\sqrt{3}}{4}a^2$

$= \dfrac{\sqrt{3}}{4}X\ 8\sqrt{3}\ X\ 8\sqrt{3}$

$= 48\sqrt{3}\ sq\ cm$

Q:Chords AB and CD of a circle intersect externally at P. If AB = 6cm. CD = 3cm and PD = 5cm, then the length PB PB is

(a) 6cm $\qquad$ (b) 4cm $\qquad\qquad$ (c) 5cm $\qquad$ (d) 6.25 cm

Sol :

AP X BP = CP X DP

$(6 + x) x = 8 X 5$

$x^2 + 6x - 40 = 0$

$x^2 + 10x - 6x - 40 = 0$

$x(x + 10) - 6(x + 10) = 0$

$x = -10 \quad , \quad x = 6$

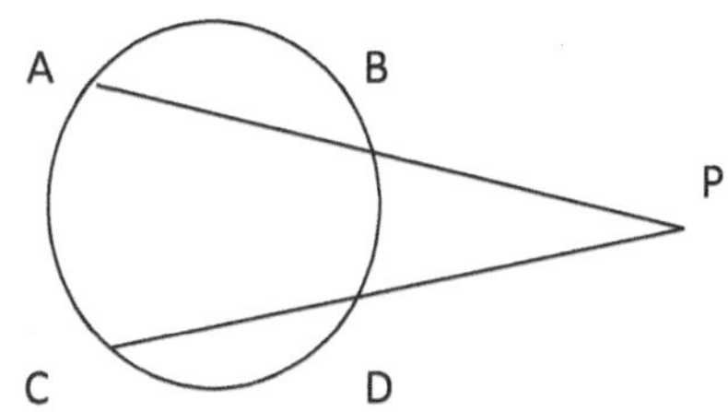

Q: the radius of a circle of a triangle whose sides are 9 cm, 12 cm, and 15cm is

(a) 13cm   (b) 3cm   (c) 6cm   (d) 9cm

Sol:

The triangle whose sides are 9cm, 12cm and 15 cm is

A right angle trianglei.e. $9^2 + 12^2 = 15^2$

Hence area of $\Delta = \dfrac{1}{2} X 9 X 12 = 54 \ cm^2$

Semi perimeter $= \dfrac{9 + 12 + 15}{2} = \dfrac{36}{2} = 18$

Radius of circle $= \dfrac{54}{18} = 3cm$

Q: the externalbisector of angle B and c of ΔABC (Where AB and AC entered to E and F) meet at point P. If angle BAC = 100⁰ then the measure of angle BPC is

(a) 50⁰   (b) 40⁰   (c) 80⁰   (d) 100⁰

Sol: Smart technique

As you know the bisector of angle externally

$BPC = 90^0 - \dfrac{1}{2} BAC$

$= 90^0 - \dfrac{100°}{2}$

$= 40^0$

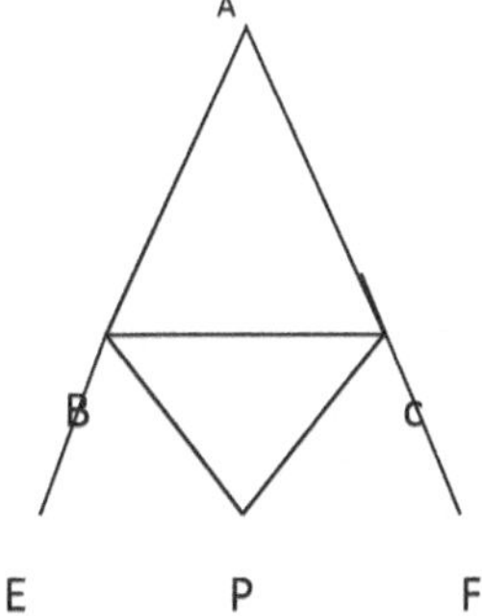

Q:if triangular field having sides 30m, 72m and 78m . The length of altitude to the side measuring 72m is

   (a) 25m   (b) 28m   (c) 30m   (d) 35m

Sol: from the given dimension, it is a right angle triangle

i.e. $30^2 + 70^2 = 78^2$

The height of altitude at the side of 72m is

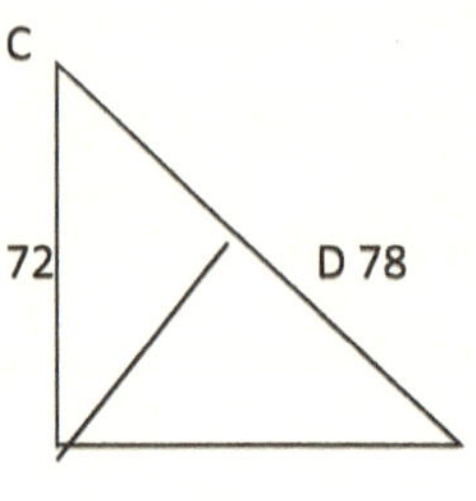

$$= \frac{1}{2} X 72 X h$$

$$= \frac{1}{2} X 30 X 72$$

$$= h = 30m$$

Q: if the perimeter of right angle isosceles triangle is $(4\sqrt{2} + 4)$cm. the length of the hypotenuse is

   (a) 4cm   (b) 6cm   (c) 8cm   (d) 10cm

Sol: Let length of two equal side be X cm

Right angle isosceles Δ

$$x + x + \sqrt{2}x = 4\sqrt{2} + 4$$

$$x(2 + \sqrt{2}) = 4(\sqrt{2} + 1)$$

$$x = \frac{4(\sqrt{2} + 1)}{\sqrt{2}(\sqrt{2} + 1)} = 2\sqrt{2}$$

Sides are $2\sqrt{2}, 2\sqrt{2}, 4$

Length of hypotenuse 4cm

Q: the internal bisectors of angle B and C of ΔABC meet at O. If angle A =80⁰, angle BOC is

   (a) 50⁰   (b) 100⁰   (c) 130⁰   (d) 160⁰

BOC = $90 + \dfrac{A}{2}$ (internal bisectior)

$$= 90 + \frac{80}{2}$$

$$= 130^0$$

Q: the radius of the incircle of a triangle which sides 15cm, 15cm and 18cm is.

  (a) 4cm   **(b) 4.5 cm**   **(c) 6cm**   **(d) 8cm**

Sol: The triangle having sides 15, 15 and

18 is called as isosceles triangle

So $h^2 = 15^2 - 9^2 = 225 - 81$

$h = \sqrt{144} = 12$

Area of the Δ is = $\dfrac{1}{2} X12X18 = 108$ cm²

radios of in circle = $\dfrac{area\ of\ \Delta\ ABC}{semi\ perimeter\ of\ \Delta\ ABC}$

$= \dfrac{108}{24} = 4.5cm$

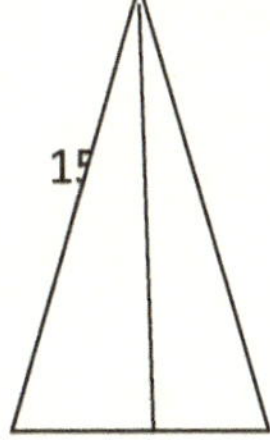

Q: perimeter of an equilateral triangle is equal to the circumference of a circle .the ratio of their areas is (use $\pi = \dfrac{22}{7}$)

  (a) $22:21\sqrt{3}$ (b) $21:22\sqrt{2}$ (c) $22:21\sqrt{2}$ (d) $21:22\sqrt{3}$

Sol: $3a = 2\pi r$ as perimetion of Δ= circmference of circle

$\dfrac{a}{r} = \dfrac{2\pi}{3}$

$= \dfrac{2X\dfrac{22}{7}X\dfrac{1}{3}}{}$

$= \dfrac{44}{21}$

The ratio of their Areass

$$\dfrac{\dfrac{\sqrt{3}}{4}a^2}{\pi r^2} = \dfrac{\dfrac{\sqrt{3}}{4}X44X44}{\dfrac{22}{7}X21X21} = \dfrac{22}{21\sqrt{3}}$$

Q: the centroid of a $\triangle ABC$ is G .the area of a $\triangle ABC$ is 60 cm². The area of $\triangle GBC$ is

(a) 30cm²   (b) 40cm²   (c) 20cm²   (d) 10cm²

Sol:

As per the figure, if we join AG, BG, CG it becomes

Three equal area based

$\triangle$. Hence area of BCG = $\dfrac{60}{3} = 20c$ m²

Q: A,B and C are three angles of a triangle . If A-B =15⁰ , B-C =30⁰, then A,B,C are

(a) 80⁰,60⁰,40⁰   (b) 70⁰,50⁰,60⁰   (c) 80⁰,65⁰,35⁰ (d) 80⁰,55⁰,45⁰

Sol:

Regular method	Smart technique
A+B+C= 180⁰------------------1 A-B=15⁰ B-C=30⁰ A-C=45⁰--------------------2 A-C+A-B= 45⁰+15⁰ 2A-B-C=60⁰--------------------3 A=180⁰-B-C -B-C=A-180⁰ 2A+A-180=60⁰ 3A=240⁰ A=80⁰ B=80⁰-15⁰=65⁰ C=180-80-65=35⁰ A,B,C = 80⁰,65⁰,35⁰	follow reverence technique to solve the question let's try Diff. of A & B =15⁰ Again the diff of B & C is 30⁰ only option C matched Hence answer is C

<u>TECHNIQUE #</u>

<u>SIMILAR TRIANGLE AND ITS RELATION</u>

Q. The areas of two similar triangle are $12cm^2$ and $48cm^2$. If the height of the smaller one is 2.1cm, then the corresponding height of the bigger triangle is

(a)12.6cm (b) 8.4cm (c) 4.2cm (d) 10.5cm (e) 1.05cm

Sol: According to triangle law

$$\frac{area\,of\,1st\,\Delta}{area\,of\,2nd\,\Delta} = \left(\frac{side_1}{side_2}\right)^2 = \left(\frac{median_1}{median_2}\right)^2 = \left(\frac{h_1}{h_2}\right)^2$$

So

$$\frac{12}{48} = \left(\frac{2.1}{x}\right)^2$$

$$12x^2 = 4.41 \times 48$$

$$x^2 = \frac{4.41 \times 48}{12}$$

$$x = 4.2\ cm$$

Q. The area of similar triangles ABC and DEF are $144cm^2\ and\ 81cm^2$ **respectively. If the longest side n triangle ABC is 36cm, then the longest side n triangle DEF is**

(a) 20cm (b) 26cm (c) 27cm (d)30cm (e) 24cm

Sol: smart technique

According to the formula

$$\frac{area\ of\ \Delta\ ABC}{area\ of\ \Delta\ DEF} = \left(\frac{Longest\ side\ n\ ABC}{Longest\ side\ n\ DEF}\right)^2$$

$$\frac{144}{81} = \frac{36^2}{X^2}$$

$$X^2 = \frac{36 \times 36 \times 81}{144}$$

$$X = \sqrt{\frac{36 \times 36 \times 81}{144}} \qquad \text{By applying smart technique}$$

$$= \frac{36 \times 9}{12} \qquad (\because \text{ all number become square root so need not to do any calculation})$$

$$=27$$

Q: The area of two similar Δs are 9cm² and 16cm² respectively. Find the ratio of their corresponding side

   (a) 3:4   (b) 4:3   (c) 2:3   (d) 3:2   (e)4:5

Sol:

Smart technique

Acc. To similar Δ formula

$$\frac{area\ of\ \Delta1}{area\ of\ \Delta2} = (\frac{side\ 1}{side\ 2})^2$$

$$\frac{9}{16} = (\frac{side\ 1}{side\ 2})^2$$

$$\frac{side\ 1}{side\ 2} = \sqrt{\frac{9}{16}}$$

$$= \frac{3}{4}$$

Q: two isosceles triangles have equal vertical angles and their areas are in the ratio 9:16 the ratio of their corresponding height

   (a) 4.5:8   (b) 8:4.5   (c)3:4   (d)4:3   (e) 3:4.5

Sol: Smart technique

Two isosceles Δ have equal verticals so both Δ are similar .

Acc.To the similar Δ formula.

$$\frac{area\ of\Delta1}{area\ of\ \Delta\ 2} = \left(\frac{h1}{h2}\right)^2$$

$$\frac{9}{12} = \left(\frac{h1}{h2}\right)^2$$

$$\frac{h1}{h2} = \sqrt{\frac{9}{16}}$$

$$\frac{h1}{h2} = \frac{3}{4}$$

Q: Given that the ratio of altitudes of two triangles is 4:5, ratio of their area is 3:2. the ratio of their corresponding base is .

   (a) 8:15   (b) 15:8   (c) 5:8   (d) 8:5

Sol: area of the triangle $= \dfrac{1}{2} X\ alt\ X\ base$

$$\frac{\frac{1}{2}X4xXbase1}{\frac{1}{2}X5xXbase\ 2} = \frac{3}{2}$$

$$\frac{2Xbase1}{\frac{5}{2}Xbase\ 2} = \frac{3}{2}$$

$$\frac{4\ base\ 1}{5base\ 2} = \frac{3}{2}$$

$$\frac{base\ 1}{base\ 2} = \frac{3}{2}$$

$$\frac{base1}{base\ 2} = \frac{15}{8}$$

Q: Given that $\triangle ABC \sim \triangle PQR.$ **If** $\dfrac{area\ of\ \triangle PQR}{area\ of\ \triangle ABC} = \dfrac{256}{441}$ **and PR = 12cm , then AC is Equal to**

   (a) $12\sqrt{2}cm$ (b) 15.75 cm (c) 15.5cm   (d) 16cm

Sol:

$$\frac{area\ of\ \triangle PQR}{area\ of\ \triangle ABC} = \left(\frac{PR}{AC}\right)^2$$

$$\frac{256}{441} = \left(\frac{12}{AC}\right)^2$$

$$\frac{12}{AC} = \sqrt{\frac{256}{441}}$$

$$\frac{12}{AC} = \frac{16}{21}$$

$$AC = \frac{12 X 21}{16}$$

= 15.75 cm

Q: the perimeters of the two similar triangles are 30cm and 20 cm respectively. If one side of first triangle is 9cm, determine the corresponding side of the second triangle.

(a) 15 cm   (b) 5 cm   (c) 6cm   (d) 13.5cm   (e) 10 cm

Sol : Smart technique

According to the similar triangle based formula, the perimeter is

$$\frac{perimeter\ of\ 1st\ \Delta}{perimeter\ of\ 2nd\ \Delta} = \frac{side\ 1}{side\ 2} = \frac{h1}{h2} = \frac{median\ 1}{median\ 2}$$

So $$\frac{30}{20} = \frac{9}{x}$$

$$x = \frac{20 X 9}{30}$$

=6cm.

TECHNIQUE

APPLICATION OF FORMULA TO FINDVOLUME AND SURFACE AREA

IMPORTANT FROMULAS:

CUBOLD:

Let length = L , breadth =b and Height = h unit, then

1. Volume = (L X b X h) cubic unit
2. Surface area = 2 (lb +bh +lh) sq unit
3. Diagonal = $\sqrt{l^2 + b^2 + h^2}$

CUBE

Let each edge of a cube be the length of a , then

1. Volume = a³ cube unit
2. Surface area = 6a²sq unit
3. Diagonal = $\sqrt{3}$a unit

CYLINDER

Let radius = r and height = h ,then

1. volume = $\pi r^2 h$ cubic unit
2. total surface area = $2\pi r(h + r)\, sq\ unit$
3. curved surface area = $2\pi rh\ unit$

CONE

Let radius = r and height = h

1. slant height l = $\sqrt{h^2 + r^2}$
2. volume = $\frac{1}{3}\pi r^2 h\ cubic\ unit$
3. total surface area = $\pi r\,(l + r)sq\ unit$
4. corve surface area = $\pi rl\ sq\ unit$

SPHERE

Let radius of schere be r , then

1. volume = $\dfrac{4}{3}\pi r^3$ cubic unit
2. total surface area = $4\pi r^2$

<u>HEMISPHERE</u>

Let radius of hemisphere r then

1. volume = $\dfrac{2}{3}\pi r^3$ cubic unit
2. total surface area = $3\pi r^2$ sq unit
3. curved surface area = $2\pi r^2$ sq unit

Q: find the length of the longest pole that can be placed in a room of 12 m long, 8m broad and 9 m height

(a) 15m   (b) 17m   (c) 19m   (d) 21m

Sol: length of longest pole = length of diagonal of them

$= \sqrt{l^2 + b^2 + h^2}$

$= \sqrt{12^2 + 8^2 + 9^2}$ (**note : use unit digit technique to obtain quick result**

$= \sqrt{144 + 64 + 81}\sqrt{*4+*4+*1} = \sqrt{*9}$

$= \sqrt{289}$ **either** 3^2 or 7^2**, hence answer is 17)**

=17

Q: water flow in to the tank 200m X 150m through a rectangular pipe of 1.5m X 1.25 @ 20kmph.In what time (in minutes) will the water rise by 2meters ?

(a) 65 min   (b) 96 min   (c) 93 min   (d) none of these

Sol: volume required into the tank = (200X150X2)m³ = 6000m³

Length of water column in min = $\dfrac{20X1000}{60} = \dfrac{1000}{3}m$

Vol. of water flow per min = 1.5X1.25X $\dfrac{1000}{3}$

= 625m³

Required time = $\dfrac{60000}{625} = 96\ min$

Q: the diagonal of the cube is $6\sqrt{3}m$. Find the surface area of the cube in m²

(a) 216   (b) 224   (c)196   (d)125

Sol: diagonal ofthe cube $=6\sqrt{3}$

$$\sqrt{3}a = 6\sqrt{3}$$

$$: a=6$$

Surface area $=6Xa^2 = 6 \times 6^2 = 216$ m²

Q: the curved surface area and the total surface area of a cylinder are in the ratio 1:2 .If the total surface area of the right cylinder is 616 cm², then its volume is

(a) 1232 cm³   (b) 1848 cm³ (c) 1632cm³ (d) 1078cm³

Sol:

$2\pi r(h + r) = 616\ then\ 2\pi rh = 308$

$2\pi rh + 2\pi r^2 = 61$

$308 + 2\pi r^2 = 616$

$2\pi r^2 = 308$

$R^2 = 308\ X\ \dfrac{7}{44} = 7\ X\ 7$

$R = 7$

$2\pi X7Xh = 308$

$2\ X\ \dfrac{22}{7}\ X\ 7\ X\ h = 308$

$h = 7$

Volume of the cylinder $= \pi r^2 h$

$= \dfrac{22}{7} X7X7X7$

$= 1078$cm³

Q: If four cubes, each of 10 cm edge are joined end to end , then find the total surface area of the resulting solid in sq cm.

   (a) 1800   (b) 600   (c) 2400   (d) 3600

Sol:

Length breadth and height of new cuboids = 40,10 and 10

Surface area = 2(40X10+40X10+10X10)

$\qquad$ = 1800 sq cm

Q: If the length of the diagonal of a cube is $\sqrt{3}cm$, then the surface area of the cube is

   (a) 192 cm²   (b) 512cm²   (c) 768cm²   (d)384cm²

Sol:

Diagonal of cube = $\sqrt{3}a$

So $\sqrt{3}a = 8\sqrt{3}$

$\qquad$ a = 8cm

Surface area of the cube =6a²= 6(8)²

$\qquad\qquad$ = 6 x 8 x 8

$\qquad\qquad$ = 384 cm²

Q: how many solid tennis balls each radius 5cm that can be molded out of a sphere of diameter 50cm?

   (a) 25   (b) 125   (c) 225   (d) 625

Sol :

Tennis ball have the spherical shape . Let x be the number of tennis ball

$$x \times \frac{4}{3}\pi \times 5^3 = \frac{4}{3} \times \pi \times 25^3$$

$$x = \frac{25 \times 25 \times 25}{5 \times 5 \times 5}$$

X = 125

Q: a hollow sphere of internal and external diameters 8 cm and 20 cm respectively is melted into a cone of base diameter 12 cm, what is the height of the cone ?

Sol :

Let height of cone h

$$\frac{1}{3}\pi 6^2 h = \frac{4}{3}\pi(10^3 - 4^3)$$

$$h = \frac{4\,X\,(1000 - 64)}{6\,X\,6}$$

$$= \frac{4\,X\,936}{6\,X\,6}$$

$$= 104\ cm$$

Q: the radii of the circular ends of a bucket of height 21 cm are 15cm and 9cm respectively. What is the volume of the bucket ?

(a) 9809 cm³   (b)b 9607 cm³ (c) 9702 cm³   (d) 9303 cm³

Sol: the circular bucket is a shape of a frustrum.

$$\text{the volume of frustum} = \frac{\pi h}{3}(R^2 + r^2 + Rr)$$

$$= \frac{\pi 21}{3}(15^2 + 9^2 + 15\,X9)$$

$$= \frac{22}{7}X7(225 + 81 + 135)$$

$$= 9702\ cm^3$$

(Note : use unit digit method to get result i.e

= 22 X (**5 +*1 + *5)

= 22 X**1

=***2   only one option which unit digit is 2

Q: the radii of the base of two cylinders are in the ratio 3:5 and their heights in the ratio 2:3 the ratio of their curved surface will be

(a) 2:5   (b) 3:5   (c) 2:3   (d) 5:3

Sol:

$$\frac{curved\ surface\ area\ of\ cylinder\ 1}{curved\ surface\ area\ of\ cylinder\ 2} = \frac{2\pi R_1 h_1}{2\pi R_2 h_2}$$

$$= \frac{3\ X\ 2}{5\ X\ 3} = \frac{2}{5}$$

Q: the radius of the base and height of a metallic solid cylinder are r cm and 6cm respectively .It is melted and recast into a solid cone of the same radius of base. The height of the cone is

(a)n 54cm   (b) 9cm   (c) 27 cm   (d) 18 cm

Sol: such type of questions, volume of both to be compared

Volume of cone = volume of cylinder

$$\frac{1}{3}\pi r^2 h = \pi r^2 . 6$$

$$h = 18\ cm$$

Q: If the area of the base of a cone is 770 cm² and the area of the curved surface 814cm² , then its volume (in cm³) is

(a) $213\sqrt{5}$ (b) $392\sqrt{5}$ (c) $550\sqrt{5}$ (d) $616\sqrt{5}$

Sol:

Base of the cone is a circle

$$\pi r^2 = 770$$

$$r^2 = 770\ X\ \frac{7}{22} = 35\ X\ 7 = 7\ X\ 5\ X\ 7$$

$$r = 7\sqrt{5}$$

Area of curved surface = 814

$$\pi r l = 814$$

$$\frac{22}{7}\ X\ 7\sqrt{5}\ X\ l = 814$$

$$l = \frac{814}{22\sqrt{5}} = \frac{37}{\sqrt{5}}$$

$$l^2 = h^2 + r^2$$

$$l^2 = h^2 + r^2 = \dfrac{(\frac{37}{\sqrt{5}})^2 - (7\sqrt{5})^2}{}$$

$$= \dfrac{37 \times 37}{\sqrt{5} \times \sqrt{5}} - 35 \times 7 = \dfrac{1369 - 1225}{5}$$

$$h^2 = \dfrac{144}{5}$$

$$h = \dfrac{12}{\sqrt{5}}$$

Volume of cone $= \dfrac{1}{3}\pi r^2 h$

$$= \dfrac{1}{3} \times \dfrac{22}{7} \times 7 \times 5 \times 7 \times \dfrac{12}{\sqrt{5}}$$

$$= \dfrac{3080}{\sqrt{5}}$$

Q: get each edge of a cube in increased by 50% find the percentage increase its surface area.

(a) 150%   (b) 125%   (c) 100%   (d) no change

Sol :

Regular method	Smart technique
Let original length = a Surface area = $6a^2$ New edge = $a + \dfrac{a}{2} = (\dfrac{3a}{2})^2$ New surface area = $6.(\dfrac{3a}{2})^2$ $= 6.\dfrac{9a^2}{4}$ $= \dfrac{27a^2}{2}$ Increase % in so A= $\dfrac{\frac{27a^2}{2} - 6a^2}{6a^2} \times 100$	each edge increases 50 % net effect on surface area $= \left(50 + 50 + \dfrac{50 \,.50}{100}\right)\%$ = 125 %

$= \dfrac{15a^2}{12a^2}X100$ $= 125\%$	

Q: a cone , a hemisphere and a cylinder stand on a equal base and have the same height . Find ratio of their volume

  (a) $1:2:4$ (b) $1:2:3$ (c) $2:3:1$ (d) $1:3:2$

Sol: let R be the radius of each height of the hemisphere = radius = R

Cone: hemisphere : cylinder

$$= \frac{1}{3}\pi R^2 h : \frac{2}{3}\pi R^3 : \pi R^2 h \quad (H = R)$$

$$= \frac{1}{3} : \frac{2}{3} : 1$$

$$= \frac{1}{3} : \frac{2}{3} : \frac{3}{3}$$

$$= 1 : 2 : 3$$

Q: there is a wooden sphere of radius $6\sqrt{3}cm$. The surface area of the largest possible cube cut out from the sphere will be

(a) 864 cm²   (b) 462 cm²   (c) $646\sqrt{3}$ cm²   (d) $464\sqrt{3}$ cm²

Sol: radius of sphere = $6\sqrt{3}$

Diagonal of cube =diagonal of sphere

$\sqrt{3a} = 12\sqrt{3}$

a =12

surface area of the cube=6a²

      =6x12x12

      =864cm2

Q. A cylinder with base radius and height 2cm is melted to form a cone of height 6cm. The radius of the cone will be

  (a) 8cm   (b) 4cm   (c) 5 cm   (d) 6 cm

Sol:

Vol. of cylinder= $\pi \times R^2 \times h$

Vol. of cone= $\dfrac{1}{3} \times \pi \times R^2 \times h$

$$\dfrac{1}{3} \times \pi \times R^2 \times 6 = \pi \times R^2 \times 2$$

$$R^2 = \dfrac{8 \times 8 \times 2 \times 3}{6}$$

R= 8 cm.

Q: the surface area of a sphere is 616 cm². If its radius is changed so that the area gets reduced by 75%, then the radius becomes

  (a) 1.6m   (b) 2.3m   (c) 2.5 m   (d) 3.5 m

Sol: Reduced surface area = 25% of 616

$$= \dfrac{1}{4} \times 616 = 154$$

$$4\pi r^2 = 154$$

$$r^2 = 154 \times \dfrac{7}{22} \times \dfrac{1}{4}$$

$$r^2 = \dfrac{7 \times 7}{2 \times 2}$$

$$r = \dfrac{7}{2} = 3.5m$$

TECHNIQUE

CIRCLE BASED FORMULA AND ITS APPLICATION

<u>Related terms and formulas</u>

If two chords intersect inside or outsideof a circle at a point then the point of intersection divides the chord in proportion on internally or eternally

i.e. **PO X OQ = RO X OS**

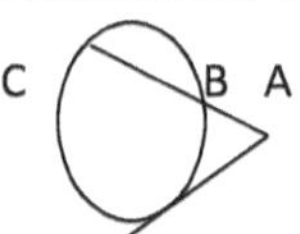

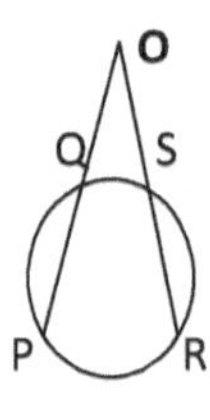

=>The line that intersects a circle at two points is called a secant

=> a line that touch a circle at a point on its circumference is called tangent.

=> If ABC is a secant and AT is a tangent

Then **AB X AC = AT²**

=>a quadrilateral having all its vertices one circumference of a circle is equal called a cyclic quadrilateral. The sum of the opposite angle of cyclic quadrilateral is always 180^0

=> length of direct common tangent is

$$AB = \sqrt{(00_1)^2 - (r_1 - r_2)^2}$$

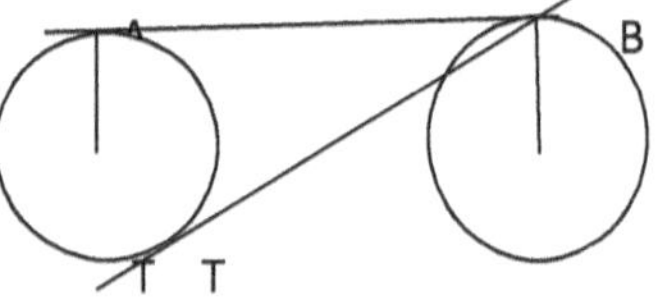

= length of transverse tangent is

$$MN = \sqrt{(00_1)^2 - (r_1 + r_2)^2}$$

=area of a sector $= \dfrac{\theta}{360} X \pi r^2 = \dfrac{1}{2} lr$

= circumference of semicircle $= \pi r + d$

Q: the distance between the centers of two equal circle of radius 3cm is 10 cm .the length of a transverse tannt is

(a) 4 cm   (b) 60m   (c) 8cm   (d) 10cm

Sol: the length of transverse tangent as per formula

$$=\sqrt{(00_1)^2 - (r_1 + r_2)^2}$$

$$=\sqrt{(10)^2 - (3+3)^2}$$

$$= \sqrt{100 - 36}$$

$$= \sqrt{64}$$

$$= 8 \, cm$$

Q: ABC is a circle with center O. P is an external point in the line AB. From P, a tangent PC has been drawn get AB=10cm, BP= 8cm, then the tangent PC is equal to

(a) 24 cm   (b) 18 cm   (c) 12 cm   (d) 10 cm

Sol:

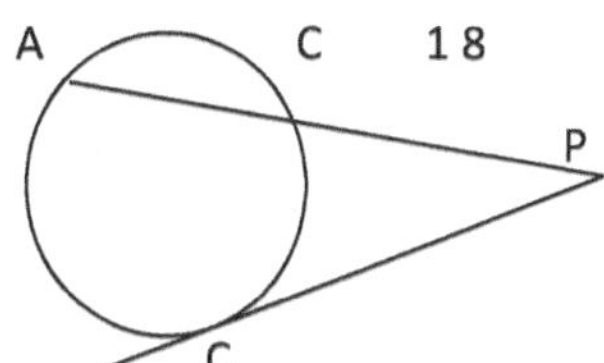

Tangent PC^2 =AP x BP

$$PC = \sqrt{18 \, X8}$$

$$= 12$$

Q: the length of the common chord of two circles of raddi 15 cm and 20 cm whose centre are 25 cm apart is (in cm)

(a) 24   (b) 25   (c) 15   (d) 20

Sol:

Let the common chard AB

Acc. To the figure

$$h^2 = (OA)^2 - (OP)^2 = (0^1 A)^2 - (0P)^2$$

$$15^2 - x^2 = 20^2 - (25 - x)^2$$

$$225 - x^2 = 400 - (625 - 50x + x^2)$$

$$50x = 450$$

$$x = 9$$

$$h = \sqrt{15^2 - 9^2} = \sqrt{225 - 81} = 12cm$$

AB =2h = 24 cm

(Note : such type of sum can be solved by understanding the question with the figure)

Q: A chord AB of length $3\sqrt{2}$ unit makes a right angle at the center O of a circle . Area of the sector AOB (in squnits) is

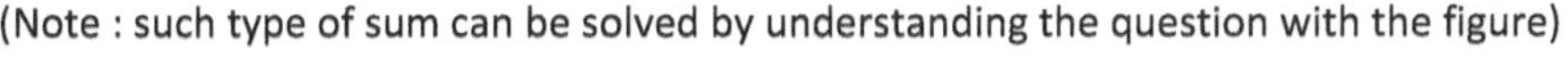

(a) 9π (b) $\dfrac{9}{2}\pi$ (c) $\dfrac{9}{4}\pi$ (d) 5π

Sol: OAB is a right angle Δ

OA =OB = r

OA²+OB²=AB²

$r^2 + r^2 = (3\sqrt{2})^2$

$2r^2 = 18$

$r = 3$

Area of sector AOB = $\dfrac{\theta}{360} \times \pi r^2$

A   B

$= \dfrac{90}{360} \times \pi \times 3^2$

$= \dfrac{9}{4}\pi$

Q: the area of a circle inscribed in a square of area 2m², is

(a) $\dfrac{\pi}{4}m^2$ (b) $\dfrac{\pi}{2}m^2$ (c) πm^2 (d) $2\pi m^2$

Sol: area of square = 2

Side = $\sqrt{2}m = diagonal\ of\ circle$

Radius of circle = $\dfrac{\sqrt{2}}{2}m$

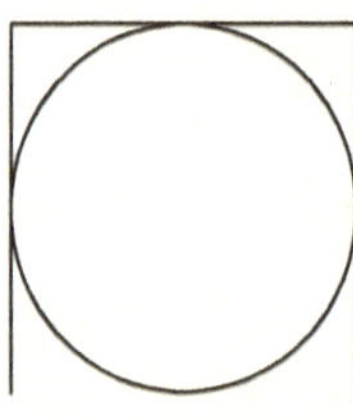

Area of the circle = πr^2

$= \pi(\dfrac{\sqrt{2}}{2})^2 = \pi \times \dfrac{2}{4} = \dfrac{\pi}{2}m^2$

Q: If the given figure PQ is the tangent of the circle .the lines segment PR intersects the circle N and R, PR= 24CM, PR=36CM, Find PN

(a) 12cm   (b) 20cm   (c) 16cm   (d) 21cm

Sol: PQ²=PN X PR

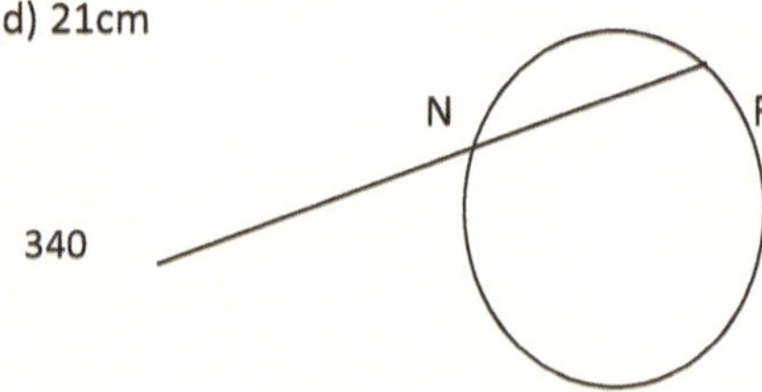

340

$xX36 = 24 X 24$

$$x = \frac{24 X 24}{36}$$

$x = 16cm$

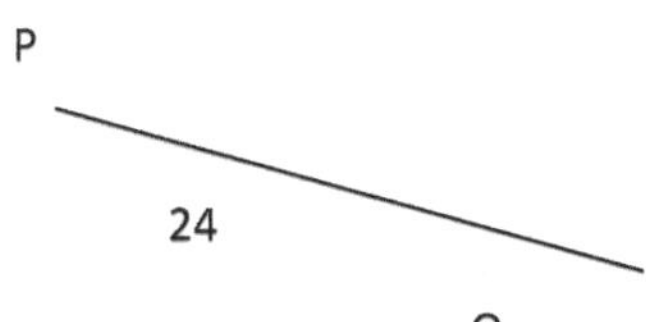

Q: the length of a tangent from an external point to a circle is $5\sqrt{3}$ unit .If radius of the circle is 5 units. Then the distance of the point from the circle is

   (a) 5 units   (b) 15 units   (c) -5 units   (d) -15 units

Sol : Tangent AB = $5\sqrt{3}$

$OA^2 = AB^2 + OB^2$

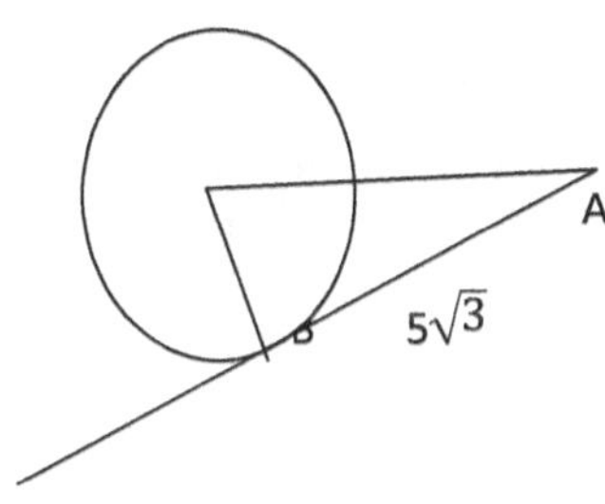

$OA = \sqrt{(5\sqrt{3})^2 + 5^2}$

$ = \sqrt{75 + 25}$

$ = 10$

OA= OD + DA

10= 5+DA

: Distance from the circle = 5 unit

Q: A point P is 13cm from the center of the circle .the length of the tangent drawn from P to the is 12cm. find the radius of the circle

   (a) 5cm   (b) 7.5 cm   (c) 25cm   (d) 8 cm

Sol: OBP is aright an angle$\triangle$ having

Right angle OBP = 90

   $OB^2 = OP^2 - PB^2$

$OB = \sqrt{OP^2 - PB2}$

$OB = \sqrt{13^2 - 12^2}$

OB = 5 CM

Q: The distance between the centre of two circle having radius 8 cm and 3cm is 13cm .the length (in cm) of the direct common tangent of the two circles is

(a) 15   (b) 18   (c) 12   (d) 16

Sol: Acc. To the formula for direct common tangent

$$= \sqrt{(00_1)^2 - (R_1 - R_2)}$$

$$= \sqrt{(13)^2 - (5)^2}$$

$$= \sqrt{169 - 25}$$

$$= \sqrt{144}$$

$= 12$ cm

Q: The distance between the centers of two circles having radii 4.5cm 3.5cm respectively is 10 cm .what is the length of the transverse common tangent of these circles?

(a) 8cm   (b) 7 cm   (c) 6 cm   (d) none of these

Sol : length of transverse tangent $= \sqrt{(00_1)^2 - (r_1 + r_2)^2}$

$$= \sqrt{(10)^2 - (4.5 + 3.5)^2}$$

$$= \sqrt{100 - 64}$$

$$= \sqrt{36}$$

$$= 6 \text{ cm}$$

Q: a chord of length 48 cm is at a distance of 18 cm from the centre of a circle .the radius of circle is

(a)m 40cm   (b) 30cm   (c) 15 cm   (d) 20 cm

Sol: the radius OA $= \sqrt{(AC)^2 + (OC)^2}$

(OAC in a right angle Δ)

$OA = \sqrt{24^2 + 18^2}$

$= \sqrt{576 + 324}$

$OA = \sqrt{900}$

    $= 30$ CM

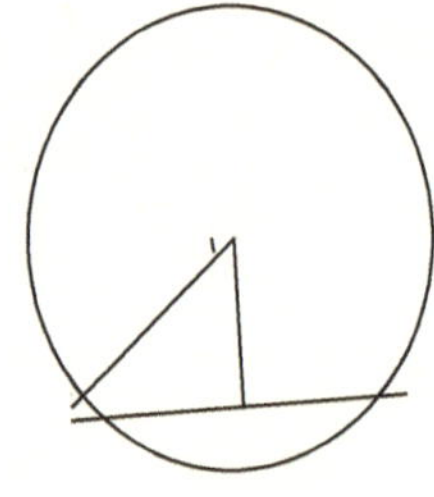

Q: A chord 12 cm is drawn in a circle of diameter 20 cm .the distance of the chord from the centre is

  (a) 60m   (b) 10cm   (c) 16cm   (d) 8cm

Sol: OAD$\triangle$ is a right angle $\triangle$

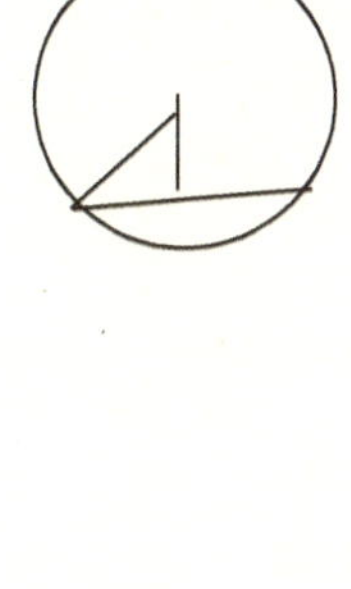

OA = 10cm as diameter is 20 cm

AD = 6 cm as cord length is 12 cm

$OD^2 = OA^2 - (AD)^2$

$OD = \sqrt{(10)^2 - (6)^2}$

$\quad = \sqrt{100 - 36}$

$\quad = \sqrt{64}$

$\quad = 8CM$

Q: The distance between the centre of the two circles with radii 4 cm and 9 cm is 13cm .the length of the direct common tangent is

Sol:

The length of jdirect common tangent of the aborn condition applied sum is

$\sqrt{(00_1)^2 - (r_1 - r_2)^2}$

$\quad = \sqrt{(13)^2 - (9 - 4)^2}$

$\quad = \sqrt{169 - 25}$

$\quad = \sqrt{144}$

$\quad = 12$

TECHNIQUE

POLYGON

Polygon related sum and its solution is qiute easy .It is a challenge for a student to apply easiest formula to solve this sum in shotest possible time. Let us have some easiest formula and its application in particular chapter.

Interior angel = $\dfrac{(n-2)180}{n} = 180^0 - exteriorangle$

Q: How many sides of a regular polygon, whose interior angle is 108^0

  (a) 4   (b) 5   (c) 6   (d) 7

Son:

Easy method	Alternate method
internal angle = $\dfrac{(n-2)180}{n}$ $108^0 = \dfrac{(n-2)180}{n}$ 180n – 108n =360 72 n = 360 n = 5	Internal angle = 108^0 External angle = 180-108 = 72^0 n= $\dfrac{360}{72}$ n = 5

Q: Eeach interior angle of a regular polygon is 150^0,the number of sides of the polygon is

  (a) 8   (b) 10   (c) 15   (d) 12   (e) none of these

Sol :

Interior angle = $\dfrac{(n-2)180}{n}$

$150^0 = \dfrac{(n-2)180}{n}$

180n -150n = 360

30n = 360

n = 12

Q : If one of the interior ang[es of a regular polygon is found to be equal to $\dfrac{9}{8}$ $times$ of one interior angles of a regular hexagon . then the number of sides of the polygon is

(a) 4   (b) 5   (c) 7   (d) 8   (e) none of these

Sol:

Interiors angle of regular hexagon = $\dfrac{(n-2)180}{n}$

$= \dfrac{(6-2)180}{6}$ (hexagon has 6 side)

$= 120^0$

Acc. To question

$\dfrac{(n-2)180}{n} = \dfrac{9}{8}X120$

180 n -135n n = 360

45n = 360

n = 8

Q: the angle of a hexagon are x, 2x-5, 2x-5, x-10 and 2x+30. Then the value of x is

(a) 45^0 (b) 60^0 (c) 80^0 (d) 30^0

Sol:

Sum of interior angle of hexagon = (6-2) 180

$$= 720^0$$

$$x + 2x - 5 + 2x - 5 + x - 10 + x - 10 + 2x + 30 = 720$$

$$9x = 720$$

$$x = 80^0$$

Q: the ratio of an interior angle to interior angle of a regular polygon is 7:2, numbers of side of the polygon is

  (a) 6   (b) 9   (c) 7   (d) 8

Sol :

Let interior angle is 7x and exterior angle 2x

$$7x + 2x = 180$$

$$x = 20^0$$

So interior angle 7 X 20 =140^0

exterior angle = 2 X 20 = 40^0

Nos of side = $\dfrac{360}{40} = 9$

Q: Each interior angle of a regular polygon is 18^0 more eight times an exterior angle .the number of sides of the polygon is

  (a) 10   (b) 15   (c) 20   (d) 25

Sol:

Acc. To question

Internal angle = 8 X exterior angle + 18

$$\frac{(n-2)180}{n} = 8X\frac{360}{n} + 18$$

$$(n-2)180 = 8\,X\,360 + 18\,n$$

$$180\,n - 18n = 8\,X\,360 + 360$$

$$162n = 360\,X\,9$$

$$n = \frac{360 \times 9}{162}$$

$n = 20$

Q: Each interior angle is double of each interior angle of a regular polygon with n sides .then the value of n is

(a) 8   (b) 10   (c) 5   (d) 6

Sol:

Easy method	Alternate method
Let interior angle x exterior angle 2x $x + 2x = 180$ $x = 60$ Nos . of side = $\dfrac{360}{60}$ = 6	Interior angle = 2X exterior angle $\dfrac{(n-2)180}{n} = 2 \, X \dfrac{360}{n}$ $180n = 2 \, X 360 + 360$ $n = \dfrac{360 X 3}{180}$ $n = 6$

Q: the interior angle of a regular polygon exceeds its exterior angle by 108^0 .the number of sides of the polygon is

(a) 12   (b) 16   (c) 10   (d) 14

Sol :

$$\frac{(n-2)180}{n} - \frac{360}{n} = 108^0$$

$$180n - 360 - 360 = 108n$$

$$72n = 720^0$$

$$n = 10$$

Q: The interior angle of a fivesided polygon are in the ratio of 2 : 3:3: 5 : 5, then the measure to the smallest angle is

(a) 20^0 (b) 30^0 (c) 60^0 (d) 90^0

Sol : sum of the angle of 5 sided polygon = $(n-2)180$

$$= 3 \, X \, 180 = 540^0$$

Angles ratio are $= 2x + 3x + 5x + 5x$

$18x = 540$

$x = 30^0$

The mea sum of smallest angle $= 2 \, X \, 30^0 = 60^0$

Q: If a regular polygon has each of its angle equal to $\dfrac{3}{5}$ time s of two right angle .then the number of side is

  (a) 3   (b) 5   (c) 6   (d) 8

Sol :

$$\frac{(n-2)180}{n} = \frac{3}{5} X 180$$

$180n - 360 = 108n$

$72 \, n = 360$

$n = 5$

TECHNIQUE

HEIGHT AND DISTANCE

Important Facts and formula

ΔABC AB = P = perpendicular

      BC = b = base

      AC = h = hypotenuse

      Angle ACB = θ

Different trigonometrically sign

$\sin \theta = \dfrac{P}{h}$ $\csc \theta = \dfrac{h}{p}$

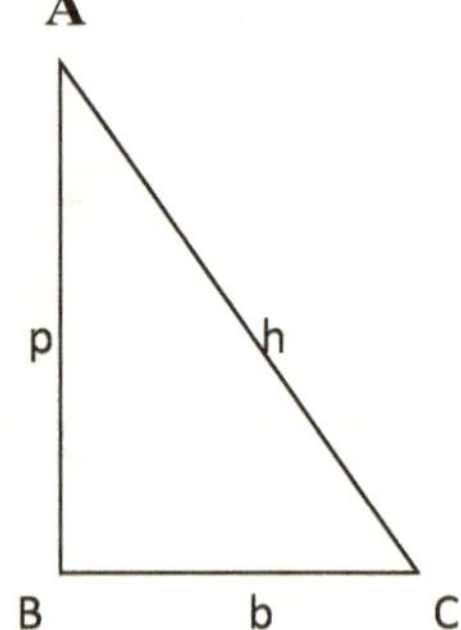

$$\cos\theta = \frac{b}{h} \qquad \sec\theta = \frac{h}{b} \qquad (\text{note ; } \sin\theta = \frac{1}{cosec\,\theta}, \cos\theta = \frac{1}{sec\theta}, \tan\theta = \frac{1}{\cot\theta})$$

$$\tan\theta = \frac{P}{b} \qquad \cot\theta = \frac{b}{p}$$

(i) $\quad sin^2\theta + cos^2\theta = 1$
(ii) $\quad 1 + tan^2\theta = sec^2\theta$
(iii) $\quad 1 + cot^2\theta = cosec^2\theta$

Different values of θ

θ^0	0^0	30^0	45^0	60^0	90^0
$\sin\theta$	0	$\dfrac{1}{2}$	$\dfrac{1}{\sqrt{2}}$	$\dfrac{\sqrt{3}}{2}$	1
$\cos\theta$	1	$\dfrac{\sqrt{3}}{2}$	$\dfrac{1}{\sqrt{2}}$	$\dfrac{1}{2}$	0
$\tan\theta$	0	$\dfrac{1}{\sqrt{3}}$	1	$\sqrt{3}$	∞
$\cot\theta$	∞	$\sqrt{3}$	1	$\dfrac{1}{\sqrt{3}}$	0
$\sec\theta$	1	$\dfrac{2}{\sqrt{3}}$	$\sqrt{2}$	2	∞
$cosec\,\theta$	∞	2	$\sqrt{2}$	$\dfrac{2}{\sqrt{3}}$	1

Angle of elevation : the angle (θ) formed between the ground (horizontal) and line of sight when an abject is seen upward

Angle of depression : the angle ($\varnothing$) former between the horizontal line and line of sight when an abject is seen downward.

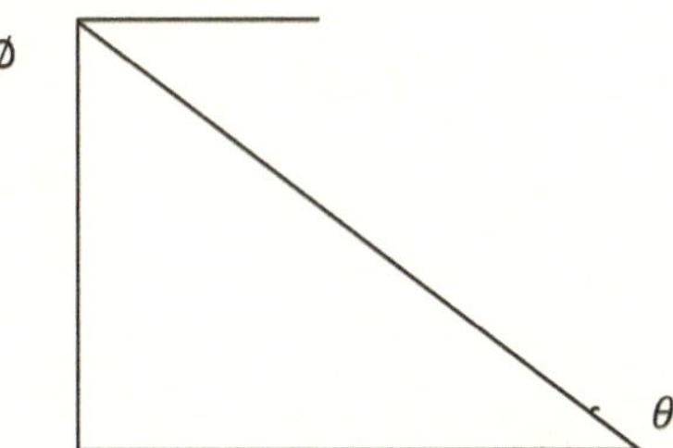

Q: If the height of a pole is $2\sqrt{3}$ metres and the length of its shadow is 2 metres. Find the angle of elevantion

(a) 30⁰   (b) 45⁰   (c) 60⁰   (d) 90⁰

Sol:

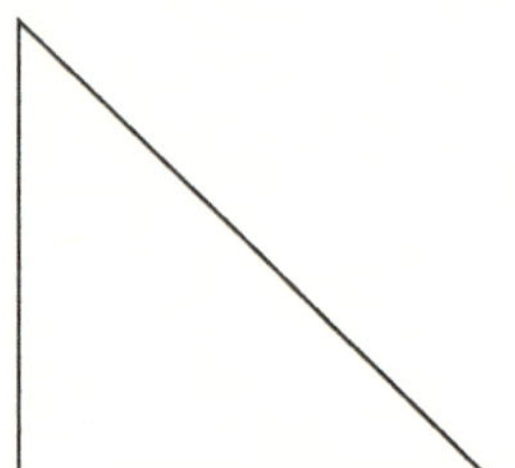

$$\tan \theta = \frac{p}{b}$$

$$\tan \theta = \frac{2\sqrt{3}}{2} = \sqrt{3}$$

$$\tan \theta = \tan 60$$

$$\theta = 60^0$$

Q: a ladder leaning against a was makes an makes an angel at 60⁰ with the gound .If the length of the ladder is 19m. Find the distance of the foot of the ladder from the wall

(a) 5   (b) 7.5   (c) 9.5   (d) 10.5

Sol: As you know

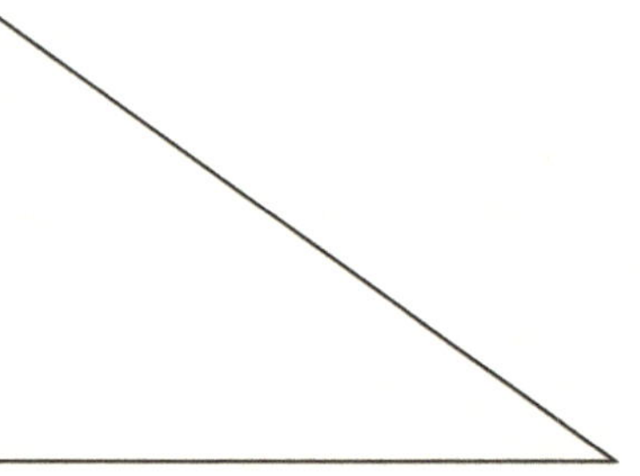

$$\cos \theta = \frac{b}{h}$$ here $\theta = 60$, $b = x$, $h = 19$

$$\cos 60 = \frac{x}{19}$$

$$\frac{1}{2} = \frac{x}{19}$$

$$x = \frac{19}{2} = 9.5\ m$$

Q: The angle of elevation of the top of a tower at a point on the ground is 30⁰. On walking 24 m towards the tower, the angle of elevation become60⁰. Find the height of the tower ($\pi = 1.73$)

(a) 18.75   (b) 19.72   (c) 20.76   (d) 20.70

Sol: Let OA = h height of tower

Walk B to C,   BC = 24 m

OC = xm

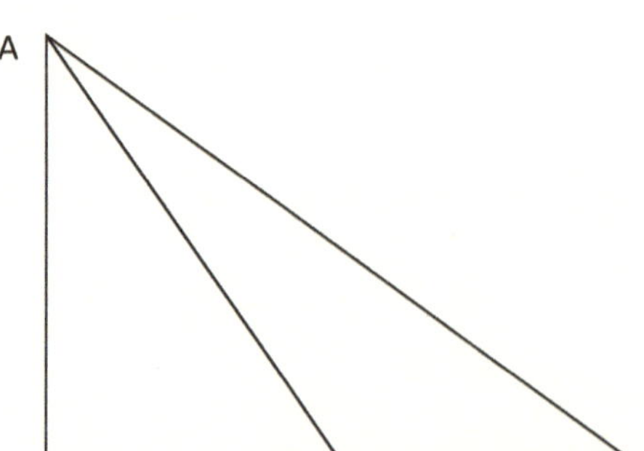

$$\text{Tan}30^0 = \frac{h}{24+x} = \frac{OA}{OB}$$

$$\frac{1}{\sqrt{3}} = \frac{h}{24+x}$$

$$\sqrt{3}h = 24 + x \ldots\ldots\ldots 1$$

$$\text{Tan}60^0 = \frac{h}{x}$$

$$\sqrt{3} = \frac{h}{x}$$

$$h = x\sqrt{3} \ldots\ldots\ldots\ldots 2$$

put the value of h in equ 1

$$\sqrt{3}.x\sqrt{3} = 24 + x$$

$$3x = 24 + x$$

$$x = 12$$

Value $h = x\sqrt{3} = 12\sqrt{3} = 12 X 1.73 = 20.76$

Q: the height of a tower is h and the angle of elevation of the top of the tower is α. On moving a distance $\frac{h}{2}$ towards the tower, the angle of elevation becomes B. the value of cot $\alpha - cotB$ **is**

(a) $\frac{1}{2}$ (b) 1   (c) $\frac{2}{3}$ (d) 2

Sol: let the distance OD =x

$$cotB = \frac{OD}{OA} = \frac{x}{h}$$

O   C   B

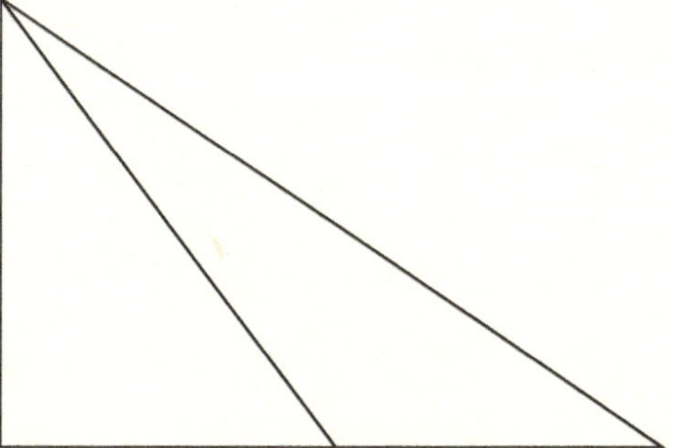

$$\cot \alpha = \frac{OB}{OA} = \frac{\frac{h}{2}+x}{h}$$

$$\cot \alpha - Cot\beta = \frac{\frac{h}{2}+x}{h} - \frac{x}{h}$$

$$= \frac{h+2x}{2h} - \frac{x}{h}$$

$$= \frac{h}{2h}$$

$$= \frac{1}{2}$$

O   h/2   D x   B

Q: a man is climbing a ladder which is inclined to the wall at an angle of 30^0 .If he ascends at a rate of 2m/sec, then he approaches the wall at the rate of

(a) 2 m/sec (b) 2.5 m/sec (c) 1.5 m / sec   (d) 1 m/sec

Sol:

Angle is formed between wall and ladder OAB = 30^0

Man ascends i.e. moves from bottom of the ladder Be = 2m

So we find the angle of elevation first

Letheangle OAB = 30^0 so angle OBA = 60^0

Man moves BC = 2 m/s

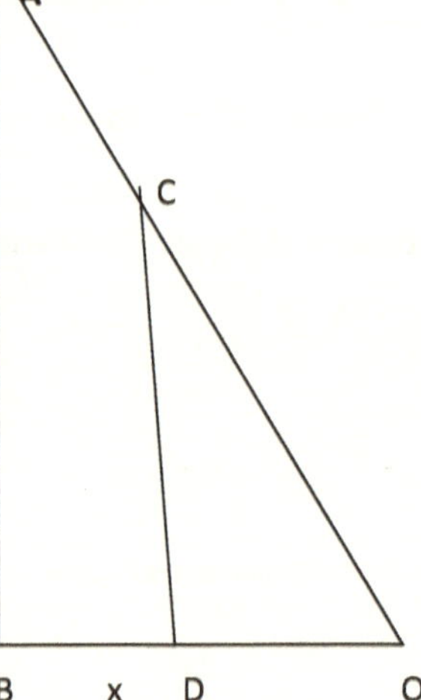

$$\text{Cos } 60 = \frac{BD}{BC} = \frac{X}{2}$$

$$\frac{1}{2} = \frac{x}{2}$$

$$x = 1 \ m/sec$$

Q : A boy flies a kite with a thread 150 meter long . If the thread of the kite makes an angle of 60^0 with the horizontal line , then the height of the kite from the ground (assuming the thread to be in a straight line) is

(a) 50 meters   (b) $75\sqrt{3}$ meters   (c) $25\sqrt{3}\ meteres$ (d) 80 meters

Sol:

$$\text{Sin} 60 = \frac{OA}{AB}$$

$$\frac{\sqrt{3}}{2} = \frac{h}{150}$$

$$h = 75\sqrt{3}\ metres$$

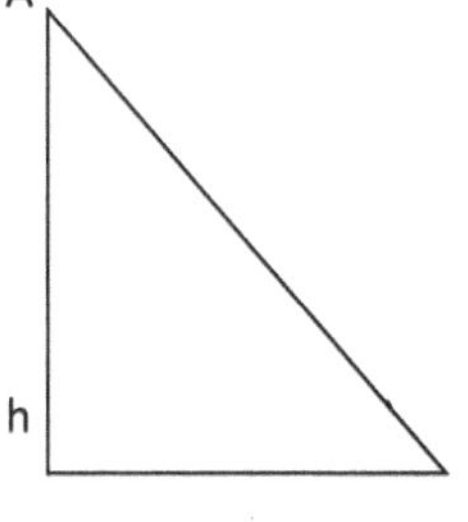

Q: the angle of elevation of a get plane from a point on the ground is 60^0. After a flight of 15 seconds, the angle of elevation changes to 30^0. If the pane is flying at constant height of 1500 $\sqrt{3}m$, find the speed of the jet plane (in m / second)

(a) 150mt   (b) 200mt   (c) 225mt   (d) 250mt

Sol:

Let A be initial and B be the final

Position of flight AC = BD = $1500\sqrt{3}$

$$\Delta APC \tan 60 = \frac{AC}{PC}$$

$$\sqrt{3} = \frac{1500\sqrt{3}}{PC}$$

Pc = 1500 m

$$\Delta BPD \tan 30 = \frac{BC}{PD}$$

$$\frac{1}{\sqrt{3}} = \frac{1500\sqrt{3}}{PC + CD}$$

$$\frac{1}{\sqrt{3}} = \frac{1500\sqrt{3}}{1500 + CD}$$

1500+CD=1500X3=4500

CD=4500-1500=3000m

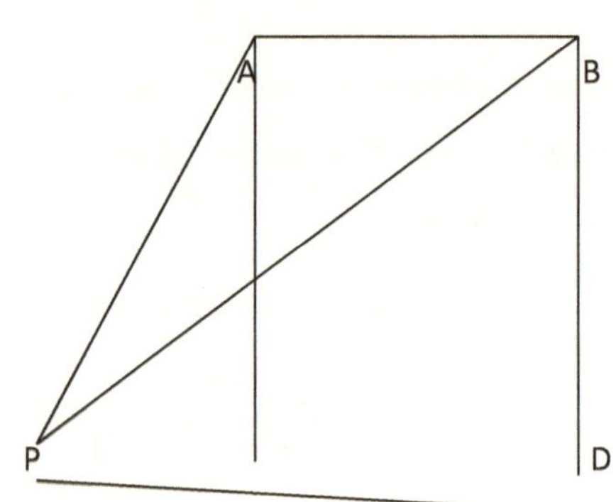

Speed of let plane = $\dfrac{3000}{15} = 200\dfrac{m}{sec}$

Q: An observer 1.5 m tall is 20m away from a tower 21.5 high, determine the angle of elevation of the top of the tower from his eye.

(a) 30⁰   (b) 45⁰   (c) 60⁰   (d) 90⁰

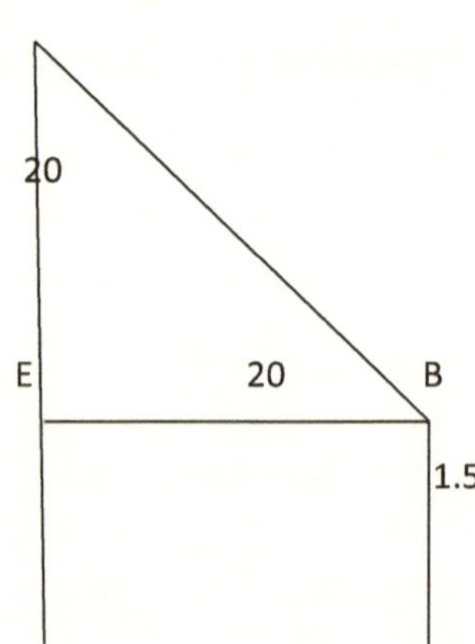

Sol:

Let AB = height of the observer = 1.5 m

CD = tower = 21.5 m

DE = CD-EC= 21.5-1.5=20m

$\Delta BDE, \tan B = \dfrac{DE}{BE} = \dfrac{20}{20} = 1$

$\tan 45^0 = 1$

$B = 45^0$

Q: the length of shadow of a tree is 16m when angle of elevation of sun is 60⁰. What is the height of the tree?

(a) 8m   (b) 16m   (c) $16\sqrt{3}$ (d) $\dfrac{16}{\sqrt{3}}m$

Sol: AB is the height of the tree

$\tan 60^0 = \dfrac{AB}{AC}$

$\sqrt{3} = \dfrac{AB}{16}$

AB = $16\sqrt{3}$

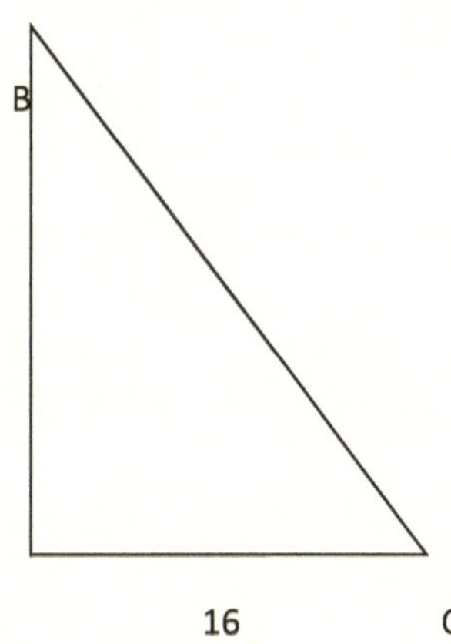

TRIGONOMETRIC RATIOS (SMART WAY TO REMEMBER)

	$\sin\theta$	$\mathrm{con}\theta$	$\tan\theta$	$\cot\theta$	$\sec\theta$	$\mathrm{cosec}\theta$
$\sin\theta$	$\sin\theta$	$\sqrt{1-con^2\theta}$	$\dfrac{\tan\theta}{\sqrt{1+\tan^2\theta}}$	$\dfrac{1}{\sqrt{1+\cot^2\theta}}$	$\dfrac{\sqrt{\sec^2\theta-1}}{\sec\theta}$	$\dfrac{1}{\mathrm{cosec}\theta}$
$\cos\theta$	$\sqrt{1-\sin^2\theta}$	$\mathrm{con}\theta$	$\dfrac{1}{\sqrt{1+\tan^2\theta}}$	$\dfrac{\cot\theta}{\sqrt{1+\cot^2\theta}}$	$\dfrac{1}{\sec\theta}$	$\dfrac{\sqrt{\mathrm{cosec}^2\theta-1}}{\mathrm{cosec}\,\theta}$
$\tan\theta$	$\dfrac{\sin\theta}{\sqrt{1-\sin^2\theta}}$	$\dfrac{\sqrt{1-\cos^2\theta}}{\cos\theta}$	$\tan\theta$	$\dfrac{1}{\cot\theta}$	$\sqrt{\sec^2-1}$	$\dfrac{1}{\sqrt{\mathrm{cosec}^2-1}}$
$\cot\theta$	$\dfrac{\sqrt{1-\sin^2\theta}}{\sin\theta}$	$\dfrac{\mathrm{con}\theta}{\sqrt{1-\cos^2\theta}}$	$\dfrac{1}{\tan\theta}$	$\cot\theta$	$\dfrac{1}{\sqrt{\sec^2\theta}}$	$\sqrt{\mathrm{cosec}^2\theta-1}$
$\sec\theta$	$\dfrac{1}{\sqrt{1-\sin^2\theta}}$	$\dfrac{1}{\cos\theta}$	$\sqrt{1+\tan^2\theta}$	$\dfrac{\sqrt{1+\cot^2\theta}}{\cot\theta}$	$\sec\theta$	$\dfrac{\mathrm{cosec}^2\theta}{\sqrt{\mathrm{cosec}^2\theta}}$
$\mathrm{cosec}\,\theta$	$\dfrac{1}{\sin\theta}$	$\dfrac{1}{\sqrt{1-\cos^2\theta}}$	$\dfrac{\sqrt{1+\tan^2\theta}}{\tan\theta}$	$\sqrt{1+\cot^2\theta}$	$\dfrac{\sec\theta}{\sqrt{\sec^2\theta-1}}$	$\mathrm{cosec}\,\theta$

Smart way to remember

How to convert $\cot\theta$ to $\sec\theta$

$$\sec\theta = \frac{\mathrm{cosec}\theta}{\cot\theta}$$

$$= \frac{\sqrt{1+\cot^2\theta}}{\cot\theta}$$

Similar way all the formulas are written

TECHNIQUE

APPLICATION OF TRIGONOMETRICAL FORMULA

Q: If sin 3A = cos (A-26^0) , where 3A is an acute angle , then the value of a is

(a) 29^0 (b) 26^0 (c) 23^0 (d) 28^0

Sol: Smart technique

The application of correct formula in specific sum is the key factor of smart technique like to perform the correct job in correct time. Trigonometrically sum can be solved in many ways but to find out which is the easiest and shortest method to solve

Quick method:

$\text{Sin} 3A = \cos(A-26^0)$

$\text{Cos}(90-3A) = \cos(A-26^0)$

$90-3A = A-26^0$

$4A = 116^0$

$A = 29^0$

Lengthy method

$\text{Sin} 3A = \cos(A-26^0)$

$\text{Sin} 3A = \sin \{90-(A-26^0)\}$

$3A = 90 - A + 26^0$

$4A = 116^0$

$A = 29^0$

Q: the value of (1+cot$\theta - cosec\theta)(1 + tan\theta + sec\theta)$ is equal to

(a) 1   (b) 2   (c) -1   (d) -2

Sol: Smart Technique

If we consider the value of θ and put in the respective place .it will become easy to get the answer. Let us try.Let us assum the volue of $\theta = 45^0$

$(1 + cot\theta - cosec\theta)(1 + tan\theta + sec\theta)$

$(1 + cot 45 - cosec45)(1 + tan45 + sec45)$

$(1 + 1 - \sqrt{2})(1 + 1 + \sqrt{2})$

$(2 - \sqrt{2})(2 + \sqrt{2})$ (a+b)(a-b) = a²-b²

$2^2 - (\sqrt{2})^2$

=4-2

= 2

Regular method

$(1 + cot\theta - cosec\theta)(1 + tan\theta + sec\theta)$

$(1 + \dfrac{cos\theta}{sin\theta} - \dfrac{1}{sin\theta})(1 + \dfrac{sin\theta}{cos\theta} - \dfrac{1}{cos\theta})$

$(\dfrac{sin\theta + cos\theta - 1}{sin\theta}) X (\dfrac{cos\theta + sin\theta - 1}{cos\theta})$

$$\frac{(sin\theta + cos\theta)^2 - 1}{sin\theta \cdot cos\theta} = \frac{sin^2\theta + cos^2\theta + 2sin\theta.cos\theta - 1}{sin\theta.cos\theta}$$

$$\frac{1 + 2sin\theta.cos\theta - 1}{sin\theta.cos\theta}$$

$$\frac{2sin\theta.cos\theta}{sin\theta.cos\theta}$$

=2

Q: the numerical value of $\dfrac{1}{1 + cot^2\theta} + \dfrac{3}{1 + tan^2\theta} + 2sin^2\theta$ **will be**

(a) 2   (b) 3   (c) 4   (d) 5   (e) 6

Sol:

Regular method	Smart technique
$\dfrac{1}{1 + cot^2\theta} + \dfrac{3}{1 + tan^2\theta} + 2sin^2\theta$	If we put the value of θ, we get the answer easily and without any paper and pen
$=\dfrac{1}{cosec^2\theta} + \dfrac{3}{sec^2\theta} + 2sin^2\theta$	Let us consider $\theta = 45^0$
	$\dfrac{1}{1 + cot^2\theta} + \dfrac{3}{1 + tan^2\theta} + 2sin^2\theta$
$=sin^2\theta + 3cos^2\theta + 2sin^2\theta$	
$=b + 3sin^2\theta + 3cos^2\theta$	$=\dfrac{1}{1 + cot^245} + \dfrac{3}{1 + tan^245} + 2sin^245$
$= 3(sin^2\theta + con^2\theta)$	$=\dfrac{1}{2} + \dfrac{3}{2} + \dfrac{2}{2}$
=3	$=\dfrac{6}{2}$

	=3

Q: If $\sin\theta + \cosec\theta = 2$, then the value of $\sin^5\theta + \cosec^5\theta$ is

(a) $\dfrac{1}{2}$ (b) 2   (c) 1   (d) 0

Sol:

Regular method	Smart technique
$\sin\theta + \cosec\theta = 2$	The standard trigonometrically formula are used for this type of sum
$\sin\theta + \dfrac{1}{\sin\theta} = 2$	(i.e if $\sin\theta + \cosec\theta = x$ then
$\sin^2\theta + 1 = 2\sin\theta$	$\sin^n\theta + \cosec^n\theta = x$
$\sin^2\theta - 2\sin\theta + 1 = 0$	**Similarly if** $\cos\theta + \sec\theta = x$ **then**
$(\sin\theta - 1)^2 = 0$	$\cos^n\theta + \sec^n\theta + \sec^n\theta = x$
$\sin\theta = 1$	if $\tan\theta + \cot\theta = x$ then $\tan^n\theta + \cot^n\theta = x$)
$\cosec\theta = \dfrac{1}{\sin\theta} = 1$	In another way , if we consider the value of θ ,
$\sin^5\theta + \cosec^5\theta$	then also easy to get the answer
$(1)^5 + (1)^2$	Let us
=1	take $\theta = 90, \sin\theta = \sin90 = 1$, $\cosec\theta = \cos$
	$\sin^5\theta + \cosec^5\theta = 1^5 + 1^5 = 2$

Q: If $\cosec\theta - \cot\theta = 2$ then $\cosec\theta + \cot\theta$ is equal to

(a) 2   (b) $\dfrac{1}{2}$ (c) 1   (d) $\dfrac{3}{2}$

Sol:

Smart technique

There is a simple formula for the above some .so we have to remember for quickness and accurate result

if $cosec\theta - cot\theta = x$ then

$$cosec\theta + cot\theta = \frac{1}{x}$$

Hence answer is $\frac{1}{2}$

Q: If $tan\theta - cot\theta = 0$, **find the value of** $sin\theta + cos\theta =$

(a) 0   (b) 2   (d) $\sqrt{2}$ (d) -2

Sol:

Smart technique	Alternate method
Consider the value of θ	$tan\theta - cot\theta = 0$
Let $\theta = 45^0$	$tan\theta = cot\theta$
$tan45 - cot45 = 1 - 1 = 0$	$tan\theta = tan(90 - \theta)$
So we confirm $\theta = 45$	$\theta = 90 - \theta$
$sin45 + cos45$	$2\theta = 90$
$\frac{1}{\sqrt{2}} + \frac{1}{\sqrt{2}}$	$\theta = 45$
$= \frac{2}{\sqrt{2}}(\frac{\sqrt{2}}{\sqrt{2}})$	$sin45 + cos45$
$= \sqrt{2}$	$= \frac{1}{\sqrt{2}} + \frac{1}{\sqrt{2}}$
	$= \frac{2}{\sqrt{2}}(\frac{\sqrt{2}}{\sqrt{2}})$
	$= \sqrt{2}$

Q:If $tan\theta + \dfrac{1}{tan\theta} = 2$, **find the value of** $\dfrac{1}{tan^2\theta + tan^2\theta}$

(a) 1   (b) 2   (c) 4   (d)$\frac{1}{2}$

Sol:

Smart method	Alernate method
$tan\theta + \dfrac{1}{tan\theta} = 2$	$tan\theta + \dfrac{1}{tan\theta} = 2$
$tan\theta + cot\theta = 2$	Squaring both side
Acc. To formula,	$(tan\theta + \dfrac{1}{tan\theta})^2 = 2_2$
if $tan\theta + cot\theta = x$ then	
$tan^2\theta + cot^2\theta = x$	$tan^2\theta + \dfrac{1}{tan^2\theta} + 2.\,tan\theta.\dfrac{1}{tan\theta} = 4$
Hence answer $tan^2\theta + cot^2\theta = 2$	
$tan^2\theta + \dfrac{1}{tan^2\theta} = 2$	$tan^2\theta + \dfrac{1}{tan^2\theta} + 2 = 4$
	$tan^2\theta + \dfrac{1}{tan^2\theta} = 2$

Q: If $2sin\theta = sec\theta,$ what is the value of $sin^4\theta + cos^4\theta$

(a) 1   (b) $\dfrac{1}{2}$ (c) $\dfrac{1}{4}$ (d) $1/8$

Sol:

Smart technique	Aternate method
$2sin\,\theta = sec\,\theta$	$2sin\,\theta = sec\,\theta$
$2sin\,\theta = \dfrac{1}{cos\theta}$	$2sin\,\theta = \dfrac{1}{cos\theta}$
$2sin\,\theta.cos\,\theta = 1$	$2sin\,\theta.cos\,\theta = 1$
$Sin2\,\theta = 1$	Value of
Assume $\theta = 45^0$	$sin^4\theta + cos^4\theta$
$Sin\ 2.45 = sin90 = 1$	$= sin^4\theta + 2sin^2\theta.cos^2\theta +$
The value of	$cos^4\theta - 2sin^2\theta.cos^2\theta$
$sin^4\theta + cos^4\theta$	

$(\frac{1}{\sqrt{2}})^4 + (\frac{1}{\sqrt{2}})^4$	$= (sin^2\theta.cos^2\theta)^2 - \frac{1}{2}.4sin^2\theta.cos^2\theta$
$=\frac{1}{4} + \frac{1}{4}$	$= (sin^2\theta.cos^2\theta)^2 - \frac{1}{2}.(2sin\theta.cos\theta)^2$
$=\frac{2}{4}$	$= \dfrac{1 - \dfrac{1}{2}}{1}$
$=\frac{1}{2}$	$=\frac{1}{2}$

Q: If 2cos² θ=3sin θ, $0 < \theta < 90^0$, then the value of sin θ is

(a) $\dfrac{\sqrt{3}}{2}$ (b) $\dfrac{\sqrt{5}-1}{\sqrt{5}+1}$ (c) $\dfrac{1}{2}$ (d) $\dfrac{1}{\sqrt{3}}$

Sol:

	Smart technique
2con² θ=3sin θ	Assume a value of θ in such a way
$2(1\text{-}sin^2\theta) = 3sin\theta$	That L.H.S = R.H.S
$2 - 2sin^2\theta = 3sin\theta$	Let $\theta = 30^0$
$2sin^2\theta + 3sin\theta - 2 = 0$	L.H.S= $\quad 2cos^2 30 = 2(\dfrac{\sqrt{3}}{2})^2$
$2sin^2\theta + 4sin\theta - sin\theta - 2 = 0$	
$2sin\theta(sin\theta + 2) - 1(sin\theta + 2) = 0$	$= 2\dfrac{3}{4} = \dfrac{3}{2}$
$2sin\theta - 1 = 0$,$sin\theta + 2 = 0$	
$sin\theta = \dfrac{1}{2}$, $sin\theta =- 2$	R.H.S = 3sin θ=3sin30= $3.\dfrac{1}{2} = \dfrac{3}{2}$
	L.H.S= R.H.S
	So $\quad \theta = 30$, $sin30 = \dfrac{1}{2}$

Q: the value of $\quad sec^2\theta - \dfrac{sin^2\theta - 2sin^4\theta}{2cos^4 - cos^2\theta}$ **is**

(a) 1   (b) 2   (c) -1   (d) 0

Sol:

	Alternate method
$$sec^2\theta - \dfrac{sin^2\theta - 2sin^4\theta}{2cos^4 - cos^2\theta}$$ $$sec^2\theta - \dfrac{sin^2\theta(1 - 2sin^2\theta)}{cos^2\theta(2cos^2\theta - 1)}$$ $$sec^2\theta - tan^2\theta \quad (cos2A = 2cos^2\theta - 1$$ $$= 1 - 2sin^2A)$$ $$= 1 + tan^2\theta - tan^2\theta$$ $$=1$$	Assume any value of θ i.e 30,45 or60. Let us take $\theta = 45$ $$sec^2 45 - \dfrac{sin^2 45 - 2sin^4 45}{2cos^4 45 - cos^2 45}$$ $$(\sqrt{2})^2 - \dfrac{(\frac{1}{\sqrt{2}})^2 - 2.(\frac{1}{\sqrt{2}})^4}{2.(\frac{1}{\sqrt{2}})^4 - (\frac{1}{\sqrt{2}})^2}$$ $$2 - \dfrac{\frac{1}{2} - 2.\frac{1}{4}}{2.\frac{1}{4} - \frac{1}{2}}$$ $$= 2-1$$ $$=1$$

Q: If $\sqrt{3}sin\theta + cos\theta = 1,$ then what will be the value of θ

(a) 30^0 (b) 0^0 (c) 45^0 (d) 60^0

Sol:

Regular method	Alternate method
$\sqrt{3}sin\theta = 1 - cos\theta$ $(\sqrt{3}sin\theta)^2 = (1 - cos\theta)^2$ $3sin^2\theta = 1 + cos^2\theta - 2cos\theta$	Lets think the θ^0 value become zero let's try $\sqrt{3}sin\theta + cos\theta$ $\sqrt{3}sin\theta + cos\theta$

$3 - 3\cos^2\theta = 1 + \cos^2\theta - 2\cos\theta$	=0+1=1 R.H.S
$4\cos^2\theta - 2\cos\theta - 2 = 0$	Hence the value of θ become zero
$4\cos^2\theta - 4\cos\theta + 2\cos\theta - 2 = 0$	
$4\cos\theta(\cos\theta - 1) + 2(\cos\theta - 1) = 0$	
$\cos\theta - 1 = 0 \;,\; 4\cos\theta + 2 = 0$	
$\cos\theta = 1 = 30^0$	
$\theta = 30$	

Q:the value of $(1 + \cos\theta)(1 - \cos\theta)(1 + \cot^2\theta)$ **is**

(a) 2   (b) 1   (c) 0   (d) $\dfrac{1}{2}$

Sol:

$(1 + \cos\theta)(1 - \cos\theta)(1 + \cot^2\theta)$

$=(1 - \cos^2\theta)(1 + \cot^2\theta)$

$=\sin^2\theta.\cosec^2\theta$

$= \sin^2\theta.\dfrac{1}{\sin^2\theta}$

$= 1$

Q: If $\sec\theta - \cos\theta = \dfrac{3}{2}$ **where** θ **is a +ve acute angle , then the value of** $\sec\theta$ **is**

(a) $-\dfrac{1}{2}$ (b) 2   (c) 0   (d)1

Regular method	Smart technique
$\sin\theta - \cos\theta = \dfrac{3}{2}$	If we consider L.H.S and assume a value of θ, we can solve it easily let's $\theta = 60^0$

$$\frac{1}{cos\theta} - cos\theta = \frac{3}{2}$$

$$1 - cos^2\theta = \frac{3cos\theta}{2}$$

$$2 - 2cos^2\theta = 3cos\theta$$

$$2cos^2\theta + 3cos\theta - 2 = 0$$

$$2cos^2\theta + 4cos\theta - cos\theta - 2 = 0$$

$$2cos\theta(cos\theta + 2) - 1(cos\theta + 2) = 0$$

$$(cos\theta + 2)(2cos\theta - 1) = 0$$

$$cos\theta = -2 \; , \; cos\theta = \frac{1}{2}$$

$$sec\theta = 2 \, , \, (\theta \; is + ve \; acqute \; angle \,)$$

$$sec\theta - cos\theta = 2 - \frac{1}{2} = \frac{3}{2} = R.H.S$$

So we assume that the value of $\theta = 60^0$

Then $sec\theta = sec60 = 2$

(solve the question on mental calculation only)

TECHNIQUE

THE METHOD OF SUBSTITUTION APPLY IN TRIGONOMETRY

Q: the value of $\dfrac{sin^3\theta + cos^3\theta}{sin\theta + cos\theta} + \dfrac{cos^3\theta - sin^3\theta}{cos\theta - sin\theta}$ is equal its.

(a) -1   (b) 1   (c) -2   (d) 0

Sol:

Regular method	Smart technique
$\dfrac{sin^3\theta + cos^3\theta}{sin\theta + cos\theta} + \dfrac{cos^3\theta - sin^3\theta}{cos\theta - sin\theta}$ $=$ $\dfrac{(cos\theta + sin\theta)(cos^2\theta + sin^2\theta - cos\theta.sin\theta)}{sin\theta + cos\theta} +$ $=$ $(cos^2\theta + sin^2\theta - cos\theta.sin\theta) + (cos^2\theta + sin^2\theta - c$ $=1 - cos\theta.sin\theta + 1 + sin\theta.cos\theta$ $= 2$ (note : $sin^2\theta + cos^2\theta = 1$)	In place of using trigonometrical formula, use numerical value of θ to get the result quick and easy. Let us put the numerical value of θ and solve Let's $\theta = 0$ $Sin\theta = sin0 = 0$ $cos\theta = cos0 = 1$ $\dfrac{cos^3\theta + sin^3}{cos\theta + sin\theta} + \dfrac{cos^3\theta - sin^3\theta}{cos\theta - sin\theta}$ $\dfrac{1+0}{1+0} + \dfrac{1-0}{1-0}$ $=\dfrac{1}{1} + \dfrac{1}{1} = 2$

Q: Find the value of $\dfrac{1}{1 + tan^2\theta} + \dfrac{1}{1 + cot^2\theta}$

(a) $\dfrac{1}{2}$ (b)1   (c) $\dfrac{1}{4}$ (d) 0

Sol:

Regular method	Smart technique

$$\frac{1}{1+tan^2\theta}+\frac{1}{1+cot^2\theta}$$ $$\frac{1}{sec^2\theta}+\frac{1}{cosec^2\theta}$$ $$cos^2\theta+sin^2\theta$$ $$=1$$	If we directly put the numerical value of θ, without using paper and pen ,will get the result let's $assume\ \theta=45$ $$tan^2\theta=tan^245=1$$ $$cot^2\theta=cot^245=1$$ $$\frac{1}{1+1}+\frac{1}{1+1}$$ $$\frac{1}{2}+\frac{1}{2}=1$$

Q: If $sec\theta-tan\theta=\dfrac{1}{\sqrt{3}}$**, the value of** $sec\theta.tan\theta$ **is**

(a) $\dfrac{4}{\sqrt{3}}$　　(b) $\dfrac{2}{3}$　　(c) $\dfrac{2}{\sqrt{3}}$　　(d) $\dfrac{1}{\sqrt{3}}$

Sol:

Regular method	Smart technique
$$sec\theta-tan\theta=\frac{1}{\sqrt{3}}\ \text{-------------- 1}$$ Then $$sec\theta+tan\theta=\frac{1}{sec\theta-tan\theta}$$ $$sec\theta+tan\theta=\sqrt{3}\ \text{------------- 2}$$ If we add 1 with 2 Then $$2sec\theta=\frac{1}{\sqrt{3}}+\sqrt{3}$$ $$2sec\theta=\frac{4}{\sqrt{3}}$$ $$sec\theta=\frac{2}{\sqrt{3}}$$ $$sec^2\theta=1+tan^2\theta\quad\text{(formula)}$$ $$tan^2\theta=sec^2\theta-1$$	In stead of using the formula , use the value of θ to get the answer As per question $$sec\theta-tan\theta=\frac{1}{\sqrt{3}}$$ We choose such a value of θ , so that the result is $$\frac{1}{\sqrt{3}}$$ Let us $assume\ \theta=30$ for confirmation $$sec\theta-tan\theta$$ $$sec30-tan30=\frac{2}{\sqrt{3}}-\frac{1}{\sqrt{3}}=\frac{1}{\sqrt{3}}$$ *then the value of .*

$$= \frac{(\frac{2}{\sqrt{3}})^2 - 1}{}$$ $$tan^2\theta = \frac{4}{3} - 1$$ $$tan\theta = 1/\sqrt{3}$$ So $$sec\theta.tan\theta = \frac{2}{\sqrt{3}}.\frac{1}{\sqrt{3}}$$ $$= \frac{2}{3}$$	$sec\theta.tan\theta$ $$= sec\theta.tan\theta$$ $$= \frac{2}{\sqrt{3}}.\frac{1}{\sqrt{3}} = \frac{2}{3}$$ Hence result is $\frac{2}{3}$

Q: $7sin^2\theta + 3cos^2\theta = 4$, **then the value of** $tan\theta$ **is (** θ **is an acute angle)**

(a) 1   (b) $\frac{2}{\sqrt{2}}$ (c) $\sqrt{3}$ (d) $\frac{1}{\sqrt{3}}$

Sol:

Regular method	Smart technique
$7sin^2\theta + 3cos^2\theta = 4$ $7(1 - cos^2\theta) + 3cos^2\theta = 4$ $7 - 7cos^2\theta + 3cos^2\theta = 4$ $7 - 4cos^2\theta = 4$ $4cos^2\theta = 3$ $cos^2\theta = \frac{3}{4}$ $cos\theta = \sqrt{\frac{3}{4}}$ $sin\theta = \sqrt{1 - \frac{3}{4}}$ $= \sqrt{\frac{1}{4}} = \frac{1}{2}$	Q is an acute angel so we consider the value θ in such a way that the value of $7sin^2\theta + 3cos^2\theta = 4$ Let us take the value of $\theta = 30$ $7sin^2\theta + 3cos^2\theta$ $= 7(\frac{1}{2})^2 + 3(\frac{\sqrt{3}}{2})^2$ $= 7.\frac{1}{4} + 3.\frac{3}{4}$ $= \frac{7}{4} + \frac{9}{4}$ $= \frac{16}{4}$

$tan\theta = \dfrac{sin\theta}{cos\theta}$ $= \dfrac{\dfrac{1}{2}}{\dfrac{\sqrt{3}}{2}} =$ $= \dfrac{1}{\sqrt{3}}$	$=4$ So we confirm $\theta = 30$ Then the value of $= tan\theta$ $= tan30$ $= \dfrac{1}{\sqrt{3}}$

Q: If $tan\theta - cot\theta = 0\ and\ \theta$ **is tre acute angle , then the value of** $\dfrac{tan(\theta + 15)}{tan(\theta - 15)}$

(a) $\dfrac{1}{\sqrt{3}}$ (b) 3   (c) $\dfrac{1}{3}$ (d) $\sqrt{3}$ (e) $\dfrac{2}{\sqrt{3}}$

Sol: smart technique

We consider the value of θ is such a way that the value of $tan\theta - cot\theta$ will be 0

Let us take the value of $\theta\ is\ 45$o

$tan45$o$_- cot45$o$_= 1 - 1 = 0$

Hence the value of $\theta = 45$

The value of $\dfrac{tan\ (\theta + 15)}{tan\ (\theta - 15)}$

$= \dfrac{tan\ (45 + 15)}{tan\ (45 - 15)}$

$= \dfrac{tan60}{tan30}$

$= \dfrac{\dfrac{\sqrt{3}}{1}}{\dfrac{1}{\sqrt{3}}}$

$= \sqrt{3}$

= 3

Q: provided $\sin(A - B) = sinA.cosB - cosA.sinB$, $\sin 15^0$ **will be**

(a) $\dfrac{\sqrt{3}-1}{\sqrt{2}}$ (b) $\dfrac{\sqrt{3}-1}{2\sqrt{2}}$ (c) $\dfrac{\sqrt{3}}{2\sqrt{2}}$ (d) $\dfrac{\sqrt{3}+1}{2\sqrt{2}}$ (e) $\dfrac{\sqrt{3}-1}{\sqrt{3}+1}$

Sol: smart technique

$$\sin(A - B) = sinA.cosB - cosA.sinB$$

$$\sin(15) = sin\ (45 - 30)$$

(Note: we obtain 15^0 by following method 1. 60^0-45^0 2. 45^0-30^0 3. 90^0-75^0 but find reliable one)

So $\sin(45 - 30) = sin45.cos30 - cos45.sin30$

$$= \frac{1}{\sqrt{2}}.\frac{\sqrt{3}}{2} - \frac{1}{\sqrt{2}}.\frac{1}{2}$$

$$= \frac{\sqrt{3}-1}{2\sqrt{2}}$$

Q: If $sin\alpha + cos\beta = 2 (o \le \beta < \alpha \le 90)$**, then** $\sin\left(\dfrac{2\alpha + \beta}{3}\right) =$

(a) $sin\dfrac{\alpha}{2}$ (b) $sin\dfrac{\alpha}{3}$ (c) $cos\dfrac{\alpha}{3}$ (d) $cos\dfrac{2\alpha}{3}$

Sol: Smart technique

If we put the value of $and\ \beta$, then it can be solved easily .

Acc. To the question the range of α , β $\beta \ge 0$

$$\alpha \le 90$$

Let us $\beta = 0^0$

$$\alpha = 90^0$$

So $sin\alpha + cos\beta$

$= sin90 + cos0$

$= 1+1$

$= 2$ R.H.S Hence B= 0 and $\alpha = 90$ in the accurate value of $\alpha \; and \; \beta$

$$sin\frac{2\alpha + \beta}{3} = sin\left(\frac{2.90 + 0}{3}\right)$$

$$= \frac{sin\frac{180}{3}}{}$$

$$= sin60$$

$$= \frac{\sqrt{3}}{2}$$

Hence $cos\,30 = cos\frac{90}{3} = con\frac{\alpha}{\beta}$

Q: If $sin\theta + cos\theta = \frac{17}{13}, 0 < \theta < 90^{0}$ **, then the value of** $sin\theta - cos\theta$ **is**

(a) $\frac{5}{17}$ (b) $\frac{3}{19}$ (c) $\frac{7}{10}$ (d) $\frac{7}{13}$

Sol:

Regular method	Smart technique
$sin\theta + cos\theta = \frac{17}{13}$ Squaring the both side $sin2\theta + cos2 \; \theta + 2sin\theta.cos\theta = \frac{289}{169}$ $2sin\theta.cos\theta = \frac{289}{169} - 1$	Trigonometry is based on formula so remembering as much as formula, becomes quite easy and time saving $If sinx + cosx = x$ **then** $sinx - cosx = \sqrt{2 - x^2}$ Apply this formula in the above sum

$$= \frac{\frac{120}{169}}{}$$

Let $sin\theta - cos\theta = x$

Squaring both side

$sin^2\theta + cos^2\theta + 2sin\theta.cos\theta = x^2$

$1 - \frac{120}{169} = x^2$

$x^2 = \frac{49}{169}$

$x = \sqrt{\frac{49}{169}}$

$sin\theta - cos\theta = \frac{7}{13}$

$x = \frac{17}{13}$

$sinx - cosx = \sqrt{2 - (\frac{17}{13})^2}$

$= \sqrt{2 - \frac{289}{169}}$

$= \sqrt{\frac{49}{169}}$

$= \frac{7}{13}$

Q: If $tanA = x + 1$ and $tanB = x - 1$, then $x^2 + \tan(A - B)$ has

(a) 1   (b) x (c) 0   (d) 2

Sol:

$x^2 \tan(A - B)$

$x^2 \frac{tanA - tanB}{1 + tanA.tanB}$

$x^2 \frac{x + 1 - x + 1}{1 + x^2 - 1}$

$= 2$

Q: If $sin\theta + 2cos\theta = 1$, then what is the value of $2sin\theta - cos\theta$ is

(a) 0   (b) 1   (c) 2   (d) 4

Sol:

Regular method	Smart technique
$sin\theta + 2cos\theta = 1$	Such large calculation cannot be possible in
Squaring both side	competitive exam in shortest possible time .so
$sin^2\theta + 4cos^2\theta + 4sin\theta.cos\theta = 1$	it have some technique to solve. Assume the
$4sin\theta.cos\theta = 1 - sin^2\theta - 4cos^2\theta$	value of θ and put in L.H.S
$(2sin\theta - cos\theta)^2$	Let's $\theta=0^0$, $sin0 + 2cos0 = 1 + 2 = 3$
$= 4sin^2\theta + cos^2\theta - 4sin\theta.cos\theta$	$\neq R.H.S$
$=4sin^2\theta + cos^2\theta - 1 + sin^2\theta + 4cos^2\theta$	$again\ assume\ \theta = 90^0$
$= 4(sin^2\theta + cos^2\theta) + sin^2\theta + cos^2\theta - 1$	$sin\theta + 2cos\theta = sin90 + 2cos90 = 1 + 0 = 1$
$= 4 + 1 - 1 = 4$	$= R.H.S$
$2sin\theta - cos\theta = \sqrt{4}$	Then value of $2sin\theta - cos\theta$
$=2$	$= 2sin90 - cos90$=2-0=2

Q: $cos\theta + sin\theta = \sqrt{2}cos\theta$ then $cos\theta - sin\theta$ is

(a) $-\sqrt{2}cos\theta$ (b) $-\sqrt{2}sin\theta$ (c)$\sqrt{2}sin\theta$ (d) $\sqrt{2}tan\theta$

Sol: Smart technique

If$cos\theta + sn\theta = x$ then

$cos\theta - sin\theta = \sqrt{2 - x^2}$

$= \sqrt{2 - (\sqrt{2}cos\theta)^2}$

$= \sqrt{2 - 2cos^2\theta}$

$= \sqrt{2}sin\theta$

Q: $\dfrac{1}{1 + tan^2\theta} + \dfrac{1}{1 + cot^2\theta}$ is

(a) 1   (b) 2   (c) $\dfrac{1}{2}$ (d) $\dfrac{1}{4}$

Sol:

Regular method	Alternate method
$$\dfrac{1}{1+\dfrac{sin^2\theta}{cos^2\theta}}+\dfrac{1}{1+\dfrac{cos^2\theta}{sin^2\theta}}$$ $$\dfrac{cos^2\theta}{sin^2\theta+cos^2\theta}+\dfrac{sin^2\theta}{sin^2\theta+cos^2\theta}$$ $$\dfrac{cos^2\theta+sin^2\theta}{sin^2\theta+cos^2\theta}$$ =1	$$\dfrac{1}{1+tan^2\theta}+\dfrac{1}{1+cot^2\theta}$$ $$=\dfrac{1}{sec^2\theta}+\dfrac{1}{cosec^2\theta}$$ $$=cos^2\theta+sin^2\theta$$ =1 (needs right approach to solve the trigonometrically sum)

Q:If $sin\,(A+B)=1$ **and** $sin\,(A-B)=\dfrac{1}{2}$**, where value of A &B between 0^0&90^0 What is the value of**sin^2A-sin^2B

    (a) 0   **(b) 1**   **(c)** $\dfrac{1}{2}$ **(d) 2**   **(e) none of these**

Sol: $sin\,(A+B)=1=sin90^0$i.e. A+B=90^0

$sin\,(A-B)=\dfrac{1}{2}=sin30^0$i.e. A-B=$30^0$

Hence A=60^0, B=30^0

$sin^2A-sin^2A=sin^260-sin^230$

$(\dfrac{\sqrt{3}}{2})^2-(\dfrac{1}{2})_2$

$=\dfrac{3}{4}-\dfrac{1}{4}$

$=\dfrac{1}{2}$

Q: **If**$tan\theta+sec\theta=4$**, then what is the value of** $sin\theta$

(a) $\dfrac{8}{17}$ (b) $\dfrac{8}{15}$ (c) $\dfrac{15}{17}$ (d) $\dfrac{23}{22}$

Sol: such type of question cannot be solved by sub situation method as no range of θ is given, so needs correct approach to solve the problem

$$\tan\theta + \sec\theta = 4$$

$$\sec\theta = 4 - \tan\theta$$

Square on both side

$$\sec^2\theta = (4 - \tan\theta)^2 = 16 + \tan^2\theta - 8\tan\theta$$

$$1 + \tan^2\theta = 16 + \tan^2\theta - 8\tan\theta$$

$$\tan\theta = \frac{16}{8} \quad \text{and} \quad \cot\theta = \frac{8}{16}$$

$$\sin\theta = \frac{1}{\operatorname{cosec}\theta}$$

$$= \frac{1}{\sqrt{1 + \cot^2\theta}} = \frac{1}{\sqrt{1 + (\frac{8}{15})^2}} = \frac{1}{\sqrt{\frac{225 + 64}{25}}}$$

$$\sin\theta = \frac{15}{17}$$

Atteranate method

If $\tan\theta + \sec\theta = x$ then value of $\sec\theta = \dfrac{x^2 + 1}{2x}$

we put the value of x, then $\sec\theta = \dfrac{4^2 + 1}{2.4} = \dfrac{17}{8}$

$$\cos\theta = \frac{8}{17} \ , \ \sin\theta = \sqrt{1 - \cos^2\theta} = \sqrt{1 - \left(\frac{8}{17}\right)^2} = \sqrt{1 - \frac{64}{289}}$$

$$\sin\theta = \sqrt{\frac{225}{289}} = \frac{15}{17}.$$

TECHNIQUE

THE ANGLE BETWEEN HOUR HAND & MINUTE HAND

Q: What is the angle between the minutes hand and hour hand in 8:30 AM in clockwise direction

  (a) 80^0 (b) 105^0 (c) 260^0 (d) 280^0 (e) 120^0

Sol:

	Smart technique
Basic rule for hour hand and minute hand	To know all such type of calculation basic rule
Hr. hand mover 360^0=12hr	should we remembered
Hr. hand move 1 hr = 30^0	The angle of hour hand at 8: 30 hr
Minutes hand move 60min =360^0	$= 30^0 \times 8.5 = 260^0$
Frinate hand man 1 min = 6	The angle of min hand in 30 min
Note:	$= 6^0 \times 30 = 180^0$
Hr. hand move 1 hr =30^0	$= 260^0 - 180^0 = 80^0$
Minutes hand move 1 min. = 6^0	

Q: what is the angle between hrs hand and min hand in 9:45 hrs?

  (a) 45^0 (b) $47\frac{1}{2}^0$ (c) $22\frac{1}{2}^0$ (d) 45^0

Sol: the angle of hrs hand = $9\frac{3}{4} X\, 30 = 9 X 30 + \frac{3}{4} X 30$

$$= 270 + 22.50$$

$= 292.5^0 = 292^0 30'$

The angle of min hand $= 45 \times 6 = 270$

The angle $= 292^0 30' - 270 = 22^0 30'$

Q: the angle formed by the hour hand and minute hand of clock at 2:15 PM is

(a) $27\frac{1}{20}$ (b) 45^0 (c) $22\frac{1}{20}$ (d) 40^0

Sol: Smart technique

Angle of hour hand in 1 hr = 30^0

Angle of hour hand in 2:15 = $2\frac{1}{4} \times 30$

$= \frac{9}{4} \times 30$

$= \frac{135}{2}$

Angle of minute hand in 60 minute = 360^0

Angle of minute hand in 15 min = $\frac{360}{4} = 90^0$

Angle between minute hand and hour hand

$= 90 - \frac{135}{2}$

$= \frac{45}{2}$

$= 22\frac{1}{2}$

TECHNIQUE

DATA INTERPRETATION THROUGH BAR CHART

Bar chart is another simplest method of data interpretation. In bar chart having two axix .i.e x- axix and y – axix. x- axix always represents class (it can be any series) and y - axix represents variable (it may be number, percentage etc.) we compare the data and answer accordingly with less calculation.

Some basic rule of bar chart

When data comparing between two variable i.e x, y with given percentage, the rules to be followed.

(a) If x is what % of y => $\dfrac{x}{y} X100$

(b) If what % of x is y => $\dfrac{x}{y} X 100$

(c) If what % y is x => $\dfrac{x}{y} X100$

(d) If x is what % more / less than y => $\dfrac{x - y}{x} X100$

(e) % change = $\dfrac{final\ value - initial\ value}{initial\ value} X100$

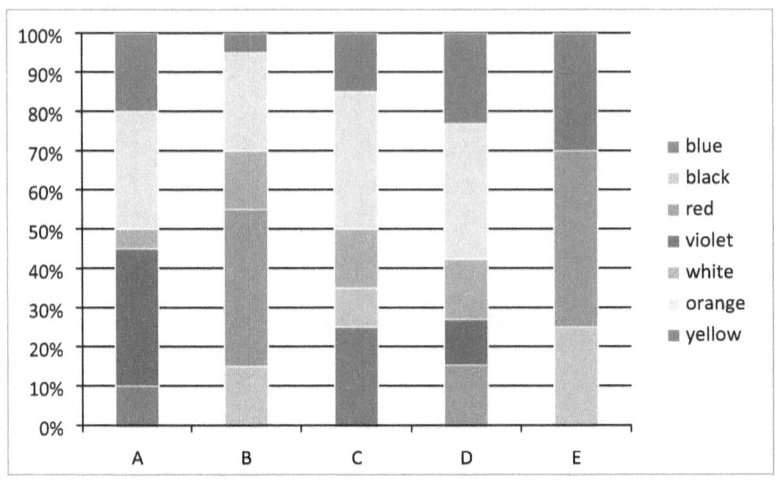

Q: The following bar diagram show the percentage of 7 coloured ball sold in 5 different shops .stdy the graph and answer the question given below

Q: the ratio of total percentage of red ball and total percentage of orange ball.

(a) 6:5   (b) 7:9   (c) 6:5   (d) 9:7   (e) 9:11

Son:

$$\frac{perentage\ of\ red\ ball}{percentage\ of\ orange\ ball} = \frac{40+20+45}{20+25+35+45} = \frac{105}{135} = 7:9$$

Q: What fraction of the total percentage of colour balls is to the percentage of total yellow ball?

(a) $\dfrac{3}{20}$ (b) $\dfrac{4}{25}$ (c) $\dfrac{13}{100}$ (d) $\dfrac{7}{50}$ (e) $\dfrac{4}{30}$

Sol: total % of yellow balls = 20+5+15+30=70

Total % of color ball = 5X100=500

Required ratio $=\dfrac{70}{500} = \dfrac{7}{50}$

Q: oIn shop A, the ratio of percentage of violet balls and yellow balls is

(a) 7:4   (b) 6:1   (c) 2:4   (d) 2:4

Sol: In shop A, % of violet balls =35

%of yellow balls = 20

Required ratio = $\dfrac{35}{20} = 7{:}4$

Q: the difference between total percentage of violet balls and total percentage of blue balls is.

(a) 15   (b) 25   (c) 40   (d) 10

Sol: Total % violet balls = 35+15=50

   Total % of blue ass = 10+25=35

Difference = 50-35 = 15

Q: annual admission of boys andgirls given in a school in 2012 study the barchart and answer the question given below

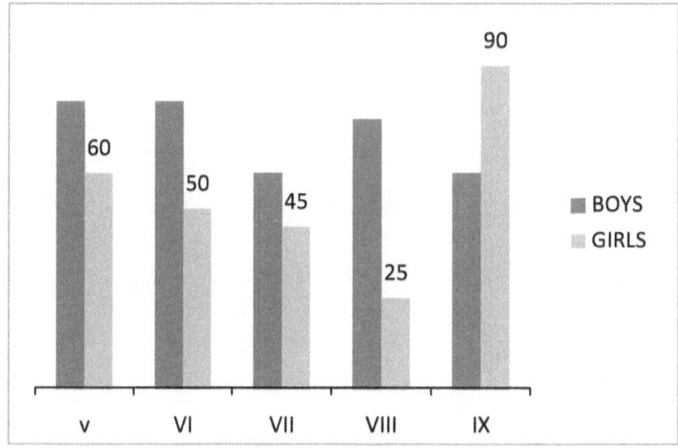

Q: in which standard in the total number of admissions in maximum

(a) V   (b) VI   (c) VIII   (d) IX

Sol: As per the graph, class IX having admission is 150 student, That is max

Q: on which standard did the least number of girls take admission?

(a) V   (b) VI   (c) VII   (d) VIII

Sol: As per the graph, class VIII having least number of girls

Q: What is the average numbers of boys who look admission in all standardstogether?

(a) 73   (b) 71   (c) 69   (d) 65

Sol: Av .number of boys in all class= $\dfrac{80 + 80 + 60 + 75 + 60}{5}$

$$= \dfrac{355}{5}$$

$$= 71$$

Q: What is the average number of girls who look admission in all class together?

(a) 54   (b) 56   (c) 58   (d) 60

Sol: Av. Number of girls on all class= $\dfrac{60 + 50 + 45 + 25 + 90}{5}$

$$= \dfrac{270}{5}$$

$$= 54$$

Q: What is the difference between the numbers of boys and the numbers of girls who took admission in all standards together.

(a) 65   (b) 75   (c) 85   (d) 95

Sol: diff. between the boys and girls =355-270

$$= 85$$

Q: the bar diagram given below shows the production (in the unit of thousand pieces) of thee types biscuits by a company in the five consecutive years. Study the diagram and answer the question.

382

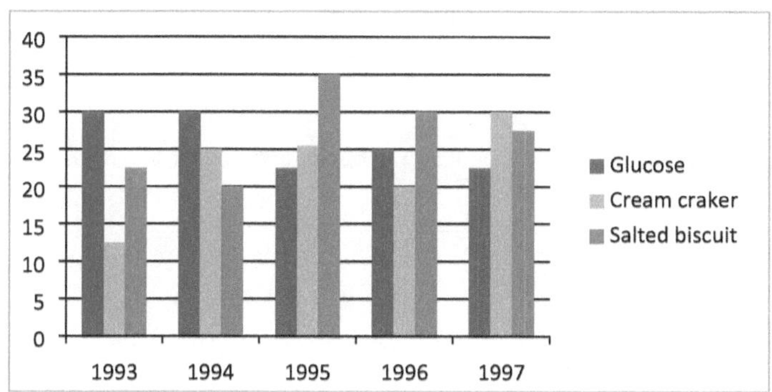

Q: the percentage drop in the number of glucose biscuit manufactured from 1994 to 1995

(a) 10   (b) 15   (c) 20   (d) 25

Sol: $\dfrac{30-22.5}{30}X100 = \dfrac{7.5}{30}X100 = 25\%$

Q: the difference (in the unit of thousand pieces) between the total numbers of cream cracker biscuits manufactured in the year 1993 , 1995 and 1997 and the total numbers of the biscuits of same type in the 1994 and 1996 is.

(a) 15   `(b) 20   (c) 25   (d) 30

Sol: the diff of cream cra biscuits

= (12.5+27.5+30) − (25+20)

= 70 -45 = 25

Q: total production of all the three types of biscuits was the least in the year

(a) **1993**   (b) 1997   (c) 1996   (d) 1993

Sol: 1993=>65 thousand   1996=>75 thousand

1997=>80 thousand   1995=>85 thousand

Q: total production of all the three types of biscuits was the maximum in the year

(a) **1995**   (b) 1994   (c) 1996   (d) 1993

Sol: 1994=> 75 thousand and rest as per Q3 compare found the year 1995

Hence 1995 her mat produtim

Q: the ratio of production of glucose biscuits and total production of biscuit in that year was maximum in

(a) 1994   (b) 1993   (c) 1996   (d) 1997

Sol: required ratio in the year

$$1993 = \frac{30}{65} = 0.46 \qquad\qquad 1995 = \frac{22.5}{85} = 0.26$$

$$1994 = \frac{30}{75} = 0.4 \qquad 1996 = \frac{25}{75} = 0.33$$

$$1997 = \frac{22.5}{80} = 0.25$$

Hence max.Ratio in the year 1993

Q: Study the following graph which shows income and expenditure of a company over the years and answer the question

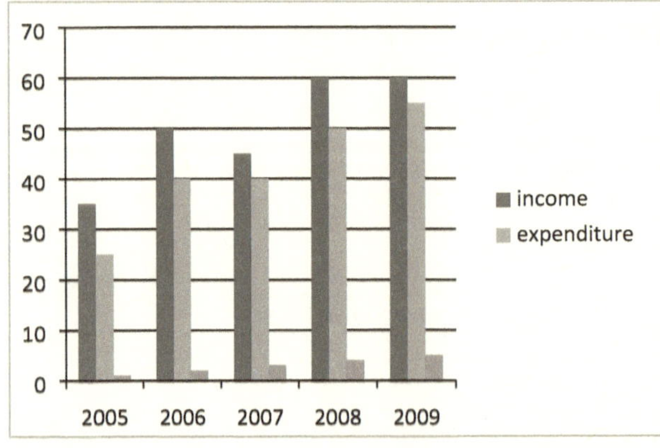

Q: the difference in profit (Rs in crores) of the company during 2007 and 2008 is

(a) 5   (b) 10   (c) 15   (d) 20

Sol: profit in 2007 = 45 – 40 = 5 crore

Profit in 2008 = 60 – 50 = 10 crore

Diff in profit in 2007 and 2008 = 10 – 5 = 5 corns

Q: on how many years was the expenditure of the company more than the average expenditure of the given years

(a) 4   (b) 3   (c) 2   (d) 1

Sol:Av.Exp. Of the given year = $\dfrac{25 + 40 + 40 + 50 + 55}{5} = 45$

No .of years more than the average is 2 i.e 2008 and 2009

Q: the percentage increase in income of the company from 2007 to 2008 is

(a) 25   (b) 30   (c) $33\dfrac{1}{3}$ (d) $42\dfrac{6}{7}$

Sol: % increase from 2007 to 2008 = $\dfrac{60 - 45}{45}X100 = \dfrac{15}{45}X100 = 33\dfrac{1}{3}$

Q: the ratio of total income to total expenditure to the company over the years is

(a) 21:25   (b) 25:21   (c) 26:21   (d) 25:22

Sol: $\dfrac{total\ income}{total\ exp} = \dfrac{35 + 50 + 45 + 60 + 60}{25 + 40 + 40 + 50 + 55} = \dfrac{250}{210} = \dfrac{25}{21}$

Q: the graph shows the demand and production of different componies. Study the graph and answer the question given below

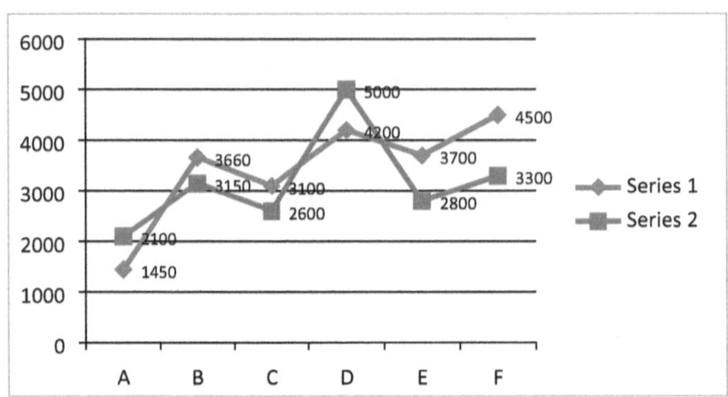

Q: the demand of company B is what percentage of the production of company F?

(a) 80%   (b) 60%   (c) 50%   (d) 70%

Sol: Demand of B = x % of production is F

$$3150 = \frac{x}{100}X4500 \quad x = \frac{3150}{45} = 70\%$$

Q: what is the ratio of the companies having more demand than production to those having more production than demand?

(a) 2:1   (b) 3:2   (c) 1:2   (d) 2:3

Sol: the required ratio = $\dfrac{A\,,\,D}{B\,,C\,,E\,,F} = \dfrac{2}{4} = \dfrac{1}{2}$

Q: What is the difference between the average demand and the average production of the companies in lakh tones approximately ?

(a) 275   (b) 325   (c) 200   (d) 250

Sol: Required average diff =

$$\frac{(1450 + 3650 + 3100 + 4200 + 3700 + 4500) - (2100 + 3150 + 2600 + 5000 + 2800 + 3300)}{6}$$

$$= \frac{20610 - 18950}{6} = \frac{1660}{6} \approx 275$$

Q: the production of company A is approximately what percentage of the demand of company C

(a) 55%   (b) 65%   (c) 50%   (d) 60%

Sol: required %

1450=x%of 2600

$$x = \frac{1450}{26} \approx 55\%$$

Q: the question based on the following bar graph.Read the graph and answer the question given below.

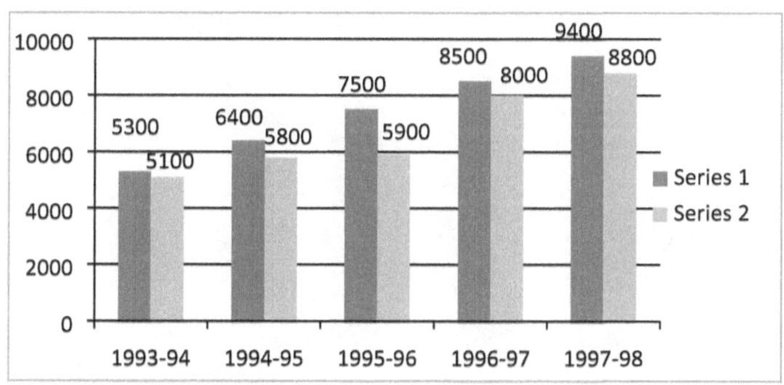

Q: In order to make profit of 10% .what should have been the gross traffic receipt (in Rs crores) in 1994-95 total expenditure remaining the some ? (approx)

(a) Rs 5667   (b) Rs 5876   (c) Rs 6444   (d) Rs 7667

Sol: Profit $= \dfrac{grose\ receipt - total\ Exp}{gross\ receipt} X100$

$$10 = \frac{x - 5800}{x} X100$$

$$10 = 100 - \frac{5800}{x} X100$$

$$x = \frac{5800 X 100}{90} = 6444\ (approt)$$

Q: what amount (in Rscrores) has the expenditure increased over the period in 1993 -94 to 1997 – 98 ?

(a) Rs 4100   (b) Rs 3900   (c) Rs 3580   (d) Rs 3700   (e) Rs 3750

Sol: the increased amount = 8800-5100 = 3700

Q: what is the percentage in the gross traffic receipt in 1995-96 as compared to 1993-94 ?

(a) 33.9%   (b) 41.5%   (c) 20.7 %   (d) 17%   (e) 16.85%

Sol: required % increase = $\dfrac{7500-5300}{5300} X100$

$= \dfrac{2200}{5300} X100 = 41.5\%$

Q: If profit =gross traffic receipts – total expenditure, then in 1996 -97 what percentage of gross traffic receipts is the profit made?

(a) 5.9%   (b) 6.4%   (c) 7.2%   (c) 8%   (e) 11%

Sol: profit in year 1996-97 = gross traffic receipt – total exp

= 8500-8000 = 500

Profit % $= \dfrac{500}{8500} X100 = 5.9\%$

Study the above bar graph showing the production of food grains (In million tons) and answer the question given below

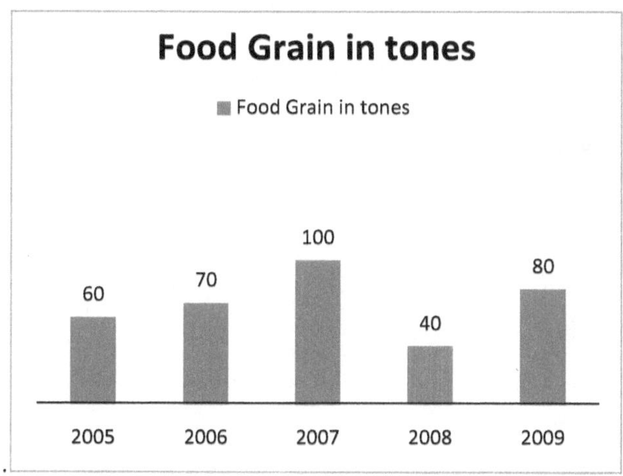

Q: what is the ratio between the maximum production and the minimum production during the given period?

(a)1:2   (b) 2:3   (c) 3:4   (d) 5:2

Sol: $\dfrac{max.\ production}{min.\ production}$ in the graph $= \dfrac{100\ tonnes}{40\ tonnes} = \dfrac{5}{2}$

Q: what was the average production of all the given years (intonnes) ?

(a)40   (b) 50   (c) 65   (d) 70

Sol: av. Production of food grains $= \dfrac{60 + 70 + 100 + 40 + 80}{5}$

$= \dfrac{350}{5} = 70$

Q: what percentage of production in 2007 is more than the production in 2008?

(a) 150%   (b) $33\dfrac{1}{3}\%$ (c) $66\dfrac{2}{3}\%$ (d) 75%

Sol: production difference between 2007 and 2008 = 100-40=60

389

More % production = $\dfrac{60}{40}X100 = 150\%$

Q: the production in the year 2006 is what percentage the total production of the given years.

Sol: total production of food grain in the given year = 350 tones

   The production in 2006 = 70tonnes

% of production = $\dfrac{70}{350}X100$

= 20%

Study the above bar graph and answer the question given below

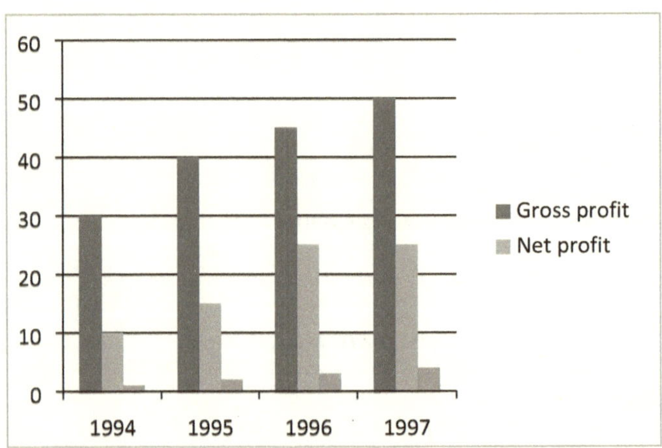

Q: the year in which the gross profit is double the net profit

(a) 1994   (b) 1996   (c) 1997   (d) 1995

Sol: As per the graph, in the year 1997, the gross profit = 50lakhs

                               Net profit = 25lakhs

Q: the percentage of net profit of 1995 as compared to the gross profit in that year is

(a) 25.5%   (b) 35.5%   (c) 37.5%   (d) 42.5%

Sol: required % = $\dfrac{15}{40} X100 = 37.5\%$

Q: the difference of average gross profit and average net profit calculated for four years is

(a) Rs 18.75 lakhs   (b) Rs 19.75 lakhs   (c) Rs 20.5 lakhs   (d) Rs. 22.5 lakhs

Sol; diff. of Av gross profit and Av. Net profit

$$= \dfrac{(30 + 40 + 45 + 50) - (10 + 15 + 25 + 25)}{4}$$

$= 22.5\ lakhs$

Q: the ratio of gross profit to net profit in which year was greatest in the given year.

(a) 1994   (b) 1995   (c) 1996   (d) 1997

Sol: the ratio $\quad 1994 = \dfrac{30}{10} = 3$

$$1995 = \dfrac{40}{15} = 2......$$

$$1996 = \dfrac{45}{25} = 1......$$

$$1997 = \dfrac{50}{25} = 2......$$

(note : further calculation need not

Required as we find the greatest ratio)

1994 has the greatest ratio

TECHNIQUE

DATA INTERPRETATION THROUGH PIE CHART

TECHNIQUE DATA INTER PRETATION THROUGH PIE CHART

Pie chart interpretation is one of the simple and easy data interpretations. If we have the knowledge of calculating the percentage which we have already discussed earlier and the correct approach of the problem.

Basic rules of pie-chart:

(a) Data given either in percentage or   degrees

(b) If data given in percentage, follow the rules

> If x is what % of y = $\dfrac{x}{y} \times 100$

> If what % of x is y = $\dfrac{x}{y} \times 100$

> If what % of y is x = $\dfrac{x}{y} \times 100$

> If x is what %   more/less than y = $\dfrac{x-y}{x} \times 100$

% charge = $\dfrac{final\ value - initial\ value}{initial\ value} \times 100$

(c) If data given in degrees, follow the rules

> The sum of degree always 360

> When value given in degree and required to change   in percentage

Eg: 36^0 *is* $x\%$ *of* 360

$$x = \frac{36 \times 100}{360} = 10\%$$

As you know $100\% = 360$

$$36^0 = 10\%$$

$$18^0 = 5\%$$

$$3.6^0 = 1\%$$

(d) When data given in percentage and required to convert in degrees

Eg: 15% *of* 360^0 *is* x *degree*

$\blacktriangleright$ $\quad x = \dfrac{15}{100} \times 360 = 54^0$

as you know $10\% = 36^0$

$$5\% = 18^0$$

Hence $15\% = 54^0$

(Note: use split method to calculate % for saving more time)

Q: The following pie chart shows the land distribution of a housing complex in degrees. If the total area of the complex is 5 acres, examine the pie chart and answer the question.

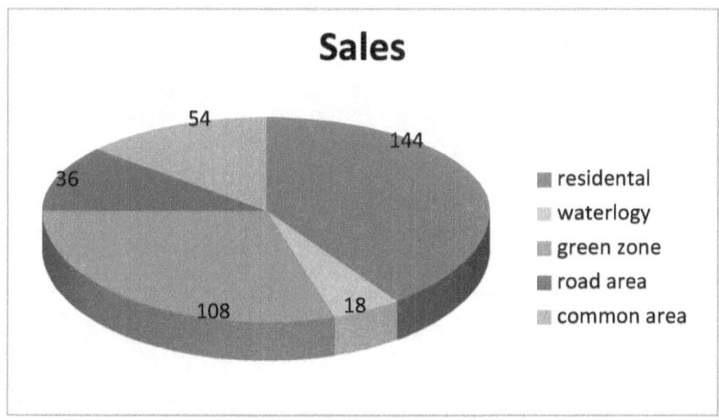

Q.1) The ratio of area allotted for residential and road purpose is

(a) 1:4 (b) 4:1 (c) 3:8 (d) 8: 3

Sol : $\dfrac{residental\ area}{road\ purpose\ area} = \dfrac{144^0}{36^0} = \dfrac{4}{1}$

Q.2) the percentage of the total area allotted to water body and green zone together

(a) 35% (b) 30% (c) 45% (c) 40%

Sol: $required\ \% = \dfrac{18^0 + 108^0}{360} \times 100$

$= \dfrac{126^0}{360^0} \times 100$

=35%

Smart technique

As your know the 36^0 = 10%

On mental calculation

18^0=5%

108^0=30%

Hence required % is 35%

Q: what percentage of waterbody is allotted for residential area

(a) 5%   (b) 6%   (c)8%   (d) 10%

Sol:

Regular method	Smart technique
Let $x\%\ of\ W.B = R.A$ $\dfrac{x}{100} X 18^0 = 144$	As you know the rule i.e $\dfrac{x}{-} X 100$ What % of y is x = y

$x = \dfrac{144}{18} X\,100$ $= 8\%$	$= \dfrac{144}{18} X100$ $= 8\%$

Q: total land allotted for residential area and commercial purpose is .

(a) $2\dfrac{1}{4}$ acres (b) $4\dfrac{1}{2}$ acres   (c) $2\dfrac{3}{4}$ acres   (d) $2\dfrac{1}{2}$ acres

Sol: total land $= \left(\dfrac{144+54}{360}\right) X5$ (total area of land = 5 acres)

$$= \dfrac{198}{360} X5$$

$$= 2\dfrac{3}{4}\ acres$$

Q: the following pie charts show the production of various food crops in two states. Study the pie chart carefully and answer the question that follows

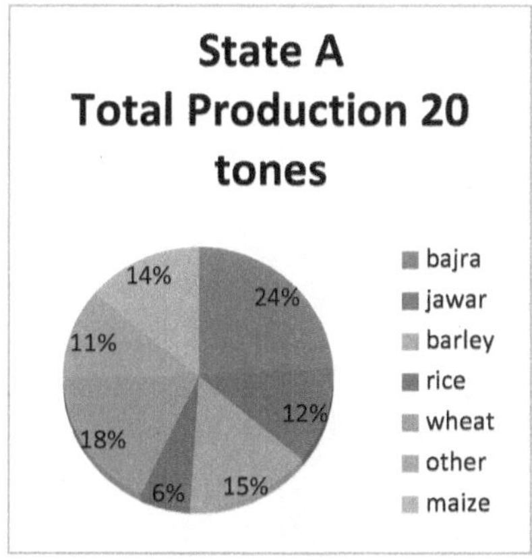

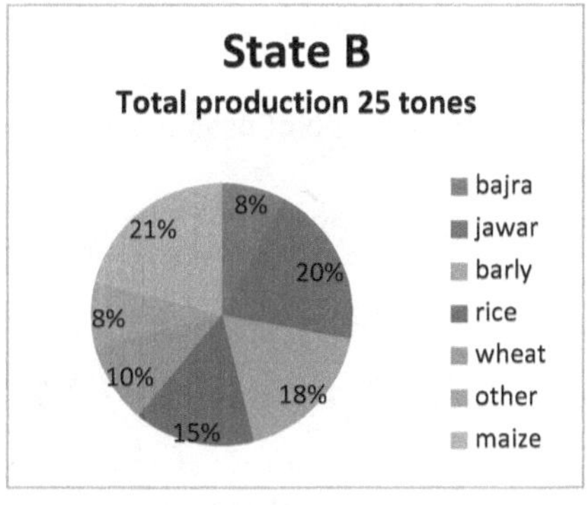

Q: what is the total production of jowar and wheat in state A

(a) 360000 tones   (b) 650000 tones   (c) 240000 tones   (d) 600000 tones

Sol: percentage of jowar and wheat is 12%+18%=30%

30% of 20,00,000= 60,0000 tones

Q: what is the production of rice and bajra in state B

   (a) 375000 tones   (b) 575000 tones   (c) 200000 tones   (d) 450000 tones

Sol: total percentage of rice and bajra in state B = 15 % +8% = 23%

 23% of 2500000= 20% of 2500000+3% of 2500000

            = 500000+75000

            = 575000 tones

Q: what is the total production of barley in state A and state B

   (a) 6000000 tones   (b) 645000 tones   (c) 750000 tones   (d) 450000 tones

Sol: 15 % of 2000000+ 18 %of 2500000

   =300000+450000

   = 750000 tones

Q: what is the ratio of production of maize in state B to that in state A

   (a) 8:15   (b) 9:8 (c) 15:8   (d) 8:9

Sol: $\dfrac{maize\ \%\ in\ state\ B}{maize\ \%\ in\ state\ A}=\dfrac{21\%\ of\ 2500000}{14\%\ of\ 2000000}=\dfrac{21/25000}{14/20000}=\dfrac{3X5}{2X4}=\dfrac{15}{8}$

(note :- when production is same in both states, only % ratio is calculated)

Q: what is the ratio of production of bajra in state A to the rice state B

   (a) 32:25   (b) 25:32   (c) 29:24   (d) 24:29

Sol: $\dfrac{bajra\ in\ state\ A}{rice\ in\ state\ B}=\dfrac{24\%\ of\ 2000000}{15\%\ of\ 2500000}=\dfrac{24X4}{15X50}=\dfrac{32}{25}$

Q: the following pie chart shows the monthly expenditure of Dr .sharma on different items. His monthly income is equal in every month and his annual income is Rs 576000. Study the chart ad answer the question given below

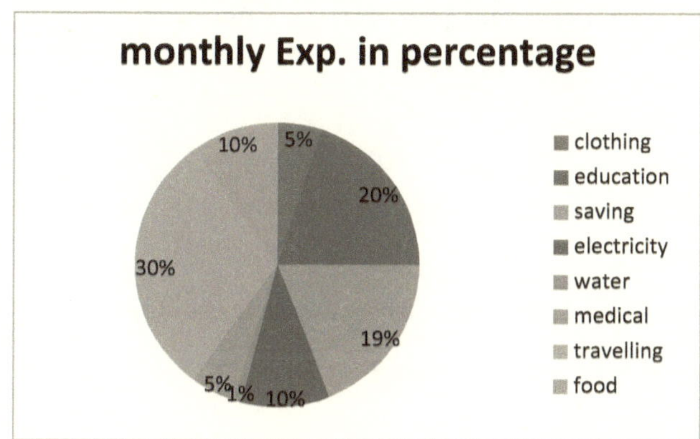

Q: how much does Dr. sharma pay on education in a month ?

(a) Rs 9760   (b) Rs 9850   (c) Rs 9800   (d) Rs 9600

Sol: Dr .sharma annual income Rs 576000

$$\text{Monthly income Rs} \quad \frac{576000}{12} = 48000$$

Spend in education = 20% of 48000= 9600

Q: what is the sum of money he spent on food and water?

(a) Rs 5200   (b) Rs 2850   (c) Rs 5280   (d) Rs 5260

Sol: the percentage of spending in food and water = 10%+1%=11%

Expenditure on food and water = 11% of 48000(10% of 48000 +1% of 48000) =48000+480)

= 5280

Q: what is the angle shown by the difference between the expenditure on travelling and the expenditure on clothes

(a) 60⁰   (b) 90⁰   (c0 100⁰   (d) 120⁰

Sol: diff. of % between travelling and clothes = 30% -5% = 25%

The difference of angle between them = 25% of 360^0

$$= 90^0 \quad (10\% \text{ is } 36^0, 10\% \text{ is } 36^0, 5\% \text{ is } 18^0 = 90^0)$$

Q: what is his monthly saving?

(a) Rs 9100   (b) Rs 9000   (c) Rs 9110   (d) Rs9120

Sol: monthly saving % = 19%

Monthly saving amount = 19% of 48000 (20% of 48000 - 1% of 48000) =36000-480=9120)

$$= 9120$$

Q: what is the ratio of expenditure on education to expenditure on food?

(a) 1:2   (b) 2:1   (c) 1:5   (d) 5:1

Sol: $\dfrac{Exp.\,on\,eduction}{exp\,on\,food} = \dfrac{20\%}{10\%} = \dfrac{2}{1}$ (note : need not quire find amount and get ratio)

Q: the pie chart shown the spending of a family on various item during the year 2017 .study the graph and answer the question given be

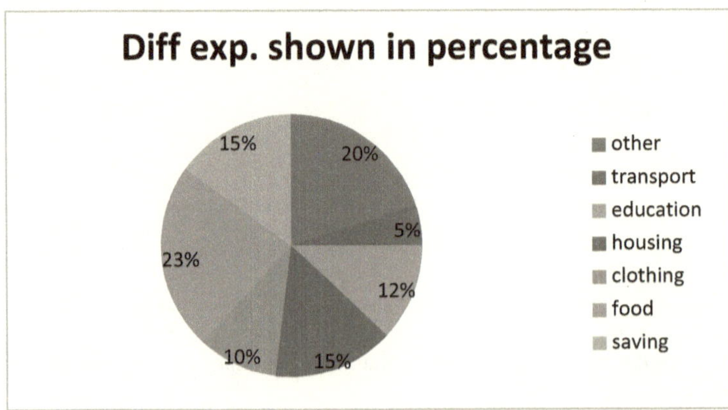

Q: If the total amount spent during the year 2017 was Rs 4600 the amount spent on food was (in Rs)

(a) 2000   (b) 10580   (c) 23000   (d) 2300   (d) 26000

Sol: Required amount 23% of 46000 (10%=4600)

$$=10580$$

Q : If the total amount spent was Rs 46000 , how much was spent on clothing and housing together ?
(inRs)

(a) 11500   (b) 2150   (c) 15000   (d) 10000   (e) 10500

Sol: Required amount 25% of 46000 $(\frac{1}{4} X\ 46000)$

$$= 11500$$

Q: the ratio of the total amount of money spent on housing to that spend on education was

(a) 5:2   (b) 2:5   (c) 4:5   (d) 5:4   (e) 3:5

Sol: required ratio $= \dfrac{houwing\ \%}{education\ \%} = \dfrac{15\%}{12\%} = \dfrac{5}{4}$

Q: the maximum amount of money spend on

(a) Food   (b) clothing   (c) housing   (d) others   (e) education

Sol: Food =23%, rest all less than that

Q: theexpenditure of transportation and others are the what percentage of total expenditure.

(a) 50%   (b) 35%   (c) 25%   (d) 30%   (e) 75%

Sol: Exp on trarsp.+other. = 5%+20%=25%

Total Exp = 100%

Exp % = 25 % of the total Exp

Q: Study the following pie chart carefully to answer the question given below

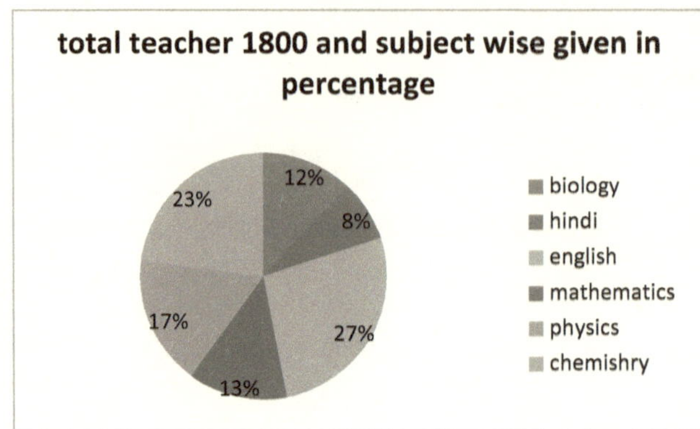

Q: If two ninth of the teachers who teachers physics , are female then number of male physics teacher is approximately what percent to the total number of teachers who teachers chemistry.

(a) 42   (b) 57   (c) 63   (d) 69

Sol: total teacher 100% = 1800

10%=180

1%=18

Remberfor all question

Total physics teacher 17 % of 1800 =306

Female teacher = $\frac{2}{9} X306 = 68$

Male teachr in physics = 306-68=238

Number of teacher in chemistry = 23% of 1800 = 414

Required % = $\frac{238}{414} X100 \approx 57\%$

Q: what is the total number of teacher teaching chemistry, English and biology?

(a) 1226   (b) 1116   (c) 1176   (d) 1096   (e) 998

Sol: total number of teachers in chemistry, English and biology

$$= \frac{23 + 27 + 12}{100}X1800 = \frac{62}{100}X1800 = 1116$$

Q: what is the difference between the total number of teachers who teach English and physics together and the total numbers of teachers who teaches mathematics and biology together.

(a) 352   (b) 342   (c) 652   (d) 653   (e) 643

Sol: required difference = $1800X\frac{(27 + 17)}{100} - 1800X\frac{(13 + 12)}{100}$

$$= 18(44 - 25) = 18X19 = 342$$

Q: what is the respective ratio of the numbers of teacher who teach mathematics and the number of teachers who teach Hindi?

(a) 13:7   (b)7:13   (c) 13:8   (d) 8:13   (e) 7:30

Sol: required Ratio = $\dfrac{1800X\dfrac{13}{100}}{1800X\dfrac{8}{10}} = \dfrac{13}{8}$

Q: on a certain country,allocation of budget to various sectors of a year per Rs. 1000 cores are represented by this pie Chart. Examine the chart and answer the fallowing question

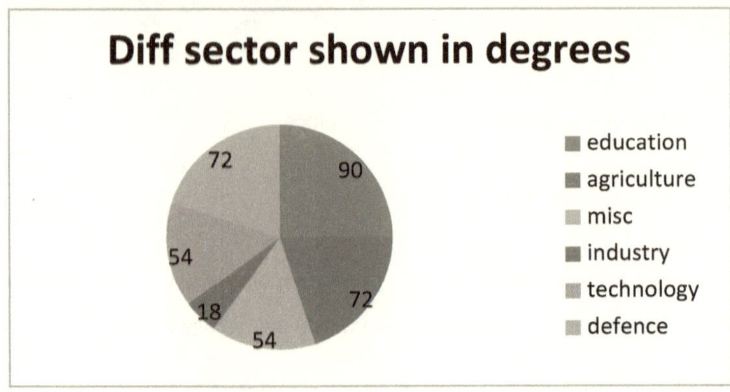

Q: the expenditure on agriculture is (in cores)

(a) 250   (b) 150   (c) 300   (d) 200

Sol: Expedition on agriculture $=\dfrac{72}{360} \times 1000$

$= 200$ acres

Q: what % of expenditure used in education, industry and agriculture

(a) 35 %   (b) 50 %   (c) 60%   (d) 65%

Sol: as you know the $36^0 = 10\%$

So calculate accordingly without using any formula,

$72^0 = 20\%$

$18^0 = 5\%$

$90^0 = 25\%$

So total % used in 50%

Q: what is the ratio of expenditure of technology and industry?

(a) 1:4   (b) 1:3   (c) 3:1   (d) 4:1

Sol: ratio $\dfrac{technology}{expenditure} = \dfrac{54}{18} = \dfrac{3}{1}$

The pie charts, given here show some auto mobile parts manufacture by on automobile company at its pune and Nagpur plant in the year 2014.Study the pie chart and answer the following question

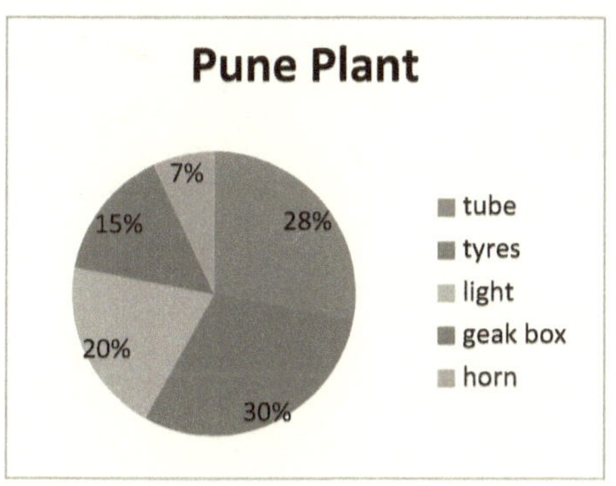

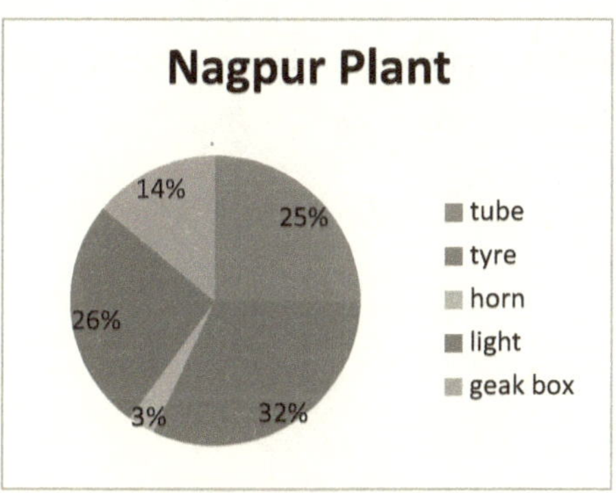

Q: If Nagpur plant produced 800000 tires, then the numbers of hounds produced by it

(a) 12000   (b) 18500   (c) 60000   (d) 75000

Sol: number of horn produced = $\dfrac{800000}{32} X3 = 75000$

Q: How much percentage more tubes produced at the pune plant than those produced at the Nagpur plant.

(a) 14   (b) 12   (c) 8   (d) 3

Sol: As your know % change = $\dfrac{final\ vacle - inition\ value}{initial\ value} X100$

$= \dfrac{28-25}{25} X100$

$$\frac{3}{25}X100 \; = 12\%$$

Q: the ratio of numbers of horns produced at nagput plant to that produced at pune plant is

(a) 3:7   (b) 7:3   (c) 10:3   (d) 7:10

Sol; this is only the ratio between the percentages, as the actual numbers produced are not required.

Hence the ratio in 3:7